EVALUATING EXPLANATIONS
A Content Theory

EVALUATING EXPLANATIONS
A Content Theory

David B. Leake
Indiana University
Bloomington, Indiana

Psychology Press
Taylor & Francis Group

New York   London

Chapter 7 is a revised version of
"Goal-Based Explanation Evaluation" by
David B. Leake (1991) *Cognitive Science.*
Copyright 1991 by Ablex Publishing Corporation.
Reprinted with permission of Ablex Publishing
Corporation

First Published by
Lawrence Erlbaum Associates, Inc., Publishers
365 Broadway
Hillsdale, New Jersey 07642

Transferred to Digital Printing 2009 by Psychology Press
270 Madison Avenue, New York NY 10016
27 Church Road, Hove, East Sussex BN3 2FA

Library of Congress Cataloging-in-Publication Data

Leake, David B.
     Evaluating explanations : a content theory / David B. Leake.
        p.   cm.
     Includes bibliographical references and index.
     ISBN 0-8058-1064-1
     1. Explanation—Computer simulation.   2. Artificial intelligence.
   I. Title.
   BF637.C45L43   1992
   153.4—dc20   91-42600
                                                               CIP

Publisher's Note
The publisher has gone to great lengths to ensure the quality
of this reprint but points out that some imperfections in the
original may be apparent.

Table of Contents

Acknowledgements

This book is a revised and extended treatment of my doctoral dissertation research at Yale University. It owes a tremendous debt to my advisor, Roger Schank: Throughout my years at Yale, he gave me the perfect combination of support, direction, and freedom, allowing me both to learn from him, and to learn to do AI on my own. He has provided invaluable assistance during and after my time at Yale; his vision and intensity of interests, both in AI and in many other areas, have enormously enriched and sharpened mine.

Chris Riesbeck served on my thesis committee, and has gone far beyond the call of duty in providing advice and encouragement in my research. Many improvements to this work are the result of his careful comments. Bob Abelson also served on my committee and provided helpful comments. Larry Birnbaum, the fourth member of my committee, taught the first AI course I took. It was an outstanding introduction, but my gratitude goes much further: I have benefited considerably from his interests, his enthusiasm, and his example as an AI researcher.

After my introduction to AI in Larry's course, I worked under Kris Hammond on a research project. I am thankful for Kris's determination to bring out my best work, and his encouragement along the way. I am very lucky to have worked under him.

I have also learned much from my collaborators on SWALE, Alex Kass and Chris Owens. Having them as colleagues and friends has made a large contribution to my life, both inside and outside of AI. Many others at the Yale AI laboratory have also contributed to my work, both individually and through their collective contribution to the laboratory's exciting and challenging atmosphere.

My parents, Roy and Alice Leake, and my sister, Patsy Leake, have offered tremendous support and encouragement at all points in my career. Caroline Verdier, my wife, has contributed to my work and home in countless ways. She has been steadfast throughout the many uncertainties and delays in the preparation of this work; her aid throughout has been invaluable. I cannot thank her enough.

I would like to thank an anonymous reviewer for Lawrence Erlbaum Associates, who provided insightful comments that guided the transformation of my dissertation into this book. I am also grateful to Hollis Heimbouch and the personnel of Lawrence Erlbaum Associates for their encouragement and assistance during the book's preparation, and to Raja Sooriamurthi for his assistance in preparing the final version.

My research at Yale was supported in part by the Advanced Research Projects Agency of the Department of Defense, monitored by the Office of Naval Research under contracts N00014–82–K–0149 and N0014–85–K–0108, and by the Air Force Office of Scientific Research under contracts 85–0343, AFSOR–87–0295 and F49620–88–C–0058. I am grateful to these agencies, and to the General Electric Forgivable Loan program, for their support. I am also indebted to Douglas Hofstadter for inviting me as a visitor to the Center for Research on Concepts and Cognition at Indiana University, where I refined many ideas presented in this book.

Overview
and Reader's Guide

Explanation plays a key role in understanding and controlling our environment. As Heider points out in his seminal study on interpersonal relations, explanation of actions allows people "to give meaning to action, to influence the actions of others as well as [themselves], and to predict future actions" [Heider, 1958, p. 123]. Likewise, explaining the material causes of events helps people to give meaning to events, and to control and predict them.

Psychology and philosophy have long studied the nature and role of explanation. More recently, Artificial Intelligence research has developed promising theories of how explanation facilitates learning and generalization. By using explanations to guide learning, explanation-based methods allow reliable learning of new concepts in complex situations, often from observing a single example.

However, the usefulness of explanation-based approaches depends not only on how explanations are used but on the framework that guides and supports explanation-based processing: on the answers to questions about when to explain, how to build explanations, what constitutes an explanation, and when an explanation applies. Explanation-based learning systems often address the first question by explaining each event for which no schema is available; the second by building explanations using backward chaining through a space of rules, starting with the state to be explained; the third by treating explanations as deductive proofs built from perfect rules; and the fourth by assuming that an explanation will apply in all contexts—that explanations are neutral—so that, if multiple explanations can be constructed for a situation, they are all equivalent.

We take a different view. By examining each question in the context of a story understanding system that explains novel events in news stories, we show that the standard framework is inadequate for explanation in complex real-world domains. We present an alternative theory: First, we contend that explanation must be selective, directed towards filling knowledge gaps revealed by anomalies. Second, we argue that there exists a theory of the content of anomalies and explanations that should be used to guide the search for explanations. Third, we claim that real-world explanations are built from uncertain inferences, making it necessary to judge explanations' goodness not just by structure, but in terms of domain knowledge. Fourth, we demonstrate that context—involving both explainer beliefs and goals—is crucial in deciding an explanation's goodness, and that a theory of contextual influences can be used to determine which explanations are appropriate. Each of these points is demonstrated with examples of the performance of ACCEPTER, a computer system for story understanding, anomaly detection, and explanation evaluation.

The following paragraphs sketch the major claims developed in this book:

Explanation should be focused on anomalies: Explanation-based understanding systems generally attempt to explain all events not already accounted for by system schemas. In everyday situations, this would result in an overwhelming number of candidate events to explain, and there is no assurance that the resultant explanations would provide useful information. For explanation-based processing to be effective, the explainer must make judicious choices of when and what to explain.

This book argues that an understander should focus explanation effort by explaining only in response to flaws and gaps in knowledge revealed by anomalies—conflicts between new information and system knowledge. When the understander's beliefs and expectations are consistent with new information, its world model provides reasonable expectations, and there is no need to explain; explanation is only needed when the system's model is deficient. In order for explanations of anomalies to enable repair of deficient knowledge, they must explain the *anomaly* rather than simply explaining the *event:* They must account not just for what happened but also for why prior understanding went awry.

Anomaly detection is pattern-based: Focusing explanation on anomalies depends on first detecting those anomalies. However, routine application of anomaly detection is only practical if it can be done efficiently, which presents a serious problem: In principle, anomaly detection may be arbitrarily expensive. Anomalies arise not only from direct conflicts between inputs and system knowledge but also from conflicts between their *ramifications;*

noticing a particular anomaly may require building long inference chains tracing ramifications until a contradiction is found. Practical anomaly detection depends on overcoming this potentially overwhelming inference cost.

Our solution to the inference problem is to avoid inference chaining entirely: We replace inference by table lookup of stereotyped patterns. Rather than inferring the ramifications of an input, our method simply searches through a series of abstraction trees for relevant patterns. Information conflicting with those patterns is considered anomalous; facts that do not conflict are accepted. This table-based approach is a radical departure from traditional methods.

Substantiating the table-based approach depends on identifying which tables are needed and establishing their generality. We do so by presenting a content theory of types of patterns that the tables must contain, and demonstrating that they provide wide coverage of everyday anomalies.

There exists a content theory of anomaly and explanation that guides explanation search: The detection of an anomaly shows that explanation is needed. The next step of the explanation process is to obtain a candidate explanation. Traditional methods build explanations by chaining through basic inference rules to account for an event. This approach can involve excessive processing cost, and may not result in explanations that actually address the anomaly to be explained. We argue instead for the case-based approach to explanation proposed by Schank [1986].

For case-based explanation construction to be effective, criteria for evaluating explanations' goodness must be translated into an indexing scheme that allows good explanations to be retrieved. We develop a theory of the content of anomaly and explanation to facilitate organization of explanations in memory, and the retrieval of appropriate candidate explanations to resolve anomalies.

Explanations are traces of plausible reasoning: In explanation-based learning research, explanations are treated as deductive proofs built from perfect rules. However, it is well known that inference rules describing real-world situations are unavoidably imperfect; they at best trace plausible but uncertain connections. Real-world explanations are generally abductive, and may be invalid; consequently it is essential to develop criteria for guiding explanation towards plausible hypotheses. This need provides additional impetus for case-based explanation: Unlike traditional explanation construction methods, which are impartial towards alternative explanatory chains, case-based explanation uses experience as a guide, focusing on explanations supported by similar prior situations.

The need to select plausible hypotheses also makes believability evaluation a crucial concern. We propose a believability evaluation method different from that in previous understanding systems: Whereas the trend in those approaches is to rank plausibility based on explanations' structure, we claim that plausibility evaluation should focus on reasonableness of their content, in light of prior knowledge and experience.

Explanation is goal-dependent: An explainer's reasons for explaining have profound effects on the information that a good explanation must provide. For example, an explainer will need different information for the goal of predicting a situation than for repairing it or preventing it. Previous research treats explanations as fundamentally goal-neutral: Understanding systems that explain often judge explanations' goodness by plausibility alone, without considering why explanation may be needed; explanation-based learning research assumes that all goals require complete explanations and treats all explanations starting from the same antecedents as equivalent when explaining. We take the opposite view, arguing that requirements for good explanations are strongly goal-dependent; needs for information determine whether partial explanations are sufficient and whether alternative explanations are in fact equivalent. We substantiate this view with a taxonomy of the goals that explanation can serve and characterizations of the widely divergent requirements that those goals impose on explanations.

The Structure of this Book

The issues we consider are relevant to readers with many interests, including understanding, anomaly detection, case-based reasoning, explanation-based learning, and explanation evaluation. To help selective readers focus on the appropriate areas, we briefly describe each chapter.

Chapter 1 discusses issues in maintaining an accurate world model in real-world domains, pointing out the central role of anomaly detection and explanation. It also introduces ACCEPTER, a computer model of routine understanding, anomaly detection, and explanation evaluation.

Chapter 2 begins with an extended trace of ACCEPTER's processing to illustrate our model of understanding and explanation. It then highlights the differences between our model and previous theories from AI, psychology and philosophy. The issues raised in this chapter are examined in detail in the following chapters.

Chapter 3 addresses the question of when to explain. It discusses the basic understanding process that provides ACCEPTER's expectations for routine events and describes the system's process for detecting anomalies when new inputs partially conflict with prior beliefs and expectations.

1 Explanation and Understanding

Two basic problems face understanders in real-world domains: recognizing what needs to be explained, and deciding whether a given explanation is sufficient. We discuss these problems and sketch the major points of the theory that this book develops to address them.

1.1 Fashioning Beliefs

When people are given new information, they seldom accept it blindly. If a politician pledges to lower taxes, or a car advertisement trumpets the high quality of a brand known for problems, people are skeptical. One possible explanation for their skepticism is that they compare new information to standard patterns and question information that conflicts. By questioning anomalous information, they can avoid mistakenly abandoning correct conclusions. Knowledge refined over long experience should not be discarded because of a freak incident: Seeing a magician levitate his assistant makes people wonder how they were fooled, rather than making them believe that the magician's supernatural power overcomes the law of gravity.

However, always clinging to old beliefs can be as dangerous as too easily abandoning them, because conflicts between old beliefs and new information can signal flaws in the old beliefs that need to be repaired. For example, suppose that someone with an unreliable car decides to replace it. In order to decide which brands to consider, he might try to judge the likelihood of various brands having problems. One heuristic people use for deciding likelihoods is the *availability* of instances with a given property: If most of the cases that can be recalled have the property, they assume that the property usually holds [Tversky & Kahneman, 1982]. If the car buyer uses this heuristic, his bad experience might make him generalize that the manufacturer of his car has bad quality control. Later, he might receive information contradicting that belief: A newspaper story could state that the manufacturer's quality control is much better than that of the competition. If he simply clung to his first generalization he would continue to avoid his original brand despite the report—and possibly buy a car that was worse.

In everyday understanding, it is impossible to avoid imperfect beliefs. Exigencies of the current situation often force conclusions to be drawn from partial or uncertain information, and even correct conclusions may be invalidated by changes in the world. Consequently, a system must be able to notice and repair those flaws in its knowledge that affect its performance.[1] In an understander, such flaws are revealed by failures to understand: by the anomalies that arise when new information conflicts with the understander's prior beliefs and expectations.

By noticing and explaining anomalies, people repair flawed knowledge and determine how to respond [Schank, 1986]. By noticing and explaining the discrepancy between his prior generalization and the newspaper story, the car buyer determines whether to revise his level of confidence in the newspaper or in his prior generalization, making his world model more accurate; he also determines which car to buy.

Likewise, Artificial Intelligence systems dealing with complex and dynamic domains must have the capacity to notice anomalous situations and react appropriately. This requires both recognizing when anomalies occur and finding a good explanation. These are difficult tasks in real-world domains, in which available information and processing resources may be limited, and where the ramifications of new information depend strongly on context— both the situation in the world, and the relationship of that situation to the system's current goals.

This book investigates when to trigger explanation, how to guide the search for explanations, and how to decide the adequacy of candidate explanations. This chapter surveys some of the territory the book will cover, beginning by discussing major issues in maintaining accurate beliefs in real-world domains. It then presents the highlights of a theory addressing those issues—a theory of how to detect potential belief problems, how to direct explanation towards resolving them, and how to assure that the resultant explanations give the information the system needs.

---

[1]Note that here and in the rest of this book, "knowledge" refers to what the understander believes and expects, which is not necessarily correct.

1.1.1 Belief in Real-World Domains

In real-world domains, understanding systems need ways to maintain reasonable views of the world, despite partial and unreliable information. Much research in story understanding has focused on how to generate a reasonable interpretation of events from partial information, but an equally important companion problem has received little attention: retracting beliefs that turn out to be incorrect [Charniak, 1978; Granger, 1980; O'Rorke, 1983]. The capability to recognize and learn from faulty beliefs is vital to the success of any real-world understanding system. No matter how good its strategies for interpreting events may be, it cannot be completely immune to being led astray by the following problems:

- **Lack of applicable knowledge:** No real-world understander can have a library of rules describing *all* features of the world that will ever be relevant; sometimes it will encounter situations outside of its prior knowledge. For example, a child going to a fancy restaurant for the first time may expect his parents to pay when they order, as they do when they take him to McDonald's.

- **Failure to notice that a situation merits attention:** Even if an understander has appropriate rules, it may not recognize that they apply. For example, even if the stock market shows classic signs of weakening, wishful thinking may make an investor miss its warning signs.

- **Application of inappropriate knowledge:** No rule about the real world can specify *all* the factors that affect its applicability—there are simply too many implicit conditions. Consequently, there is always a possibility that applied knowledge will not be appropriate. For example, clocks in airports and train stations are usually kept quite accurate, but this generalization may fail without warning—in one airport, many passengers missed their flights because the clocks had not been reset after the previous night's time change.

- **Changes in the world:** Even if an understander applies the correct knowledge when it first interprets a situation, the situation may change. For example, a luxurious house may change overnight from a good investment to a bad one, if the state decides to put a freeway through its front yard.

Because no real-world system can maintain perfect beliefs, the best that can be hoped for is to notice any problems that arise and to generate appropriate repairs. These are the belief maintenance issues faced by understanders of everyday events.

1.2   Maintaining Beliefs During Understanding

Belief maintenance depends on two things: deciding *when* beliefs need to be updated, and deciding *how* to update them. We consider these problems in the context of an understanding system that must maintain accurate beliefs and expectations despite partial information. In addition, we assume that the understander is part of a system with some overarching task (e.g., planning) that places additional requirements on the understanding process through task-specific needs for information. Thus our theory is one of belief maintenance in goal-driven understanding.

Our theory of goal-driven understanding involves four component processes: (a) routine understanding, (b) anomaly detection, (c) construction of explanations, and (d) evaluation of candidate explanations, to assure that the explanation selected provides sufficient information for the explainer to accomplish system goals.

Before looking at each of these processes in detail, we give a simple example of how the processes interact in a goal-based understander. Suppose Mary is waiting for the 12:20 bus to the airport, and the time is now 12:40. Failure of the bus to arrive is a failure of Mary's expectations and shows that her beliefs need to be revised. However, the importance of the failure does not arise from the abstract goal to have an accurate world model. Instead, it is important because it may affect her concrete plans and goals: She may be in danger of missing her plane. The explanation effort is motivated by her need to understand the situation in order to get to the airport on time.

Obviously, in order to respond to the unexpected problem, her routine understanding must include *anomaly detection*. If she did not notice the anomaly of the bus's failure to appear and simply waited at the bus stop, she might miss her flight. When she notices the delay, she needs to *construct an explanation*, in order to determine the appropriate response. If she explains the delay by a recent schedule change by the bus company, but knows that the bus should arrive in 5 minutes, she may wait. If she explains it by a bus strike, she needs to take a taxi. If the delay is caused by roads being closed to let a presidential motorcade cross the city, a taxi may not be faster, and she needs to take the subway instead.

As she looks for an explanation, she needs to be able to *evaluate candidate explanations*, to reject implausible candidates. For example, if a passerby explains the bus's failure to appear by the transit authority's cancellation of that route, she should reject that explanation if she saw a bus stop there earlier in the day. In addition, she must elaborate explanations that fail to give sufficient information. For example, if a passerby tells her that the bus broke down a few blocks away, it would be useful to know the cause of the breakdown, to estimate the delay before the bus could restart its route. Thus each of the four component processes in goal-driven understanding plays a crucial role.

1.3   Routine Understanding

Routine understanding is simply the integration of new information into prior knowledge. Recognizing the coherence of ideas is part of this integration: A program does not understand "Mary won a million dollars and took a trip around the world" unless it knows that her new wealth probably enabled the trip. The construction of chains representing such causal links is an important way to establish textual coherence [Schank, 1975].

One way to facilitate forming causal connections between events is to pre-package common chains in schemas or knowledge structures that can be applied as a unit to guide routine understanding [Schank & Abelson, 1977]. Once a knowledge structure has been selected to package an event, the appropriate causal connections are available with very low inference cost. Many AI models of understanding consider it primarily a process of finding an appropriate knowledge structure into which to fit the event, and applying that knowledge structure [Charniak, 1978; Cullingford, 1978; DeJong, 1979; Kolodner, 1984; Lebowitz, 1980; Minsky, 1975; Schank & Abelson, 1977]. A very simple example of this process is making sense of the sentence "Mary ordered lobster," by recognizing it as part of a restaurant meal. Once the knowledge structure for restaurant meals has been activated, it provides connections between Mary's ordering and likely prior events (we can assume that she entered the restaurant, and that she received a menu) as well as leading us to expect certain future events (such as her being served) without having to infer them from scratch.

As previously mentioned, much research effort has been devoted to the problem of selecting a knowledge structure to package an event, but little effort has been devoted to resolving problems that arise after a knowledge structure has been selected. These problems may be conflicts between external information and system beliefs and expectations, or conflicts between expectations that arise from multiple knowledge structures that are active simultaneously. For example, an understander might have a schema for the behavior of fraternity members at parties that includes excessive consumption of alcohol, as well as a schema for athletic training which prohibits such behavior. If both schemas were active simultaneously for a single person, accurate expectations would depend on noticing and resolving the conflict: deciding whether the person would refuse drinks, or would perform less well than normal in the next day's game.

> Understanding a fact requires more than placing it in a knowledge structure in memory: it depends on placing it in memory and *reconciling it with other active knowledge.*

Reconciling old and new information requires detecting when conflicts arise, in order to resolve them. This is the process of anomaly detection.

1.4   Detecting Anomalies

Intuitively, an anomaly is something that surprises us. Consequently, it might appear that being anomalous is a property of events in themselves. However, given any surprising event, we can imagine background knowledge that would render it mundane. It would usually be surprising for an elephant to trap someone in a telephone booth, but not within the context of a TV show like *Candid Camera*. In Chapter 3, we argue that being anomalous is a property of the interaction between events and context: Any particular fact can be anomalous or nonanomalous, depending on the situation and on the processing we are doing. A new fact is anomalous if we cannot reconcile it with other knowledge provided by the context that guides our understanding.

> Anomalies are conflicts between aspects of our active knowledge.

The success of anomaly detection depends on two things. First, it depends on applying a wide enough range of checks to detect a large proportion of conflicts. Second, it depends on restricting verification effort so that anomaly detection does not overburden the system's processing resources.

1.4.1   Anomaly Detection Must Consider Many Perspectives

Any event can be understood from many different perspectives; which one is appropriate depends on the active goals of the understander. If a friend buys something in a store, our explanation might focus on his motivation, to refine our expectations for his behavior—if he buys $10 worth of fishing lures, we may hypothesize that fishing is one of his hobbies. To the managers of a competing store, other aspects of the situation would be important: They might ask why he bought the lures where he did, rather than at their store, or why the price was so low.

If we were looking for a job, or if the cashier was a friend, we might instead explain why the cashier worked there as opposed to somewhere more pleasant. Or if the item being bought was itself new to us, we might ask for details on why it was preferable to standard models or how its uses or quality compared with those of similar products we had encountered, in order to decide whether we wanted to buy it. Each of these perspectives focuses on different gaps in the understander's knowledge, requiring different explanations.

However, previous understanding systems generally interpret situations from a single viewpoint. For example, SAM [Cullingford, 1978], FRUMP [DeJong, 1979], IPP [Lebowitz, 1980], and GENESIS [Mooney, 1990] activate schemas according to static criteria based on information such as the actor's location or the action being performed. (In learning systems such as IPP and GENESIS, the schema library changes, but for a given situation and state of the schema library, the same schema will always be selected.) Likewise, systems that generate explanations from scratch do so from fixed perspectives; for example, PAM [Wilensky, 1978], the explanation component of GENESIS, and Wimp [Goldman & Charniak, 1990] all have the fixed focus of accounting for the actor's plan.

In a complex situation, many aspects may be important to the understander simultaneously, each for a different reason. Each reason gives a perspective that shapes what the understander expects and how it understands. In the preceding example, someone might both be looking for a job and trying to decide where to buy fishing lures; these goals would require noticing and explaining different aspects of the situation.

> An evaluator must be able to verify a situation from many perspectives.

The richness of possible perspectives for understanding has been recognized in systems such as BORIS [Dyer, 1983] and FAUSTUS [Norvig, 1983] which simultaneously understand events in terms of a rich range of types of properties. The central question that arises is the potential cost involved: Which of the many possible perspectives actually merits an anomaly detection system's consideration?

1.4.2 Anomaly Detection Must Be Selective: Basic-Level Checks

Identifying all belief problems requires checking not just for direct conflicts between new information and prior beliefs but also for conflicts between all their ramifications. This level of verification involves enormous processing cost. Of course, failure to do sufficient anomaly detection has costs as well: Overlooking an anomaly allows faulty beliefs to stand, possibly leading to mistaken decisions that have serious repercussions. Therefore, ways are needed to achieve a reasonable level of verification without incurring excessive cost.

Previous research does not attempt to strike a balance between anomaly detection thoroughness and understanding efficiency: One is achieved at the expense of the other. For example, the story understanding system FRUMP blindly trusts its predictions. Although this gives considerable efficiency, the system has no capacity to detect understanding problems.

Rieger [1975] has investigated an approach closer to the other extreme: In Rieger's program, ramifications of each input are inferred until they are either confirmed by other beliefs or a conflict is found. This process gives thorough anomaly detection in principle but in practice is overwhelmingly expensive due to the combinatorial explosion of ramifications to consider. Belief maintenance systems (e.g., [Doyle, 1979]) achieve thoroughness in identifying indirectly conflicting beliefs *after* an initial direct conflict has been found, by recording all dependencies among the beliefs they derive and using the dependencies to guide belief revision. Some work has used dependency records to guide retraction of faulty beliefs generated during story understanding [Charniak, 1978; O'Rorke, 1983], but noticing that a new input conflicts with a system belief may still in principle require arbitrarily expensive inference chaining.

In this book, we strive for a middle ground: a sensible tradeoff between efficiency and thoroughness. When a system has goals in the world, accurate beliefs are not an end in themselves but a means to better performance; verification costs must be balanced against the value of the information they provide.

For example, if someone states a figure for the gross national product of Honduras, we will notice a problem if the figure is wildly unlikely, but if it is vaguely reasonable we will probably not try to verify further that it is true— the exact figure is unimportant to our actions. However, if a general in an early warning radar post sees a signal that seems to indicate the start of a nuclear attack, careful testing is essential before deciding that an attack has started and initiating a response.

> A real-world anomaly detection scheme should not verify indiscriminately: It should focus on facts worth checking.

One possible strategy would be to thoroughly verify only the beliefs that enter into important decisions. However, this approach would be mistaken. Detecting surprising situations early can save effort later, even if they are not important to current goals. A person without a car would have no direct motivation to notice the high price of parking when he visits New York, but knowing the price could prove useful in the future—for example, when deciding whether to drive to town with a friend or to take the train. If a system only tried to understand and verify information that was relevant to its current goals, it would miss information that might be helpful in the future. By the time the system noticed a problem, it might be much harder to make alternate plans. Once someone has driven to New York and noticed the high price of parking, it is too late to do anything but pay.

Consequently, an anomaly detection system needs routine checks that are sensitive enough to identify major problems but efficient enough not to impair processing. Further checks should be performed only when an input is implausible—when the standard checks find problems—or when additional certainty is important to the system's goals. This book focuses on issues related to routine checks; it does not address the question of how goals determine the thoroughness of anomaly detection.

We call the needed checks *basic level* checks. The idea of these checks is that there is a level at which anomaly detection maximizes the amount of return per unit of effort. Although fine grained checks would detect additional anomalies, they give proportionately less return, because they need to check specialized aspects of the situation that will be irrelevant to many situations. Consequently, only a screening by basic checks is worthwhile during routine processing.

> Evaluators need a basic level of verification that can efficiently find most problems.

In order to implement a basic verification level, we need a way to detect problems without extensive inference.

1.4.3 Controlling Inference in Anomaly Detection

In principle, looking for conflicts between new information and old beliefs is an explosive inference problem: many levels of ramifications of old and new information might have to be checked before finding a conflict. This book presents a solution to that inference problem: replacing the inference process with table lookup. Rather than inferring the consequences of new inputs, a program can check their reasonableness by searching an abstraction hierarchy of stereotyped patterns, looking for explicitly stored information. Inputs that conflict with this information are anomalous; inputs that are confirmed are considered reasonable. When no relevant information is found, the verification effort simply fails.

> Verification effort can be controlled by using table lookup: restricting verification of inputs to comparison with prestored patterns in memory.

In order to develop and evaluate this approach, we need to answer three questions: which tables are needed, what information they contain, and how effectively those tables cover the space of possible anomalies. We examine these questions in Chapters 3 and 4.

1.5   Learning by Explaining Anomalies

When anomalies are detected, an understander needs to revise its knowledge to account for the surprising circumstances. This can involve both changing its view of the current situation, and learning new schemas or rules to improve its performance in similar future situations. Crucial to the process of forming new schemas is identifying the important features of the new events.

Much research in machine learning has centered on inductive learning methods, which form category descriptions by generalizing from correlations between the features in sample category instances (see Dietterich and Michalski [1983] for a comparative review). However, because inductive methods base their generalizations only on correlations, spurious correlations can lead them astray. On limited sets of data, inductive learners often make faulty generalizations, some of which are very unlikely to be considered by people. For example, when the inductive learner IPP processed stories about two bombings in India, each of which resulted in two deaths, it generalized that bombings in India always kill two people [Lebowitz, 1980]. In addition, unlike people, who often learn from single episodes, inductive systems are helpless to deal with single-example learning. (For further discussion of these problems and others, see Schank at al. [1986].)

Explanation-based learning (EBL) is an alternative method that avoids the problems of inductive approaches. Given an example category member, an explanation is built to show *why* the example belongs to the category, and that explanation is used to distinguish its important features from coincidental ones. Consequently, EBL systems can often learn useful generalizations from a single episode or category instance [DeJong & Mooney, 1986; Mitchell et al., 1986].

For example, if two football teams are expected to be evenly matched, but one team wins overwhelmingly in their latest game, an explanation of the anomalous margin will show which features are responsible. If the winning team did better than expected because of playing particularly hard, in order to avenge an insult from the other team's quarterback, that explanation of the victory can be generalized to form a rule to improve future predictions: A competitor's desire for revenge can make it play above its normal level. The explanation makes it possible to discount coincidental features such as a new chant the players recited before the game, the cold weather when the game was played (even if weather was also cold the day of the only previous lopsided victory), and the number of people in the stadium: It shows that desire for revenge is the key factor in understanding the rout.

The intuitive and practical appeal of explanation-based methods has made them the subject of much research in AI. For concept recognition tasks, explanations of why an exemplar belongs to a concept are used to formulate concept descriptions in terms of easily observable features, to allow the recognition of concept members at low cost. For example, from an instance of a cup and knowledge of its function as a graspable container for liquid, explanation-based generalization can determine that important features for recognizing other cups include handles (which make cups graspable) and appropriate concavities (which make them containers for liquid) [Winston et al., 1983; Mitchell et al., 1986]. For schema acquisition, EBL systems explain why an observed plan is successful and use the explanation to guide abstraction in building plan schemas with wider applicability [DeJong & Mooney, 1986; Mooney, 1990; Segre, 1988]. In addition, some psychological support has been provided for the role of explanation in human schema acquisition [Ahn et al., 1987] and in the ability to predict outcomes [Pazzani, 1990, pp. 174–177].

In this book we investigate how explanation-based processing can be applied most effectively in an understanding system: how to detect the anomalies that signal the need for explanation, and how to guide the search for worthwhile explanations of those anomalies.

1.5.1 Why explanation should be anomaly-driven

Deciding when to learn is an important part of learning effectively. However, research on explanation-based learning usually concentrates on the process arising after decisions of what to learn have been made externally (e.g., [Mitchell et al., 1986]). In systems that do decide for themselves when to learn, the standard approach is to learn in response to every observed instance of successful behavior that is not already characterized by a system schema, as in [Mooney, 1990; Segre, 1987]. We take a different view: that explanation effort should be applied more selectively. A real-world domain is likely to contain so many potential subjects for explanation that it would be overwhelmingly expensive to attempt to explain without additional focus; in addition, much of that learning could be irrelevant to actual system tasks. Our view, like that of Hammond [1989a], is that explanation effort should be applied primarily in response to problems: when inadequacies in previous knowledge cause the system to fail at its task. For a system doing routine understanding, there is no reason to explain as long as new information seems reasonable—as long as prior knowledge is consistent with new information. Explanation is only needed when understanding fails: when the system encounters an anomaly.

The explanation process should be triggered by anomalies.

By explaining only in response to anomalies, a system can avoid unnecessary effort. In addition, the explanation construction problem is simpler, because explanation of unexpected failures can be a more focused process

than explanations of success. An explanation of a failure needs only to identify the unexpected problems, rather than to account for all the factors on
which the success depended [Hammond, 1989a].

1.5.2 The need for explanation evaluation

It is obvious that the results of any explanation-based method can only be as
good as the explanation used as its starting point. In the preceding example
of explaining a team's victory, it would be disastrous to explain the victory
by the team's special chant: In that case, explanation-based learning would
cause us to expect victories by teams that chant, or perhaps those that have
bizarre customs. A generalization of a bad explanation is even worse than
the bad explanation itself, because use of the resultant rule will lead the
system astray more often. Consequently, any explanation-based system needs
ways to assure that it starts from explanations that will guide it to the right
conclusions.

The need for evaluation is especially great in creative explanation systems.
Because explanation builds new structures extending the explainer's ability
to process new situations, explanation is in principle a creative process.[2] Of
course, in any situation it is possible to offer explanations at very different
levels of creativity, ranging from extremely straightforward to highly creative.
Schank [1986] argues that in order for explanation construction to realize its
full creative potential, its processing should be relatively unconstrained, risk-
ing unreasonable results in order to have the potential of creative ones as
well. Sometimes, this will lead to breakthroughs; other times it will lead to
completely invalid hypotheses. Evaluation of explanations is vital to distinguish between the two, so that a system can benefit from inspired leaps and
avoid being mislead by those that are merely bizarre.

1.6   What Is a Good Explanation?

In our view, evaluation of explanations for anomalous events must consider
three factors: the explanation's plausibility (or believability), its relevance to
the anomaly, and its usefulness. We introduce these factors next. In Chapter
2, we present a detailed comparison of our criteria to those of previous theories
of explanation evaluation.

Plausibility: Because anomalies highlight surprising events, a natural goal
for explanation of anomalies is to demonstrate why the anomalous situation

---

[2]The relationship between creativity and explanation is beyond the scope of this book
but is discussed in Schank and Leake [1989] and treated extensively in Schank [1986].

actually makes sense—why it is a reasonable consequence of prior circumstances. To give a convincing account, the explanation must provide a plausible derivation of the situation from reasonable causes.

Explanation-based learning treats explanations as deductive proofs built from correct rules [Mitchell et al., 1986]. In that framework, any explanation with the proper form is guaranteed to be valid—no additional plausibility checks are needed. This book examines issues of everyday explanations, which are abductive accounts involving uncertain premises and imperfect rules. For any real-world situation, it is possible to build countless explanations with appropriate structure, only some of which are plausible.

Given any event to explain, and any event as a candidate for its cause, a person can probably think of a way to derive the event from the candidate cause, even when the candidate cause is unlikely to actually be related.[3] For example, despite the implausibility of any connection between a rise in the price of pork futures, and an opera-goer getting a parking ticket, we can imagine many ways in which they could be connected, such as:

> When the price rose, a local investment club knew it would reap large profits, so its members decided to celebrate in a fine restaurant near the opera. Members took all free parking spaces, making area parking impossible to find. The opera-goer decided to park illegally rather than miss the curtain. As a result, the opera-goer got a parking ticket.

This explanation has a reasonable *form* but is not especially plausible, and we could imagine many alternative explanations as well.

Many explanations can be generated for any event, and only some of them are plausible.

AI methods for choosing the most plausible explanation often use content-independent structural criteria (e.g., [McDermott, 1974; Ng & Mooney, 1990; Pazzani, 1988; Thagard, 1989]). Instead, we argue for a model of plausibility evaluation that considers an explanation's content as well as its form, relying primarily on the explanation's consistency with the explainer's prior knowledge.

Our model of explanation evaluation also differs from traditional approaches in giving vital importance to factors beyond plausibility. While

---

[3]While most of our examples involve explanations of what caused an event, note that explanations may also trace a noncausal derivation of why its occurrence should be believed. For example, we may explain the *belief* that a horse is in good physical condition by having read about its condition in a newspaper, even though the newspaper account has no effect on the horse's condition.

many approaches consider the "best explanation" to be simply "the explanation most likely to be valid," we claim that the notion of a "best" explanation is meaningless without considering the overarching task—the best explanation is the one that best satisfies the explainer's needs for information. Need-based considerations are reflected in our remaining two criteria.

Relevance: Research on explanation-based schema acquisition has treated explanation as context-neutral, with the same event always explained in the same way regardless of other circumstances. However, people with different previous knowledge may require very different explanations of a single situation. For example, if a car that was badly assembled breaks down soon after being bought, a plausible explanation might be "the car was badly assembled." If the buyer had not known of the assembly problems before the breakdown, that explanation might be relevant. To the unknowing buyer, the anomaly might be that the car failed prematurely for a new car, and the explanation provides new information showing why the car did not live up to new-car expectations. However, if the buyer *had* known about the bad assembly before buying the car and had concluded that none of the defects would affect the car's performance, the anomaly would be different: It might be that events conflicted with the previous conclusion. Because prior reasoning already took assembly problems into account, "the car was badly assembled" provides no new information. An explanation relevant to the anomaly would have to show why the buyer's assessment of the severity of the assembly problems was wrong—perhaps the combination of multiple defects had unexpected ramifications.

> To be relevant to an anomaly, explanations must resolve the belief conflict underlying the anomaly.

Usefulness: Even when an explanation is plausible and relevant to the anomaly, it may not be useful. "The car was badly assembled" is not a very helpful explanation for a driver who is stranded on the side of the highway and wants to repair the car to drive to the next town. To accomplish the repair goal, the driver needs information that will point to the specific defects that need repair.

> Good explanations must serve the explainer's overarching goals.

Often, explainers need to accurately characterize specific types of causes of an event (e.g., the defect that caused a car to break down). However, even accuracy may take second place to usefulness. For example, consider the following scene from the movie *Breaking Away:*

> A used-car salesman is taking a prospective buyer out on a test drive. He stops suddenly to avoid a cyclist, and the car dies. He tries frantically to start it, but he can't. He explains to the buyer: "Damn. You know what I did. I think I put premium gas in this baby by mistake. It hates expensive gas."

Although the salesman does not believe the explanation, it is excellent for his purposes: Not only does it divert blame from the car's mechanical condition, but it also introduces a new factor to sway the buyer towards buying it, that it is inexpensive to operate. Thus the fundamental criterion for goodness of explanations is simply whether the explainer can use them successfully. The role of explanation is not to enumerate plausible causes of an event: It is to provide the information that is needed for the explainer's goals.

1.7   Constructing Explanations

The traditional approach to explanation construction is to build each explanation from scratch by chaining together basic rules or operators. A problem with this method is well known: the combinatorial explosion of alternatives to consider makes it extremely costly for all but simple cases [Rieger, 1975].

Schank [1986] proposes an alternative approach: explaining by retrieving and adapting previous explanations stored in memory. This process is an application of case-based reasoning (CBR), an approach that is the subject of growing investigation [Ashley, 1990; Bareiss, 1989; Carbonell, 1986; Hammond, 1989a; Kolodner, 1987; Koton, 1988; Schank, 1983; Schank, 1986; Simpson, 1985; Sycara, 1987]. Case-based explanation allows an explainer to reuse prior effort, and offers the potential advantage of generating explanations more likely to be valid, because similar past experience supports them.

In principle, case-based systems improve performance with experience: as their case libraries grow, they are more likely to have applicable prior cases in memory. Whether this is borne out in practice depends on how the cases are organized in memory—whether retrieval can be guided towards the right cases. How to focus retrieval is a well-known problem being addressed by many different approaches for different tasks (for a summary of some approaches, see Hammond [1989b], pp. 25-44).

We address the retrieval issues in case-based explanation by developing a theory of anomaly and explanation that can be used to organize explanatory information in memory. This vocabulary organizes both specific explanations, and general information to aid in constructing explanations when no relevant prior cases are available. We return to the design of the vocabulary, and present a particular theory of anomaly characterization, in Chapters 5, 6, and 7.

1.8   Implementing the Theory

We have implemented our theory in the computer program ACCEPTER, which performs pattern-based anomaly detection and dynamic, need-driven explanation evaluation. The purpose of ACCEPTER is to be a first-order test of our theory, to test the theory's contributions and limitations.

ACCEPTER is a story understanding program. As it understands, it monitors its understanding for anomalies, and responds to the anomalies it finds by characterizing them to facilitate search for explanations. It retrieves explanations indexed under similar anomalies, and evaluates the retrieved explanations according to their relevance to the anomaly being explained and their usefulness for overarching goals.

> ACCEPTER explains in order to fill specific gaps in its knowl-
> edge and judges explanations in terms of goals to be served
> by the explanation effort.

ACCEPTER only addresses issues of anomaly detection/characterization and explanation evaluation, rather than including a component to conduct explanation adaptation; the program is designed to be embedded within a larger case-based explanation system that would use information from AC-CEPTER to guide its adaptation. Ideas on ACCEPTER's role in such a system have been tested in SWALE [Kass, 1986; Kass & Leake, 1988; Leake & Owens, 1986; Schank & Leake, 1989], a case-based explanation system which performs retrieval and adaptation of explanations in memory, based on the anomaly characterizations that ACCEPTER generates.

Likewise, although ACCEPTER generates its own goals to repair flawed beliefs, it relies on an overarching planning system to decide which additional goals explanation should serve. In the current stand-alone implementation of ACCEPTER, the system's goal-based evaluation procedures are exercised by having a human user select general tasks for the explanation to serve, such as preventing an outcome in the future or repairing an undesirable state.

Figure 1.1 summarizes ACCEPTER's basic understanding process. The program takes as input a story in which each fact is represented either in terms of the primitives of Conceptual Dependency (CD) theory [Schank, 1972], or in terms of MOPs (Memory Organization Packages) [Schank, 1982], which represent stereotyped action sequences in terms of CD primitives and other

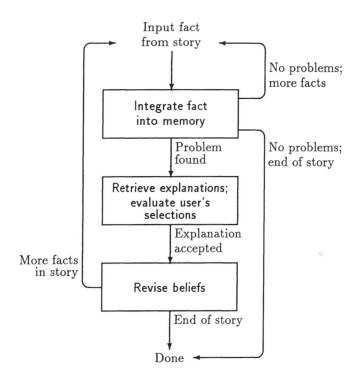

FIG. 1.1.   ACCEPTER's basic understanding process.

MOPs. (MOPs are described in detail in section 3.2.1.) ACCEPTER processes one fact of a story at a time, sequentially building up expectations for succeeding events.

As ACCEPTER integrates each fact of a story into memory, it uses pattern-based anomaly detection to detect any anomalies that arise. The anomalies it finds are presented to the user, along with candidate explanations retrieved from ACCEPTER's library of standard explanations. Those explanations are stored in the program's memory as *explanation patterns* (XPs) [Schank, 1986], which are belief dependency chains tracing how the anomalous state or event (called the explanation's consequent) can plausibly be inferred from a set of assumptions (called the explanation's antecedents). We describe XPs' structure more fully in section 8.1.1. For compactness, in examples we will sometimes call a set of facts an "explanation" of an event, but we consider the actual explanation to be the entire dependency chain.

ACCEPTER's XP library is organized by anomaly types. It selects explanations to retrieve by characterizing the current anomaly according to its anomaly type, and retrieving explanations for similar types of anomalies. It presents the retrieved explanations to a human user, who successively selects those for ACCEPTER to evaluate. Little effort has been expended on the user interface; it would be desirable to allow the user to interactively specify modifications to repair the problems ACCEPTER finds, but in the present version it is necessary to add variants of explanations to the explanation library in order to allow that cycle to be pursued. However, ACCEPTER has been used as part of a case-based explanation system that adapts its own explanations, guided by ACCEPTER's problem characterizations; we describe that process in Chapter 2.

The following sections sketch each of the ACCEPTER's processing phases in more detail, illustrating them with brief traces of program output. The following chapter contains a trace of a complete ACCEPTER run.

1.8.1   Routine Understanding and Anomaly Detection

Because anomalies are failures of the beliefs and expectations built during routine understanding, any theory of anomaly detection needs to be based on a theory of what it means to understand. ACCEPTER understands routine events in terms of expectations based on prestored schemas; its expectation-based processing is modeled on the routine understanding process used in SAM [Cullingford, 1978]. When a fact is placed in an existing schema, the schema provides a routine explanation for the event.

However, ACCEPTER's schema activation is different from SAM's, and more dynamic: Rather than basing schema activation solely on the situation being described, it tries to activate schemas focusing on the situation's ramifications *on known actors*. The same situation will be understood in different ways, depending on which of the involved actors the system has encountered previously and is tracking during its processing. For example, ACCEPTER generates different schemas to understand a horse-racing victory if it is already tracking the jockey (in which case it considers the win's effect on the jockey's career) than if it is tracking the horse (in which case it considers the race in terms of the horse's future).

ACCEPTER's schema activation is actor-oriented.

ACCEPTER's anomaly detection monitors the reasonableness of the expectations and beliefs provided by its routine understanding. It implements a theory of when routine explanation is insufficient, and how tests for problems can be integrated into the understanding process by using table lookup to control verification inference. Its tables contain patterns for actor-based stereotypes, prohibitions, functional limitations, and the normative role-fillers associated with common actions (we describe them in detail in Chapter 4).

When processing a new fact, ACCEPTER applies pattern-based tests to detect potential problems and uses more thorough (though still restricted) tests to characterize the problems those tests find.

ACCEPTER uses a three-phase process to accept new information. In the first phase, it compares new information with prior beliefs and active expectations. To facilitate conflict detection, ACCEPTER represents both expectations for events that should happen, and prohibitions—predictions that certain events will *not* happen, because they conflict with other active knowledge. When expected events fail to occur, or prohibited events take place, the failure is symptomatic of problems in the system's model.

The following output shows the first phase of ACCEPTER's routine understanding, for the input *Audi does quality control on its cars.*[4]

```
Processing:  There is a M-QUALITY-CONTROL with AUDI as its
INSPECTOR.

Doing routine understanding of input ...

Phase 1:  Trying to recognize fact as known or expected.

          Checking if "AUDI'S M-QUALITY-CONTROL" is already known,
          or conflicts with facts in memory.
          ... No relevant belief found.

          Checking if "AUDI'S M-QUALITY-CONTROL" is expected from
          (or prohibited by) active MOPs.
          ... No relevant expectations found.
```

The fact of Audi's quality control is not already known or expected, nor does it directly contradict an explicit prior belief or expectation. Consequently, ACCEPTER begins the second phase of its processing: pattern-based anomaly detection. When new information does not directly relate to information in memory, ACCEPTER decides whether it is likely to be inconsistent with old information by comparing it to standard patterns explicitly represented in memory. In that way, ACCEPTER detects likely problems without the cost of computing and comparing the ramifications of old and new information.

> ACCEPTER uses pattern-based checks to identify potential problems with low processing cost.

---

[4]As stated earlier, all stories are input to the system in a conceptual representation. In what follows, we show the English equivalents of the actual inputs. In this and following program examples, some output has been edited for readability.

The output that follows traces the stereotypes that ACCEPTER considers when deciding whether Audi's quality control is routine or whether further explanation is needed. It first looks at stereotypes associated with both action and actor, to see if the combination is reasonable. After finding a general confirmation, it looks for specific limitations of the current role-fillers compared with the normal fillers for their roles, to see if those limitations might cause problems. Because no relevant limitations are found, ACCEPTER accepts the quality control as routine.

```
Phase 2:  Judging plausibility by comparing to patterns.
   Checking if the role-fillers of "AUDI'S M-QUALITY-CONTROL"
   are reasonable.

      Checking if action/actor combination makes sense.

         Checking behavior patterns of AUDI and abstractions,
         to see if INSPECTOR of M-QUALITY-CONTROL is a usual
         role.

            Looking under AUDI-CORPORATION for patterns.
            ... No relevant patterns under AUDI-CORPORATION.

            Looking under MANUFACTURING-COMPANY for patterns.
            ... No relevant patterns under MANUFACTURING-COMPANY.

            Looking under FOREIGN-COMPANY for patterns.
            ... No relevant patterns under FOREIGN-COMPANY.

            Looking under HIGH-PERFORMANCE-PRODUCT-COMPANY
            for patterns.

         ... AUDI'S M-QUALITY-CONTROL CONFIRMS expectations
         from the role-filling pattern
         "HIGH-PERFORMANCE-PRODUCT-COMPANYs routinely fill role
         INSPECTOR in M-QUALITY-CONTROL".

         Checking AUDI for limitations compared to generalized
         MANUFACTURING-COMPANYs, to see if they cause problems
         filling the role INSPECTOR of AUDI'S M-QUALITY-CONTROL.

         Searching up the abstraction net for limitations

         ... No relevant limitations found.
```

Unless there is an anomaly, understanding is adequate: no further explanation is needed. Because nothing about the input fact is surprising, ACCEPTER simply installs the fact in memory and generates routine expectations for the events it suggests: Audi manufacturing some object and inspecting it to assure that the product has no defects:[5]

```
Phase 3:   Installing input in memory and updating expectations.

  Activating expectations/prohibitions from AUDI'S
  M-QUALITY-CONTROL.
     Expectations:
        AUDI AS MANUFACTURER OF MANUFACTURED-OBJECT-199.
        AUDI'S M-INSPECTION.
     Prohibited states/events:
        MANUFACTURED-OBJECT-199'S LOW MECHANICAL-CONDITION.
```

1.8.2 Finding an Anomaly

The facts that ACCEPTER stores during routine understanding, and the expectations based on those facts, become the context in which new inputs are understood. The following output shows processing of a new input that conflicts with the context built during the processing just discussed: the fact that Joe's Audi was recalled in the 1987 Audi recall.

```
Processing input:
   There is a M-CAR-RECALL with JOE as its CAR-OWNER,
   AUDI as its MANUFACTURER, and AUDI'S CAR as its CAR.
```

The first phases of routine understanding for this information detect no problems. The recall was not known or expected, but recalls by car companies are fairly common, so there is no immediate conflict with stereotypes. However, when the system considers the standard components of a recall, it detects an anomaly. The steps in ACCEPTER's MOP for automotive recalls are that a car has a defect, its owner takes it to be repaired, the company repairs it, and the owner takes it back. Existence of the defect that initiates the

---

[5]ACCEPTER generates names for unnamed objects by concatenating the object type and a unique identifying number. For example, the following output sample refers to the manufactured object as MANUFACTURED-OBJECT-199.

recall conflicts with a prior expectation: that Audi's quality control prevents defects.[6]

Phase 3:   Installing input in memory and updating expectations.

  Activating expectations/prohibitions from AUDI'S M-CAR-RECALL.
    Expectations:
      AUDI'S CAR'S LOW MECHANICAL-CONDITION.
      JOE'S PTRANS.
      AUDI'S M-REPAIR.
      JOE'S PTRANS.

  Recursively using routine understanding to check believability
  of expectations/prohibitions from AUDI'S M-CAR-RECALL.

  Checking expectation for AUDI'S CAR'S LOW MECHANICAL-CONDITION
  from AUDI'S M-CAR-RECALL.

  Phase 1: Trying to recognize fact as known or expected.

    Checking if "AUDI'S CAR'S LOW MECHANICAL-CONDITION"
    is already known, or conflicts with facts in memory.

    ... No relevant belief found.

    Checking if "AUDI'S CAR'S LOW MECHANICAL-CONDITION"
    is expected from (or prohibited by) active MOPs.

      Problem detected installing "AUDI'S CAR has
      LOW as its MECHANICAL-CONDITION" in memory:
      the prohibition of MANUFACTURED-OBJECT-199'S
      LOW MECHANICAL-CONDITION due to AUDI'S M-QUALITY-CONTROL.

      Specifying the anomaly characterization: Since
      a plan to prevent it was in effect, the event
      is a PLAN-EXECUTION-FAILURE problem.

Anomaly detected!
  AUDI'S CAR'S LOW MECHANICAL-CONDITION CONFLICTS-WITH prohibition
  for MANUFACTURED-OBJECT-199'S LOW MECHANICAL-CONDITION due to
  AUDI'S M-QUALITY-CONTROL.

---

[6]The following output uses the Conceptual Dependency Theory primitive PTRANS to represent the change of location of an object.

Thus ACCEPTER infers from the recall that Joe's Audi is defective, which conflicts with its expectation that Audi's quality control prevents defects. The conflict reveals that explanation is needed to repair the faulty reasoning that led to the erroneous expectation.

1.8.3 Searching for explanations

Because ACCEPTER's choice to explain is motivated by the need to repair failed reasoning, an explanation will only satisfy its needs if it accounts for the reasoning failure. Consequently, ACCEPTER may require very different explanations of the same event, depending on context.

> ACCEPTER focuses its explanation effort on filling current gaps in its knowledge.

ACCEPTER's dynamic focusing of explanation differs from that of traditional explanation-based understanding systems, which always focus on a predetermined aspect of the situation: the actors' goals. A system that always focused on actors' goals might explain the recall by *the manufacturer ordered the recall in order to avoid bad publicity.* However, although that explanation might be a good account of the motivation involved, it is irrelevant to the current anomaly, which is that quality control failed. By searching for explanations that account for the anomaly, rather than accepting any explanation of the current event, ACCEPTER assures that its explanations will provide the information it needs.

ACCEPTER's process of explanation search is memory-based: It characterizes the anomaly to be explained and uses that characterization as an index for retrieving explanatory information. Its anomaly characterizations organize a memory of prior explanations, represented as XPs; they would also be appropriate to organize general *explanation strategies* [Hammond, 1987] for broad classes of anomalies.

> ACCEPTER characterizes anomalies to index into explanatory information stored in memory.

For example, the characterization of the problem with Audi's quality control is *plan execution failure: quality control.* An XP retriever could use this characterization as an index to retrieve XPs accounting for quality control breakdowns, such as *too few inspectors, product deteriorated between inspection and sale,* or *quality control can't catch problems that only arise in rare situations.* After forming the characterization, ACCEPTER does not do further selection: It presents the user with a list of all XPs stored in its library under the anomaly class, and the user selects the explanation from that set to consider.

1.8.4 Evaluating Candidate Explanations

Once an XP is suggested, its goodness must be decided. As observed before, plausibility is often important—a doctor will want to be extremely certain of the explanation for a problem before ordering surgery to correct it.

As previously mentioned, AI research on plausibility evaluation concentrates on the form of the explanation, rather than the content of the beliefs it involves. Some evaluation schemes favor explanations requiring the fewest new assumptions [McDermott, 1974; Pazzani, 1988]; other schemes use structural criteria to judge explanations' coherence [Ng & Mooney, 1990; Thagard, 1989]. Such structural judgments are the only way to assess plausibility in the absence of domain information, but in a familiar domain, the *content* of an explanation can be crucially important. For example, the explanation that a child is absent from school because of illness would usually be more plausible than one attributing the absence to kidnapping, even if each explanation requires only one new assumption, simply because of our world knowledge that illness is more likely than kidnapping.

ACCEPTER judges plausibility based on its world knowledge. It rejects hypotheses that conflict with its knowledge of common events; it believes explanations if their hypotheses are consistent with its prior beliefs, active expectations, and stereotypes about the world.

> ACCEPTER bases its plausibility evaluation on its prior beliefs and its knowledge of standard patterns.

Beyond Believability: How Goals Drive Evaluation

ACCEPTER is driven by two types of goals. First, it is driven by its goal as an understander to make sense of the stories it processes and account for anomalies in order to repair flaws in its world model to avoid future understanding failures. Second, it is driven by additional goals, selected by an external user, to gather information needed to respond to the surprising situation.

Accounting for Anomalies to Avoid Future Failures

Avoiding future understanding failures requires explaining why expectations failed. ACCEPTER's explanation retrieval scheme guides the search for explanations towards those likely to give useful information, because ACCEPTER's anomaly characterizations organize explanations by the failures they explain.

However, it is still necessary to verify that a retrieved explanation actually does account for why current reasoning went wrong. ACCEPTER judges this by checking whether the explanation shows factors that led to the surprising situation but were overlooked or assumed false when the original prediction was formed. The failure to consider those factors accounts for why the faulty expectation was generated, and shows how to avoid future failures: The system can check for those factors in the future, and by expecting the current situation, rather than the previously expected one, whenever they hold. Chapter 8 describes ACCEPTER's relevance evaluation in more detail.

Finding Information for Overarching Goals

Expectation failures show that the world is different from what was expected, and that difference may have serious ramifications for what will happen in the future. If someone owns a stock and sees that its price is twice what he thought it was, he will not be content with the explanation "an unusually large number of people wanted to buy it," even though that explanation is relevant to the change. A useful explanation will give him the information needed to update his plans for buying and selling—the news underlying the change in sentiment about the company's potential.

Integrating goals into the evaluation process requires a theory of the tasks that an explanation can serve, and of how those tasks are translated into heuristics for evaluating explanations. Criteria for a number of tasks are implemented in ACCEPTER. The program's user selects the tasks to influence evaluation, and the system judges the explanation according to criteria based on those tasks.

For example, consider the following hypothetical explanations for the Audi recall. Each answers the question "why was there a defect, despite Audi's quality control?"

1. The mechanical problems resulted from the car being manufactured by Acme Car Company, under contract as a supplier. Acme has bad quality control, leading to the defect.

2. The defect resulted from a flaw in the transmissions, which are not checked by Audi's quality control department.

Neither explanation holds for the actual recall incident, but it would in principle be possible for both the explanations to fit the facts of a recall. However, the following output shows that even if both were valid, they would not be equally useful to a mechanic. A mechanic needs to find a current state that can be repaired; causes of the problem that happened in the past but no longer affect the situation cannot be repaired. Consequently, attributing the problem to prior subcontracting and bad quality control is insufficient from the mechanic's point of view:

```
Checking detail for repair.
  To aid in repair, explanation must show a cause that:
    1. Is repairable.
    2. Is predictive of the problem occurring.
    3. Will not be restored by another state if repaired.

    Checking whether some antecedent satisfies the following
    tests:  CAUSAL FORCE TEST (does fact cause consequent?),
    REPAIRABILITY, PREDICTIVENESS, and INDEPENDENT CAUSE.

      Applying test for REPAIRABILITY to AUDI'S
      PRODUCTION-CONTRACT to ACME.

        Searching up abstraction net for pointers to standard
        repair plans.

        ... test failed.

      Applying test for REPAIRABILITY to ACME'S NOT
      M-QUALITY-CONTROL.

        Searching up abstraction net for pointers to standard
        repair plans.

        ... test failed.

      ... Detail is unacceptable.
```

The second explanation involves two factors that continue to contribute to the car's bad condition: the transmission's bad condition, and the fact that it is part of the car. ACCEPTER finds that a plan exists for correcting one of them, so that a repair can be done:

```
Applying test for REPAIRABILITY to TRANSMISSION-743'S
PART-OF-RELATIONSHIP to AUDI'S ENGINE.

  Checking repairability of features of TRANSMISSION-743'S
  PART-OF-RELATIONSHIP to AUDI'S ENGINE.

    Searching up abstraction net for pointers to standard
    repair plans.
```

```
AUDI'S ENGINE AS CONTAINER OF TRANSMISSION-743'S
PART-OF-RELATIONSHIP to AUDI'S ENGINE is repairable, since
CONTAINERs of PART-OF-RELATIONSHIPs can usually be repaired
by the standard plan REPLACE-COMPONENT.

... test passed.

... Detail is acceptable.
```

However, to a new car buyer the usefulness of the two explanations would be reversed: An explanation that predicts quality control problems in an entire line of cars is more useful than one that only identifies the defect in a single car. Thus static evaluation criteria are insufficient; what determines an explanation's goodness will change with changing explainer goals.

> ACCEPTER's explanation evaluation dynamically reflects current overarching goals.

1.9   Significance for Explanation-Based Systems

The preceding examples sketch ACCEPTER's ability to detect problems without costly inference and its capability for dynamic explanation evaluation. They illustrate how our theory extends the capabilities of explanation-based systems in three areas:

Detecting when to learn: In order to learn effectively, a system needs to focus learning on important gaps in its knowledge. In an understander, these gaps are revealed by anomalies. However, the inference involved in detecting anomalies is in principle enormously expensive. The more complex the domain, the more anomaly detection is needed, but the more costly anomaly detection becomes. We present a solution to the problem of inference cost in anomaly detection: Replacing inference by table lookup. The success of such an approach depends on being able to identify a limited set of tables providing sufficient coverage of anomalies; we develop a theory of the specific types of tables needed to detect everyday anomalies and substantiate their generality.

Guiding explanation construction: Our theory of anomaly types provides a means for organizing explanations by the anomalies they resolve, to guide search for explanations stored in memory. This makes it practical to replace traditional chaining methods of explanation construction with case-based explanation, facilitating explanation construction and increasing the quality of the explanations produced.

Learning useful things from an explanation: Once a system finds a gap in its knowledge, it needs to fill it in order to avoid future problems. Explanation-based approaches are powerful tools for dealing with new situations, but they do not assure that an explainer will learn useful concepts— they cannot give good results if applied to explanations that are invalid or that fail to provide the information the explainer needs. We show how a system can reject explanations that are implausible or fail to focus on the important parts of the situation, in order to do useful learning from explanations.

The value of goal-based evaluation goes beyond allowing explainers to reject explanations that do not satisfy their needs: It extends the range of situations that a program can deal with, by giving a way for programs to apply explanation-based learning to situations that are too complex for them to explain completely. Consequently, the theory contributes in an additional area:

Learning from partial explanations: EBL systems require complete deductive proofs as the starting point for their learning; they do not learn from situations in which, due to lack of information or other factors, only a partial derivation can be built.[7] However, people learn from situations even if they cannot construct a definitive explanation. For example, suppose someone notices that her car sometimes fails to start on cold days and decides that the cold is one of the factors contributing to the problem. She has not found necessary conditions for failure to start, because it probably fails to start under other circumstances as well; she has not found sufficient conditions, because the failure is intermittent even in cold weather. Nevertheless, she can learn what she needs to know from her partial explanation. Because she knows that cold is one of the factors involved, she can prevent the problem by keeping her car in the garage on cold nights.

Sometimes an explanation must show sufficient conditions in order to account for the feature being explained; sometimes such thoroughness is unnecessary. Systems that treat explanations as being neutral to the overarching task must always apply the same criteria, which will necessarily be too strong

---

[7]Note that although use of an approximate domain theory may make it easier for EBL systems to construct explanations, EBL always requires explanations to show sufficient conditions for concept membership according to the domain theory being used.

for some tasks in order to be strong enough for all uses. Our goal-based evaluation criteria give a dynamic way to determine whether a partial explanation gives adequate information. The ability to use partial explanations allows systems to learn in complex situations that they cannot completely explain, extending the applicability of explanation-based approaches to complicated situations that are not well understood—in which learning may be needed most.

1.10   The Following Chapters

The problems this book confronts can be summarized as deciding what to explain and deciding how to explain it, under the constraints that face understanders in complex and uncertain domains. Resolving these issues is central to making effective use of explanations to understand, learn from, and respond to novel situations.

In the following chapter, we put our ideas into perspective by tracing in more detail their ramifications for the behavior of a computer model, and by comparing them with previous viewpoints on explanation and explanation evaluation. In later chapters, we elucidate the theory for each step of the understanding and explanation processes: anomaly detection, search for explanations, and evaluation of the candidate explanations retrieved.

2 Perspective on the Theory

We place our theory in perspective of both its practical and theoretical ramifications. From a practical point of view, we describe how AC-CEPTER can guide explanation in a case-based explanation system, and illustrate the system's processing. We then take a more theoretical view, highlighting how our theory relates to previous views on explanation from Artificial Intelligence, psychology, and philosophy.

ACCEPTER is designed as part of a bigger system. Its main functions—anomaly detection, anomaly characterization, and explanation evaluation—are important because of their effect on the performance of an explanation system using them to provide guidance. In this chapter, we place our theory in context, showing why ACCEPTER confronts the problems it does, and the significance of the methods it applies.

Early versions of ACCEPTER were developed as part of SWALE,[1] a story understanding program developed at the Yale Artificial Intelligence laboratory [Kass, 1986; Kass & Leake, 1988; Leake & Owens, 1986; Schank, 1986; Schank & Leake, 1989]. SWALE uses schema-based understanding to understand routine events. When it encounters anomalous events, it uses case-based reasoning to construct explanations that resolve the anomalies. It then adds the new explanations to its memory, learning them to facilitate future explanation of similar situations.

---

[1] System With Automatic Learning by Explanation

Within SWALE, ACCEPTER focuses understanding effort in three ways. First, it decides when explanation is needed: its anomaly detection process identifies gaps in system knowledge. Second, ACCEPTER decides the focus of SWALE's search for explanations: ACCEPTER's anomaly characterizations guide retrieval and adaptation of candidate explanations. Third, ACCEPTER decides when SWALE should stop explaining: it evaluates when an explanation is sufficient.

> ACCEPTER's theory guides both explanation construction and evaluation.

The theory of explanation underlying ACCEPTER contrasts with many previous assumptions. Our theory calls for focusing explanation on anomalies, rather than explaining all episodes that are beyond system schemas; for detecting anomalies by table lookup, rather than by inference; for treating explanations as traces of plausible reasoning, rather than as deductive proofs; and for treating explanations' goodness as dependent on goals and circumstances, rather than as context-neutral. In this chapter, after describing what ACCEPTER does we discuss its relation to previous AI research along each of these dimensions. We then turn briefly to psychological and philosophical perspectives on explanation, sketching their relationship to the principles we advocate.

2.1   The SWALE Project

Work on the SWALE project was inspired by observing how students at the Yale AI lab tried to explain a story in the news: the story of the racehorse Swale. In 1984, Swale was the best 3-year-old racehorse. He won the Kentucky Derby by $3\frac{1}{4}$ lengths, the biggest margin in a decade. Although he lost the Preakness, he immediately took the lead when he ran in the Belmont Stakes, and never relinquished it, winning by four lengths. After Swale's Belmont win, his career winnings were $1.5 million, and his market value was estimated at $50 million.

After Swale's outstanding Belmont performance, his owners decided to give him the summer off and then prepare him to compete against older horses in the lucrative Breeder's Cup. Eight days after the Belmont win, Swale was in high spirits after a morning gallop. As he was being groomed, a worker near Swale's barn heard "a funny sound" [Vecsey, 1984] and saw Swale fall. Swale was dead.

The death was so shocking that it made the front page of the *The New York Times*. Many people, both experts and casual observers, attempted to explain Swale's death—how could a young horse in peak condition have died with no warning?

Many explanations were hypothesized, including death from the stress of training, death from foul play, and even Swale being killed by his owners to collect on his insurance. Two days after Swale's death, *The New York Times* published an article devoted to questions and answers about common theories. That article deepened the mystery by showing that each explanation was unlikely: Swale died at a time when he was being given only easy workouts; he had been carefully guarded, and no one could think of any outsider who would have had a motive to kill him (the next race was 9 months away, ruling out killing him to fix a race); and Swale was underinsured, so the death caused a large financial loss for his owners [Crist, 1984a].

Issues in Real-World Explanation

One of the reasons Swale's death is an interesting example is because it demonstrates how different real-world explanation is from the idealized models used in EBL research:

- In EBL, explanations are deductive proofs. In the Swale episode, the best explainers could hope for was to build plausible hypotheses. Despite extensive effort, no definitive explanation of the death was ever found.[2]

- In EBL research, only a single explanation is presented to the learner. In the Swale episode, not only were many alternative explanations generated, but the choice between them was crucial—for example, accusations of foul play could have serious consequences.

- In the limited domains used by most EBL models, it is feasible to construct explanations by undirected chaining through a space of rules or operators. In the Swale episode, there were countless factors that *might* have been involved in the death. Consequently, the combinatorial explosion of possibilities would have swamped a system that explained by simple backwards chaining from the death, making explanation construction infeasible.

- EBL systems treat explanation construction as goal-independent, assuming that the rules from which explanations are built are neutral to

---

[2]Almost a month after the death, microscopic analysis revealed evidence supporting heart failure, an explanation that had been hypothesized early on but rejected for lack of confirmation in the original autopsy. When the new evidence appeared, a pathologist reported "We can't say, 'Yes, this killed Swale,' but it's possible ...I'm afraid this is as far as we'll be able to take it" [Crist, 1984c]. As a prescient veterinarian said shortly after Swale died: "Sometimes horses die on you and you never know why" [Crist, 1984b].

how those explanations are used. In the Swale episode, different explainers of the death had different uses for their explanations, making them need to trace different kinds of connections (e.g., veterinarians sought chains of immediate physical causes, and detectives sought possible motivational chains for wanting Swale dead).

Our theory of explanation responds to each of these points, but for the moment we restrict our consideration to the first three: building plausible explanations from uncertain rules, guiding choice between alternatives, and controlling the cost of explanation construction. Our solution to all three is to base explanation on experience.

A Case-Based Approach to Explanation

The Yale students who attempted to explain Swale's death had no specialized knowledge of racehorses, but the death reminded them of prior episodes they had encountered—the premature deaths of people and pets. After being reminded, they often hypothesized that similar causes applied to Swale. For example, the Swale story reminded one student of the death of the runner Jim Fixx, who died when his running overtaxed a hereditary heart defect. This made the student wonder if Swale died of similar causes: whether Swale had a heart defect that caused his racing to trigger a heart attack.

Swale's death reminded another student of the death of Janis Joplin: Both Swale and Joplin were young superstars who died at their peak. The cause of Joplin's death was an overdose of recreational drugs, which immediately suggests a bizarre hypothesis—perhaps Swale too was taking drugs to escape the stress of stardom. Although this is absurd, the Janis Joplin reminding suggested another explanation that was more plausible: Because a horse could not have administered drugs to himself, perhaps someone else did. Asking who might have given Swale drugs brings to mind stories of horses drugged by their trainers to improve performance and suggests a more reasonable hypothesis for the death: Swale died because his trainer accidentally administered an overdose of performance-enhancing drugs.

The students' hypotheses were generated by case-based explanation, the process of explaining by remembering and adapting explanations of similar prior cases. Experts as well tried to explain the death by applying past cases: One veterinarian's immediate reaction to the news was "this sounds like an aneurysm. I've seen this sort of thing before." [Cress, 1984]

Case-based explanation focuses explanation construction. For example, the veterinarian constrains his search for explanations by considering not *all* possibilities that might cause Swale's death, but those that have actually caused similar deaths in his experience. Rather than having to chain through all possible causes of an event, a case-based explanation system reuses the chains built for prior events. This method exploits regularities in the world, assuming that if new and old situations are similar their explanations should be similar as well; given this assumption, case-based explanation will help to hypothesize reasonable explanations. Some support for use of this assumption in human explanation is provided by experiments by Read and Cesa [1991] in which subjects rate explanations of expectation failures more favorably if they are reminded of previous analogous expectation failures and explanations.

Despite the intuitive attractiveness of these arguments, however, the effectiveness of the case-based explanation process is not guaranteed: It depends on being able to develop effective retrieval and adaptation mechanisms. If the wrong case is retrieved, the system may be guided towards an inapplicable explanation, making adaptation expensive (perhaps more costly than reasoning from scratch). If adaptation is poorly directed, it may never produce an applicable case. In this book we present a theory of how to guide explanation retrieval and judge the candidate explanations that are retrieved; Kass [1990] addresses the question of how to guide the adaptation process.

2.1.1 SWALE's Design

Case-based explanation requires four main steps, each of which was done by the students trying to explain Swale's death. First, the students determined what needed to be explained. Second, they recalled an old explanation for a similar situation. Third, they noticed any applicability problems. Finally, if the explanation did not apply, they tried to adapt it to repair the problems. The SWALE system was designed to model this process by detecting and characterizing anomalies, retrieving explanations stored in memory, evaluating candidate explanations, and adapting them to fit new episodes. In addition, the SWALE system learned the explanations it generated, extending the range of situations it could explain beyond those possible with straightforward application of the explanations stored as explanation patterns (XPs) in its memory.

The SWALE system was implemented as three modules:

- ACCEPTER, an early version of the current system, is the main program of SWALE. It does routine understanding, detects and characterizes anomalies, searches for XPs indexed under the anomaly characterizations, evaluates candidate XPs, updates memory to reflect the explanations that are accepted, generalizes adapted XPs,[3] and integrates

---

[3]In response to the imperfect nature of domain theories for real-world events, SWALE restricts routine generalization to variablizing the facts in the explanation; further generalization is done only to the extent necessary to accommodate examples the system has seen. See Schank and Leake [1989] for a full description.

the new XPs into its memory, indexing them under characterizations of the anomalies they explain.

- The EXPLORATORY SEARCHER (written by Chris Owens) is called upon to retrieve candidate XPs when ACCEPTER's XP search fails. It uses two retrieval strategies: searching for explanations indexed by unusual features of the event, and searching for folkloric explanations for the event.

- The TWEAKER (written by Alex Kass) adapts candidate XPs that fail to apply or do not provide sufficient information. It has a library of repair strategies, indexed by problem type, and uses ACCEPTER's problem characterizations to select the adaptation strategies to apply.

Figure 2.1 summarizes the steps in SWALE's understanding process; the module communication is shown schematically in figure 2.2. Here our primary interest is how SWALE motivates ACCEPTER's functions, so we will not discuss SWALE further. However, a more thorough summary of the system and its function can be found in Kass et al. [1986] or Schank and Leake [1989].

2.2   ACCEPTER Overview and Sample Run

Initial research on SWALE identified many issues in retrieval, adaptation and evaluation. As the component modules of SWALE became increasingly large and complex to address those issues, the system grew unwieldy. Consequently, it was decided to split the system into independent programs focusing on particular issues within the SWALE framework [Kass, 1990; Leake, 1988a; Owens, 1991]. The current version of ACCEPTER preserves the basic functions of the ACCEPTER module in SWALE, but relies on a human user to perform some of the functions of the other SWALE modules. Given an anomaly, ACCEPTER retrieves all XPs indexed under the anomaly type and relies on the user to select one of that set to evaluate; when problems are found, ACCEPTER outputs its problem characterization to the user instead of to the TWEAKER. The user can then call upon ACCEPTER to evaluate a new XP that repairs or avoids the original problem.

To illustrate ACCEPTER's capabilities, this section sketches the examples ACCEPTER processes and then traces a complete ACCEPTER run, beginning with routine understanding and ending with explanation evaluation. This demonstrates both the system's processing of a novel story, and the interaction between system and user. In the following chapters, we examine in detail the issues underlying each phase of the system's processing.

1. **ANOMALY DETECTION**

   ACCEPTER attempts to fit fact into memory.

   - If no problems, done.
   - Else characterize anomaly.

2. **XP SEARCH**

   ACCEPTER searches for XPs indexed under anomaly type.

   - If success, go to XP ACCEPTING.
   - Else EXPLORATORY SEARCHER applies unusual feature and folkloric explanation search.

3. **XP ACCEPTING**

   ACCEPTER evaluates candidate XP.

   - If problems, go to XP TWEAKING.
   - Else update memory to reflect assertions of XP.
   - If TWEAKER adapted XP, go to XP INTEGRATION.
   - Else done.

4. **XP TWEAKING**

   TWEAKER adapts XP and sends results to XP ACCEPTING.

5. **XP INTEGRATION**

   ACCEPTER generalizes and stores XP, indexed under anomaly type.

FIG. 2.1.   SWALE's algorithm for processing an input fact.

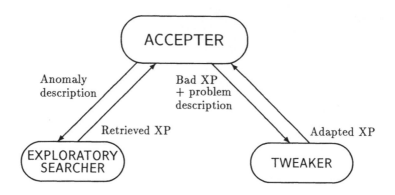

FIG. 2.2.   Communication between SWALE's modules.

2.2.1   Range of Program Examples

ACCEPTER processes about 20 simple (1–4 line) stories about anomalous events. These stories include stories of deaths, damage, and destruction from the news, including the death of Swale, the death of basketball star Len Bias (who died the day after being first choice in the basketball draft), the explosion of the Space Shuttle Challenger, two stories of the accidental shootdown of an Iranian airliner by the American warship Vincennes (one story reflecting initial news reports that the ship had shot down an attacking military plane, and the other reflecting the story after all facts were known), and the recall of *Audi 5000* cars for transmission problems). They also include other stories designed to exercise portions of the system, such as a fictional story about the victory of a lame racehorse, and stories about a student who flies first class, a Quaker who is also a Marine, a student who uses a frying pan to drive nails because he does not own a hammer, a policeman who sells cocaine, an airliner that leaves from the wrong departure gate, and an athlete who takes drugs during training.

At the start of each ACCEPTER run, the user is presented with a list of available stories from which to choose a story to process. Facts of the story are understood sequentially, with understanding of each fact forming the context for understanding the next, until an anomaly is found.

When an anomaly is detected, ACCEPTER retrieves XPs that are indexed as relevant to the anomaly type, and the user selects one of those XPs for evaluation. ACCEPTER's XP library contains about 20 XPs; these are intended to illustrate and test the system's evaluation capabilities, rather than to cover all the anomalies that ACCEPTER detects. Consequently, the system may retrieve many XPs for a given anomaly, or none at all. Also, a given XP may be applicable to an anomaly type that arises in multiple stories. For example, *exertion + heart defect causes fatal heart attack* might apply to either the death of Swale, or to the death of the athlete Len Bias. In all, ACCEPTER evaluates about 30 instantiated XPs. Its evaluation criteria are goal-based and depend on the task to be served by the explanation effort. Criteria for five tasks are implemented, and the user selects which of them should guide evaluation; each of the 30 instantiated XPs can be evaluated for any of the tasks.

2.2.2 Trace of Processing for the Challenger Disaster

The following output traces ACCEPTER's processing of the story of space shuttle Challenger's explosion. In January of 1986, after a series of successful space shuttle launches, the Challenger was launched from the Kennedy Space Center in Florida. Soon after an apparently successful liftoff, the Challenger exploded in flight, killing its crew of seven astronauts. An enormous effort was begun to explain the disaster in order to increase shuttle safety.

Numerous factors were implicated in the explosion. Joints in the solid rocket boosters (SRBs) were sealed with rubber O-rings, and it was determined that the O-ring seals had failed, allowing flames from a booster to escape and reach the main rocket. The seal failure was attributed to unusually cold weather on the launch day, which chilled the seals and made them brittle, preventing them from sealing properly when the boosters flexed during launch. An engineer had foreseen the danger before launch and attempted to prevent the flight, but had been overruled—consequently, NASA's failure to heed the warnings was blamed as well. Other implicated factors included the tendency of NASA workers to automatically follow orders, and the priority NASA gave to schedule over safety [Adler et al., 1988].

ACCEPTER's Challenger story consists of conceptualizations representing the following facts:

> Challenger was an American spacecraft.
> Challenger was launched at Kennedy Space Center.
> Challenger exploded.

Our trace begins by showing ACCEPTER's routine processing of the first two lines of the story, and its detection of an anomaly in the third. It then traces ACCEPTER's evaluation of a candidate explanation for the explosion. All text was generated by the program, using a very simple template-based generator; fillers for template slots are printed in capital letters. ACCEPTER can trace its processing at different levels of detail; the following output was generated at a medium level, with some output omitted for reasons of space. In later chapters we often return to this example, sometimes with more complete traces of particular steps, to elaborate on the system's processing.

2.2.3   Routine Understanding and Anomaly Detection

ACCEPTER's routine understanding is divided into three phases. In the first phase, the system tries to recognize the input as something previously believed, or expected from active MOPs—if so, the input can be merged with the previous structure, and no further verification needs to be done. ACCEPTER has no background knowledge about Challenger, so this phase of processing fails.

```
Processing:   There is a SPACECRAFT with USA as its SPONSOR, and
              CHALLENGER as its NAME.

Applying routine understanding process to CHALLENGER ...

   Phase 1:  Trying to recognize fact as known or expected.

      Checking if "CHALLENGER" is already known, or conflicts
      with facts in memory.

      ... No relevant belief found.

      Checking if "CHALLENGER" is expected from (or prohibited
      by) active MOPs.

      ... No relevant expectations found.
```

When it cannot recognize an input, ACCEPTER moves to the second phase of its processing: checking its reasonableness compared to stereotyped patterns. ACCEPTER's memory contains one pattern that is relevant to Challenger: Superpowers tend to sponsor spacecraft. This confirmation makes ACCEPTER accept the Challenger information as reasonable:

```
Phase 2:  Judging plausibility by comparing to patterns.

   Checking if the role-fillers of "CHALLENGER" are reasonable.

      Checking if action/actor combination makes sense.

         ... CHALLENGER CONFIRMS expectations from the role-filling
         pattern "SUPERPOWERs routinely fill role SPONSOR
         in SPACECRAFT".
```

ACCEPTER then tries to activate a knowledge structure to package Challenger, and to provide expectations to guide future understanding. It finds a candidate package—the MOP SPACE-MISSION—and checks its reasonableness, by recursively applying its routine understanding process. It finds no problems and activates that MOP's expectations.

```
Phase 3:  Installing input in memory and updating expectations.

  Checking if a packaging MOP can be instantiated for "CHALLENGER".

    A possible package for CHALLENGER is "SPACE-MISSION".

    Verifying whether SPACE-MISSION is a reasonable package.

    Applying routine understanding process to USA'S
    SPACE-MISSION ...
    ⋮
      Activating expectations/prohibitions from USA'S
      SPACE-MISSION.

        Expectations:
          CHALLENGER'S SPACE-LAUNCH.
          ASTRONAUT-26'S SPACE-WALK.
          CHALLENGER'S RE-ENTRY.
      ⋮

    Accepting "There is a SPACE-MISSION with ASTRONAUT-26
    as its ASTRONAUT, CHALLENGER as its SPACECRAFT, and
    USA as its SPONSOR" to package "CHALLENGER".

The information about CHALLENGER has been accepted
in context BELIEF-SET-6.
```

Because no problems have been found, ACCEPTER processes the next line of the story: Challenger's launch at Kennedy Space Center. This fact satisfies an expectation from the MOP for Challenger's space mission.

```
Processing:  There is a SPACE-LAUNCH with KENNEDY-SPACE-CENTER
             as its LOCATION, and CHALLENGER as its SPACECRAFT.

Applying routine understanding process to CHALLENGER'S
SPACE-LAUNCH ...
```

Phase 1: Trying to recognize fact as known or expected.

Checking if "CHALLENGER'S SPACE-LAUNCH" is already known,
or conflicts with facts in memory.

... No relevant belief found.

Checking if "CHALLENGER'S SPACE-LAUNCH" is expected from
(or prohibited by) active MOPs.

The fact "CHALLENGER'S SPACE-LAUNCH" satisfies the
expectation for CHALLENGER'S SPACE-LAUNCH from USA'S
SPACE-MISSION.

The fact "CHALLENGER'S SPACE-LAUNCH" has been installed
in the expectation for CHALLENGER'S SPACE-LAUNCH from
USA'S SPACE-MISSION.

No further verification is needed for the parts of the launch that were expected. However, there was no expectation for when or where the launch would take place, so ACCEPTER uses routine understanding to check those features. However, no problems are found.

The values for LOCATION, and TIME of CHALLENGER'S SPACE-LAUNCH
are not accounted for by the expectation, and will be
checked for reasonableness.
⋮

The information about CHALLENGER'S SPACE-LAUNCH has been accepted
in context BELIEF-SET-6.

The system next processes the final line of the story, which is the explosion. There is no expectation for the explosion, nor an explicit expectation against the explosion. However, indexed under **device** in ACCEPTER's memory is knowledge that, for any device, explosion is usually prohibited by normal device function: Explosion is a stereotyped failure mode. Consequently, the explosion is anomalous.

Processing: There is an EXPLOSION with CHALLENGER as its OBJECT.

```
Phase 2:  Judging plausibility by comparing to patterns.
  ⋮
Anomaly detected!

DEVICE-FAILURE:  CHALLENGER'S EXPLOSION CONFLICTS-WITH
expectations for normal device behavior.
```

This output shows that the anomaly is characterized according to the *source* of the failed expectation, in this case the device specification.

2.2.4 Evaluating a Candidate Explanation

When ACCEPTER detects an anomaly, it uses the anomaly characterization to guide explanation retrieval, retrieving all explanations in its XP library for similarly characterized anomalies—in this case, those accounting for similar device failures.[4] It then presents the explanations to the user, who selects one to evaluate. Before this program run, three XPs for DEVICE-FAILURE of a rocket were installed in ACCEPTER's library: that its booster seals became brittle because of cold, causing them to fail and leading to explosion; that a competitor sabotaged the rocket to preserve market share in the space business; and that a country sabotaged it to prevent its mission.[5]

```
Retrieving explanations indexed as relevant to DEVICE-FAILURE.

Possibilities for explaining DEVICE-FAILURE:
    1:  SRB-BURNTHROUGH
    2:  SPACE-COMPETITOR-BLOWS-UP-COMPETING-CRAFT
    3:  COUNTRY-BLOWS-UP-SPACECRAFT-TO-STOP-MISSION
    4:  QUIT

Item number? 1

Candidate explanation selected:  SRB-BURNTHROUGH.
```

---

[4]ACCEPTER's retrieval considers only one anomaly at a time. Another strategy would be to perform coordination of anomalies [Schank, 1986], searching for explanations that simultaneously resolve as many anomalies as possible.

[5]Although these explanations are designed for the Challenger episode, some similar candidate explanations could result from adapting XPs for prior episodes. For example, sabotage by a foreign power to stop the mission could be suggested by being reminded of the mysterious explosion of Greenpeace's "Rainbow Warrior" in New Zealand in 1985—French intelligence agents sabotaged it to stop its mission protesting French nuclear testing.

ACCEPTER begins its evaluation by generating a new memory context to use
when installing the explanation in memory, so that hypotheses from different
explanations can be kept distinct from each other, and from the background
knowledge used to evaluate the explanations.

```
Generating new subcontext BELIEF-SET-30 of BELIEF-SET-29 to
use as context for evaluating SRB-BURNTHROUGH.
```

It then checks the explanation's relevance, plausibility, and level of detail.

Checking Relevance

ACCEPTER's relevance checks have two parts. First, ACCEPTER checks
to see if the explanation accounts for the occurrence of the event's surprising
features. Second, it checks whether the explanation shows why the system's
reasoning went wrong—why beliefs underlying the expectation failed. If both
conditions are satisfied, the explanation is sufficient to show why the new
situation should be believed, and to guide repair of knowledge gaps that kept
the system from predicting correctly.

To check whether the explanation accounts for the surprising features,
ACCEPTER compares the consequent of the explanation against the surprising information. The XP traces how all features in its consequent are
inferred from its premises, so a match means that the XP gives a derivation for the surprising features. In the following output, ACCEPTER checks
whether the explanation that the booster seals burned through accounts for
the particular type of device failure: Challenger's explosion.

```
Checking if explanation is relevant to anomaly type DEVICE-FAILURE.

    Part 1:  Checking if explanation derives surprising event
    features.

        Need to account for CHALLENGER'S EXPLOSION, which is a
        failure of normal device behavior.

        Matching CHALLENGER'S EXPLOSION and explanation's
        consequent ...

        The explanation accounts for the surprising event.
```

To account for the system's reasoning failure, the system needs to find where its beliefs went wrong. The basic process for doing this is to examine the explanation's premises, looking for premises that contrast with the prior beliefs that led to its failed expectation. If the explanation shows that there is a cause that was not believed to hold, or that was overlooked, the explanation shows how the system went wrong. If the system assumed something that was false, it can repair the assumption; if it was overlooking an important factor, it can start considering that factor in the future.

To find its reasoning failure, the system needs access to its old reasoning—what led it to form an expectation. For failures of MOP-based expectations, ACCEPTER checks whether any of the explanation's premises deviate from normal conditions for the MOP. For device failures, it tries to reconstruct the likely source of the expectation: It assumes that the behavior was expected because of the device design and tries to find a MOP describing that design. If part of the current structure or use deviates from normal, according to the design, and that deviation caused the device failure, the anomaly is accounted for.

```
Part 2:  Checking if explanation shows why the reasoning underlying
the expectation failed.

   Reconstructing the likely source of expectation that failed.

   Since problem is DEVICE-FAILURE, the failed reasoning probably
   involves the structure or use of CHALLENGER.

   Searching up hierarchy for design MOP.
   Found the MOP ROCKET-DESIGN under ROCKET.
   CHALLENGER'S ROCKET-DESIGN probably led to expectations
   for CHALLENGER's normal function.

   Checking whether explanation shows factors that were not
   considered for CHALLENGER'S ROCKET-DESIGN.
```

Once the reasoning underlying the expectation has been reconstructed, AC-CEPTER checks whether the explanation shows features that deviate from that reasoning. To do this, it generates a new memory context containing only standard patterns and the specific information taken into account when building the expectation. If the explanation includes any premises that are distinctive from the previous view of the situation, those premises can be used as predictive features for similar outcomes in the future. If the explanation only includes factors that are normal or expected, more elaboration is needed. For example, "high pressure in the booster caused the booster to rupture" is a true partial explanation of the Challenger disaster, but is not sufficient for prediction because the high pressure existed in each successful launch as well.

In the next output, ACCEPTER compares each factor in the explanation to the factors in a normal launch to judge whether the factor is routine. For each comparison, it generates relevant expectations for a routine launch (in the output, the sequence of different expectations is indicated by the sequence of different identifying numbers for the objects and relationships described). The factors in the explanation are then matched against normal factors. In this way ACCEPTER verifies that it is normal for the boosters to be part of a space shuttle, that the boosters normally include O-rings, and that the O-rings are normally made of rubber. It also determines that the explanation includes a factor that is not a standard part of space shuttle launches: that the O-rings were cold because of the unusually cold launch day. This factor explains why the Challenger launch deviates from the routine launch that was expected. Because the explanation has already been determined to account for the explosion's occurrence, ACCEPTER outputs that the explanation resolves the anomaly.

```
Using routine understanding to check whether SOLID-ROCKET-31'S
PART-OF-RELATIONSHIP to CHALLENGER is standard in context
of CHALLENGER'S ROCKET-DESIGN.

   Building up new memory context with expectations
   from CHALLENGER'S ROCKET-DESIGN.

   Integrating SOLID-ROCKET-31'S PART-OF-RELATIONSHIP
   to CHALLENGER into that context.

   SOLID-ROCKET-31'S PART-OF-RELATIONSHIP to CHALLENGER
   satisfies expectation for SOLID-ROCKET-33'S PART-OF-RELATIONSHIP
   to CHALLENGER from CHALLENGER'S ROCKET-DESIGN, so
   it's routine.

Using routine understanding to check whether SOLID-ROCKET-31'S
O-RING is standard in context of CHALLENGER'S ROCKET-DESIGN.
   ⋮
   SOLID-ROCKET-31'S O-RING satisfies expectation for
   SOLID-ROCKET-36'S O-RING from CHALLENGER'S ROCKET-DESIGN, so
   it's routine.
```

```
Using routine understanding to check whether SOLID-ROCKET-31'S
O-RING'S RUBBER MATERIAL is standard in context of CHALLENGER'S
ROCKET-DESIGN.
   ⋮

   SOLID-ROCKET-31'S O-RING'S RUBBER MATERIAL satisfies
   O-RING'S RUBBER MATERIAL, so it's routine.


Using routine understanding to check whether SOLID-ROCKET-31'S
O-RING'S COLD TEMPERATURE is standard in context of
CHALLENGER'S ROCKET-DESIGN.
   ⋮

   SOLID-ROCKET-31'S O-RING'S COLD TEMPERATURE isn't expected
   from CHALLENGER'S ROCKET-DESIGN, or from standard
   stereotypes, so it's distinctive.


SRB-BURNTHROUGH resolves the anomaly, by accounting both for
why the surprising part of the situation happened, and why
predictions went wrong.
```

Checking Believability

If an explanation is relevant, ACCEPTER checks its plausibility. To do so, it applies its routine understanding and anomaly detection process to the story the explanation describes: It integrates the explanation's antecedents into memory and then traces through the inference links they support to see if they present a reasonable chain of events.

Initial premises of the Challenger explanation include that the boosters were part of Challenger, that the boosters contain O-rings, that the O-rings were made of rubber, that the O-rings were cold, and that a launch order was given. ACCEPTER tests the plausibility of each of these antecedents, given its background knowledge. For example, it can accept the premise that the solid rocket boosters are contained in the shuttle, based on standard expectations for space shuttle design:

```
Integrating the antecedent SOLID-ROCKET-31'S PART-OF-RELATIONSHIP
to CHALLENGER into memory.

   The fact "There is a PART-OF-RELATIONSHIP with SOLID-ROCKET-31
   as its CONTAINED-PART, and CHALLENGER as its CONTAINER"
   satisfies the expectation for SOLID-ROCKET-43'S
   PART-OF-RELATIONSHIP to CHALLENGER from CHALLENGER'S ROCKET-DESIGN.
```

Each of the explanation's antecedents is reasonable.

ACCEPTER next traces through the causal chain in the explanation, verifying each step in its derivation of the explosion. For example, it considers the SRB explosion is reasonable, given the high pressure of the SRB and the fact that it was sealed with a brittle seal:

```
Integrating the antecedent SOLID-ROCKET-31'S EXPLOSION into
memory.

Applying routine understanding process to SOLID-ROCKET-31'S
EXPLOSION ...

The fact "There is an EXPLOSION with SOLID-ROCKET-31
as its OBJECT" satisfies the expectation for SOLID-ROCKET-31'S
EXPLOSION from
BRITTLE-SEAL+CONTAINER-SEAL+CONTENTS-PRESSURE=>CONTAINER-EXPLOSION.
```

The SRB explosion in turn accounts for the explosion of Challenger, because the SRB was a part of Challenger. Consequently, the explanation provides a plausible derivation of the explosion.

Checking Detail

The final phase of evaluation checks whether the explanation provides enough information for the explainer's purpose. The user can select any of five implemented purposes to guide evaluation:

```
Checking explanation's detail.

Purpose for which explanation might be used:
     1:  Predict event in the future
     2:  Prevent the outcome in the future
     3:  Repair the current situation
     4:  Assign blame
     5:  Assign responsibility
     6:  QUIT

Item number? 1
```

In this example, the purpose of prediction has been selected. An explanation is useful for making predictions if it identifies factors that will be useful for predictive features in the future. To do so, all nonroutine factors should be knowable in advance of the event (either by casual observation, or by applying standard tests), should happen long enough before the event to be useful (predicting the explosion seconds before it happens would not be useful, but predicting it a few minutes before would allow the launch to be cancelled), and should reasonably lead to a prediction of the outcome. In addition, at least one of the factors should be unusual compared to the normal situation, so that future predictions can distinguish between the anomalous situation and what was previously expected.

Evaluation for prediction begins with the user being asked how much warning is needed. (ACCEPTER uses a coarse-grained temporal representation, distinguishing only simultaneous events and event separations of minutes, hours, days, weeks, or years.) The user is then asked how much verification effort (tests or casual observation) is acceptable.

```
Checking detail for prediction.
  To aid in prediction, explanation must satisfy:
    1. Each antecedent must either be
        a. predictive, and knowable early enough to be useful.
        b. routine.
    2. At least one of the predictive antecedents is distinctive.

How early must prediction be done, for prediction to be useful
(MINUTES, HOURS, DAYS, WEEKS, or YEARS)? minutes

Checking detail for predicting CHALLENGER'S EXPLOSION MINUTES
before it happens.

How much effort is acceptable when predicting? (OBSERVATION,
or TESTS)? observation
```

ACCEPTER then examines the antecedents of the original explanation to see if they are satisfactory. (If not, it checks whether the explanation contains a satisfactory subexplanation.)

```
Checking whether each antecedent satisfies test(s) for either:

    1. KNOWABILITY, TIMELINESS (is fact at least MINUTES
    before CHALLENGER'S EXPLOSION?), and PREDICTIVENESS.

    2. STANDARDNESS.
```

Testing CHALLENGER'S SPACE-LAUNCH with test set 1.

Testing: KNOWABILITY, TIMELINESS (is fact at least
MINUTES before CHALLENGER'S EXPLOSION?), and PREDICTIVENESS.

   Applying test for KNOWABILITY to CHALLENGER'S
   SPACE-LAUNCH.

      Searching up abstraction net for observability
      information.

      CHALLENGER'S SPACE-LAUNCH is probably observable,
      since it is a type of ACTION, and ACTIONs are
      usually observable.

      ... test passed.

   Applying test for TIMELINESS (is fact at least
   MINUTES before CHALLENGER'S EXPLOSION?) to CHALLENGER'S
   SPACE-LAUNCH.

      Summing temporal separations along belief-support
      chain connecting CHALLENGER'S SPACE-LAUNCH
      to CHALLENGER'S EXPLOSION.

         CHALLENGER'S SPACE-LAUNCH leads to ROCKET-IGNITION-46
         immediately.

         ROCKET-IGNITION-46 leads to GAS-44'S HIGH
         PRESSURE MINUTES afterwards.

         GAS-44'S HIGH PRESSURE leads to SOLID-ROCKET-31'S
         EXPLOSION MINUTES afterwards.

         SOLID-ROCKET-31'S EXPLOSION leads to CHALLENGER'S
         EXPLOSION immediately.

      ... CHALLENGER'S SPACE-LAUNCH is MINUTES BEFORE
      CHALLENGER'S EXPLOSION.

      ... test passed.

   Applying test for PREDICTIVENESS to CHALLENGER'S
   SPACE-LAUNCH.

```
Checking the connection between CHALLENGER'S
SPACE-LAUNCH and CHALLENGER'S EXPLOSION.

  Testing if CAUSAL-MOP-SCENE:LAUNCH=>IGNITION
  satisfies test for LINK PREDICTIVITY.

  Testing if CAUSAL-MOP-SCENE:IGNITION=>HIGH-PRESSURE
  satisfies test for LINK PREDICTIVITY.

  Testing if BRITTLE-SEAL+CONTAINER-SEAL+CONTENTS-PRESSURE=>
  CONTAINER-EXPLOSION
  satisfies test for LINK PREDICTIVITY.

  Testing if EXPLOSION-IN-COMPONENT=>EXPLOSION-IN-WHOLE
  satisfies test for LINK PREDICTIVITY.
... All links are acceptable.

... test passed.
```

Each of the other antecedents leading to prediction of the explosion (the cold temperature, and the fact that the SRB is part of Challenger) is also timely and knowable.

The final evaluation phase verifies that at least one antecedent is distinctive, making it possible to use that antecedent as a predictive feature.

```
Checking whether some antecedent satisfies the following tests:
DISTINCTIVENESS.

Checking whether CHALLENGER'S SPACE-LAUNCH satisfies
test(s) for "DISTINCTIVENESS".

  Applying test for DISTINCTIVENESS to CHALLENGER'S SPACE-LAUNCH.

    Using routine understanding to check whether CHALLENGER'S
    SPACE-LAUNCH is standard in context of CHALLENGER'S
    ROCKET-DESIGN.

      Building up new memory context with expectations
      from CHALLENGER'S ROCKET-DESIGN.

      Integrating CHALLENGER'S SPACE-LAUNCH into
      that context.
```

```
        CHALLENGER'S SPACE-LAUNCH satisfies the role-filling
        pattern "ROCKETs routinely fill role SPACECRAFT
        in SPACE-LAUNCH", so it's routine.
        ... test failed.
      ⋮
Checking whether SOLID-ROCKET-31'S O-RING'S COLD TEMPERATURE
satisfies test(s) for "DISTINCTIVENESS".

   Applying test for DISTINCTIVENESS to SOLID-ROCKET-31'S
   O-RING'S COLD TEMPERATURE.

   Using routine understanding to check whether SOLID-ROCKET-31'S
   O-RING'S COLD TEMPERATURE is standard in context
   of CHALLENGER'S ROCKET-DESIGN.

      Building up new memory context with expectations
      from CHALLENGER'S ROCKET-DESIGN.

      Integrating SOLID-ROCKET-31'S O-RING'S COLD
      TEMPERATURE into that context.

   SOLID-ROCKET-31'S O-RING'S COLD TEMPERATURE isn't
   expected from CHALLENGER'S ROCKET-DESIGN, or
   from standard stereotypes, so it's distinctive.
   ... test passed.
 ⋮
 SRB-BURNTHROUGH has sufficient detail for PREDICTION.
```

The final evaluation takes into account all the components of the evaluation process:

```
                     EVALUATION RESULTS

Summarizing evaluation of SRB-BURNTHROUGH to explain CHALLENGER'S
EXPLOSION has the problem DEVICE-FAILURE.

Explanation is relevant to anomaly:
it DERIVES-SURPRISING-EVENT-FEATURES, and ACCOUNTS-FOR-FAILURE.

Plausibility is POSSIBLE.

Detail is ACCEPTABLE for PREDICTION.
```

Because the explanation is satisfactory, ACCEPTER updates its picture of the situation by changing its main understanding context to the one that includes the beliefs included in the explanation.

```
Accepting "SRB-BURNTHROUGH" to explain the anomaly "DEVICE-FAILURE:
CHALLENGER'S EXPLOSION CONFLICTS-WITH expectations for normal
device behavior"

BELIEF-SET-49 is the memory context reflecting the explanation's
premises.

Resetting main understanding context from BELIEF-SET-28 to
BELIEF-SET-49.

End of story.
```

2.3   Comparison to Views from AI

The preceding trace illustrates our model of how explainer needs and knowledge influence explanation. In our model, explanation is triggered by anomalies; those anomalies are characterized to guide retrieval of explanations; and retrieved explanations are evaluated for relevance to the anomaly, for plausibility, and for usefulness for overarching goals. We now turn to the significance of that model compared to previous theories. We begin by comparing its tenets to other Artificial Intelligence perspectives on fundamental issues of explanation: when and what to explain, what explanations are, how they are built, how to overcome imperfections in the explainer's domain theory, and how to evaluate the goodness of candidate explanations. Because explanation evaluation has also received much attention in psychology and philosophy, we close the chapter with a comparison of our ideas to some major currents from those areas.

2.3.1   When and What to Explain

As discussed in section 1.5, explanation-based methods are powerful tools for focusing learning. However, whether a system that uses them will actually benefit depends strongly on decisions of when to learn. It has been widely observed that not all explained situations lead to useful generalizations [DeJong, 1986; Mooney, 1990; Segre, 1988], and has been demonstrated that rules acquired through EBL can even degrade performance due to the cost of deciding which of the learned rules to apply [Etzioni, 1990; Minton, 1988].

In response to the need to focus learning, criteria have been developed for deciding whether to learn from a new explanation [DeJong, 1986; Minton, 1988; Mooney, 1990]. However, these criteria are applied only after an explanation has been built—they restrict generalization and storage of explanations, but do not restrict explanation construction. In explanation-based schema acquisition, systems explain whenever they lack schemas characterizing observed events, which may occur frequently in everyday situations. The result is construction of large numbers of explanations that may not lead to useful learning. Construction of even a single explanation can be extremely expensive (see section 2.3.4), so needless construction of explanations may result in considerable wasted effort. Consequently, we propose that focus is needed *before* an explanation is constructed, to determine whether to explain at all.

> Explanation construction should be done selectively.

The remainder of this section considers issues in guiding selective explanation.

Failure-driven explanation: If a system's performance is satisfactory, there is little motivation for it to refine its knowledge. However, if a system fails to perform its task, learning is needed to avoid similar future failures. Learning from failures is also easier to perform effectively than learning from satisfactory performance, because the failure provides a precise focus for explanation [Hammond, 1989a]. These arguments provide support for failure-driven learning, a process that has been investigated from many perspectives in AI [Bhatnagar & Mostow, 1990; Birnbaum et al., 1990; Chien, 1989; Hammond, 1989a; Hayes-Roth, 1983; Leake, 1988a; Minton, 1988; Riesbeck, 1981; Schank, 1982; Sussman, 1975]. A major premise of this book is that an understander's explanation should be failure driven.

The task of a story understanding system is to maintain a coherent model of the facts it processes and their likely consequences. Given this task, its understanding is sufficient as long as the new information is consistent with prior beliefs and expectations; failures occur when expectations or beliefs prove false. Anomalous states and events show that the system's model is inadequate; explaining the problem allows repair of current beliefs and avoidance of problems that those erroneous beliefs might cause in similar future situations.

> Explanation should be triggered by anomalous states and events.

Explaining events versus explaining anomalies: Any state or event may be explained in many different ways. Traditional explanation construction approaches are context-neutral: They either generate arbitrary chains of rules, or always explain from a single fixed perspective. For example, explanation systems for story understanding generally explain events in terms of the actor's motivation (e.g., [DeJong, 1986; Mooney, 1990; Wilensky, 1978]).

In human explanation, however, context has a profound effect on how a given set of events is explained. For example, if we encounter an automobile recall for the first time, we will try to explain different things if different aspects of the recall conflict with our prior expectations. If we previously thought the manufacturing company had perfect quality control, we would need to explain how the defects could slip through; if we knew that the company's president forbade repairing defects for free, we would need to explain how the president's policy was circumvented; if we expected the company to take care of the problem by sending checks to each owner to have the repair done privately, we would need to explain why the company decided to handle the recall through its dealers.

> Good explanations must account for the anomalous features of the situation being explained.

This view follows that reflected by systems such as ALFRED [Riesbeck, 1981] and CHEF [Hammond, 1989a], which also focus their explanation on the anomalous features of a situation.

Assuring relevance to anomalies: Because not all explanations are relevant to a given anomaly, an explanation system needs to assure that its explanations are relevant to the anomaly at hand. ALFRED and CHEF depend on their explanation construction processes to produce relevant explanations, but a case-based explainer cannot: A case-based explainer may reuse prior explanations built in other contexts and for other anomalies. Consequently, a case-based explainer needs the capacity to explicitly test a candidate explanation's relevance to the current anomaly.

In the CHEF domain, information about the reasons for holding an expectation is usually unavailable, so the only requirement for relevant explanations is that they account for the anomalous features of an event. In explaining everyday anomalies, however, another factor must be considered: whether the explanation accounts for the flaws in the reasoning leading to the expectation. For example, consider explaining the Challenger disaster. An explainer that looked for a derivation of the anomalous part of the launch (the explosion) without considering prior expectations would generate *some* explanation of the explosion, perhaps "cold weather made the seals brittle." If it had not considered the effects of the cold weather before the launch, this explanation would be sufficient: it shows where system reasoning went wrong—the cold was overlooked—and resolves the anomaly. However, if the weather *had* been taken into account, and the seals were expected to be brittle without ill effects, "cold weather made the seals brittle" would be an inadequate explanation—it does not show where reasoning went wrong. A system that does not consider the reasoning underlying failed expectations has no way to know that the explanation is relevant in the first situation, but not in the second.

> Systems that explain the surprising feature, without considering *why* it is surprising, may generate irrelevant explanations.

ACCEPTER's search for explanations reflects both the anomalous features of the situation and why they are anomalous. In addition, after a candidate explanation has been generated, ACCEPTER's evaluation process explicitly evaluates its relevance to the anomaly.

2.3.2 Anomaly Detection

Despite the importance of explaining anomalies, anomaly detection has received little attention in AI research. Information that fails to fit expectations is often treated as irrelevant rather than as indicative of problems, without any attempt to resolve the disparity.

For example, in conceptual analyzers such as ELI [Riesbeck, 1975], semantic expectations guide the process of filling conceptual cases in CD conceptualizations. When components of a situation clash with expectations, as in the sentence "John ate a computer," ELI simply ignores the unusual components. It leaves the slot for what John ate unfilled, and does not connect the unusual role-filler to its representation of the action of eating. Likewise, schema-based understanding systems such as SAM and FRUMP are not sensitive to expectation failures. Once FRUMP selects a script to apply to a situation, it blindly applies it, no matter how many following events fail to fit the script's expectations. When SAM cannot fit an input into its active scripts, it instantiates a new script to accept it, but it makes no effort to reconcile the already active scripts with the new one. IPP does have the capability to detect one type of problem—events that were not accounted for by its active schemas—but cannot identify other classes of problems.

The view reflected by ALFRED and CHEF is much closer to ours. Those systems notice and explain expectation failures, and use the explanations to improve their understanding. Those systems, however, like others that detect understanding problems (e.g., [Charniak, 1978; O'Rorke, 1983]), rely on a very straightforward anomaly detection method: They check for direct conflicts between new inputs and prior beliefs. Unfortunately, not all anomalies are so simple to detect. Identifying a belief problem may depend on considering how new information relates to implicit ramifications of explicit inputs or system knowledge.

For example, consider the anomaly of the Challenger explosion. It seems unlikely that before the launch an understander would have had an explicit expectation that Challenger would *not* explode—just as it would not have generated explicit expectations that Challenger would not catch fire and would not disintegrate. The explosion is anomalous because it conflicts with ramifications of very general expectations for the safety of Challenger's design, so detecting the anomaly requires first recognizing the explosion as an implicit failure of those expectations.

Few systems attempt to detect anomalies beyond direct conflicts between individual beliefs. Two exceptions are Rieger's [1975] memory system, which detects indirect conflicts by building inference chains from inputs and comparing them to beliefs in memory, and Charniak's [1986] Wimp, which decides whether abductive assumptions are reasonable by using a theorem prover to attempt to prove that they are false, and accepting them if the proof attempt fails. However, any chaining-based method suffers from a basic problem identified in Rieger's work: The combinatorial explosion of alternatives to consider makes processing cost overwhelming. One of the main contributions of this book is its development of an alternative to inference-based anomaly detection approaches: avoiding the inference cost of anomaly detection by replacing inference chaining with pattern-based anomaly detection.

2.3.3   What Explanations Are

Artificial Intelligence research on explanation shows wide agreement on the basic form that should be used to represent explanations: networks that trace dependencies between pieces of knowledge, according to particular rules or operators.[6] However, despite this agreement on form, there are important differences concerning what explanations represent.

In EBL research, explanations are treated as deductive proofs built from perfect rules (e.g., [Hirsh, 1987; Kedar-Cabelli, 1987; Minton, 1988; Mitchell et al., 1986; Mostow & Bhatnagar, 1987]). However, everyday explanations lack this certainty. First, everyday explanation is primarily abductive rather than deductive; we elaborate on this distinction in section 2.5. Second, even when everyday explanations derive an event from known premises, they are only plausible reasoning chains; our explanation patterns trace not the ne-

---

[6]We consider here only explanations of novel situations; routine explanations are often built by identifying a fact with an existing knowledge structure such as a script or MOP.

cessity of a conclusion but only how belief in certain hypotheses supports belief in others. In representing the propagation of plausible beliefs, XPs resemble Pearl's plausible inference networks [Pearl, 1988b], although with two main differences: the support relationships in XPs are qualitative rather than quantitative, and the set of influences considered is determined by analogy to specific prior cases.

When explanations are plausible accounts rather than deductive proofs, they highlight certain features of a situation without any assurance that they state *all* the conditions needed for the event to occur (which would of course be impossible in everyday domains). For example, we consider that the following chain of states, events, and causes constitutes a possible explanation for the Challenger explosion: *Weather at the launch site was cold, leading to the booster rockets on the launch pad being cold, leading to the rubber booster seals within the shuttle becoming brittle, leading to improper fit of the seals, leading to escape of flames from the booster, leading to the explosion.* These connections rely on many implicit assumptions that might be violated in a given instance. For example, the connection between cold weather and the shuttle becoming cold depends on factors such as the absence of shelter and heaters at the launch pad, but this is not stated explicitly by the rules in the explanation.

Treating explanations as uncertain chains makes it essential to have criteria for evaluating the plausibility of competing explanations; we discuss our plausibility evaluation methods in section 2.3.6. Likewise, it becomes important to have methods for guiding explanation construction towards the most reasonable explanations possible, rather than accepting an arbitrary explanatory chain; we argue in the following section that case-based reasoning is an appropriate method for guiding explanation construction.

2.3.4 Explanation Construction

AI systems traditionally build explanations by chaining through a space of rules or operators. However, the combinatorial explosion of possibilities to consider makes unguided methods extremely expensive for building complex explanations. This problem is widely acknowledged, and many ideas have been proposed for reducing chaining cost during search for explanations, such as combining of top-down and bottom-up processing [Wilensky, 1978], limiting the amount of chaining allowed [Mooney, 1990], heuristics to limit the branching factor of search [Hobbs et al., 1990], using marker-passing to propose candidate paths [Charniak, 1986; Norvig, 1989], and making simplifying assumptions about the explanations [Bhatnagar & Mostow, 1990; Chien, 1989; Tadepalli, 1989]. Nevertheless, controlling search cost remains a fundamental problem.

In addition, even if an explanation is found, it may not be useful. Traditional explanation construction approaches are neutral to why explanation is done, so the resultant explanations may not provide the information the explainer needs. (One exception is the research of Krulwich et al. [1990], which argues for incorporating goal-based considerations into the chaining framework.)

As we discuss in Chapter 1, our view stands in contrast to approaches based on chaining through a space of rules or operators: We advocate case-based explanation construction. The idea of this process is to facilitate construction of new explanations by reusing prior reasoning—in familiar situations, it should be possible to generate even complex explanations at low cost, by minor adaptation of prior explanations. In addition, because the resultant explanations are supported by prior experience, they should be more likely to be valid than arbitrary explanatory chains. Case-based explanation also allows explanation to be focused on filling information needs: Indices for retrieving explanations can reflect not just the event but also the focus for explanation.

The effectiveness of any case-based reasoning process depends on retrieving appropriate stored cases. In case-based explanation to resolve anomalies, effective retrieval depends on being able to characterize anomalies so that anomalies with similar characterizations will require similar explanations. If this can be done, explanations can be organized in memory by the anomaly characterizations, making it possible to retrieve appropriate explanations given only information about the anomaly. A major component of this book develops the requisite indexing vocabulary to organize explanations of anomalies.

2.3.5 Dealing with Imperfect Theories

EBL depends on starting with a perfect domain theory. In real-world domains, however, EBL is impeded by the impossibility of having such a theory. Mitchell et al. [1986] describe three imperfect theory problems: If the domain theory is incomplete, it may be impossible to prove concept membership; if the theory is inconsistent, it may be possible to construct mutually incompatible proofs, resulting in conflicting concept definitions; if the theory is intractable, construction of the needed proofs may be prohibitively expensive. In ACCEPTER's domain of real-world news stories, all these problems are unavoidable, so successful performance depends on how effectively they can be overcome.

Approaches to the intractable theory problem generally depend on making simplifying assumptions to facilitate explanation construction [Bhatnagar & Mostow, 1990; Chien, 1989; Doyle, 1986; Tadepalli, 1989], and refining the explanations when those assumptions result in problems. This reduces the cost of explanation construction, but does not totally alleviate the problem: Even the simplified explanations may be expensive to construct by the traditional explanation methods those approaches use.

Approaches to inconsistency and incompleteness focus primarily on repairing the flaws in a theory. For example, Dietterich and Flann [1988] propose a method for repairing domain theories that allow multiple incompatible explanations. Their technique, induction over explanations, uses induction over a set of positive and negative training examples to guide theory repair. Rajamoney [1988] advocates experimentation to determine how to extend or repair a domain theory in response to multiple incompatible explanations, or in response to the inability to construct any complete explanation; Carbonell and Gil [1990] present another model of experimentation-based theory revision.

Unfortunately, however, these theory refinement methods are not always usable. For example, it may be necessary to act before having observed multiple examples, forcing use of an imperfect theory before it can be repaired by induction over explanations. Likewise, performing experiments to choose between explanations may be undesirable, impractical, or impossible. We would not want to perform a series of space shuttle launches to decide what went wrong with Challenger, and, even if we did, we could not be sure of replicating all the important conditions in our experiments unless we already knew the explanation for the problem.

We take a different approach to the imperfect theory problems: We develop criteria to improve the system's application of the current theory as it stands, despite the theory's imperfections. Our solution to the incompleteness problem is a theory of when partial explanations can be used without decreasing their reliability; this makes it possible to learn useful things, even if a complete explanation cannot be built. We discuss this approach in section 2.3.8.

Our approach to the inconsistent theory problem has two parts. First, our model judges candidate explanations in an explicit evaluation phase, choosing between conflicting explanations according to their plausibility in light of prior knowledge. Second, to focus initial explanation construction on explanations likely to appy, we advocate case-based explanation. When it is possible to construct multiple explanations, case-based explanation favors candidates supported by prior experience. As discussed previously, if the explainer's world is relatively stable, it is often reasonable to assume that usual past causes of an event are likely causes in the present as well.

Our approach to the intractable theory problem also relies on case-based reasoning: We argue that explanation construction in real-world domains can be made tractable by exploiting the domains' structure, adapting prior explanations of similar situations rather than explaining from scratch. In the following chapters, we develop a theory of anomaly and explanation for everyday events and show how that theory makes possible efficient and effective retrieval of stored explanations.

2.3.6   Evaluating Plausibility

In an EBL system with a perfect domain theory, any explanation will be valid. However, when multiple incompatible explanations can be built, plausibility becomes a crucial concern. Consequently, many understanding systems evaluate the plausibility of explanations. Their evaluation is comparative, based on the explanations' form, and is strongly influenced by Occam's razor: They favor the "minimal" explanation according to some minimality criterion [Ram & Leake, 1991]. For example, McDermott [1974] suggests favoring explanations that depend on the fewest new hypotheses; Granger [1980] suggests favoring explanations that postulate as few actor goals as possible; and Wilensky [1983] suggests favoring explanations that account for an action with the shortest possible chains. Likewise, forms of minimality criteria are advanced by Hobbs et al. [1990], Kautz and Allen [1986], and Peng and Reggia [1990]. Other work proposes an alternative structural criterion: favoring explanations with the most cohesive internal structure [Ng & Mooney, 1990; Thagard, 1989].

One problem with comparative approaches is that we may need to know more than comparative plausibility. If we are given a set of candidate explanations, we need to decide not just which is best, but whether any one is reasonable. Especially if candidate explanations are generated iteratively, criteria are needed for recognizing when the current explanation is sufficiently good to forgo additional search.

Even for comparative evaluation, purely structural methods may not accurately reflect plausibilities. In familiar domains, plausibility of explanations seems to depend strongly on the explanations' content: An explanation requiring the two assumptions "John ate supper" and "John watched TV" would generally be more plausible than one requiring the single assumption "John is a Martian."

Plausibility evaluation methods that consider explanations' content often use external information to rule out incorrect explanations. Experimentation to rule out incorrect hypotheses has been the subject of much research [Carbonell & Gil, 1990; Doyle, 1986; Pazzani, 1988; Rajamoney, 1988], but as previously discussed, performing experiments is frequently infeasible.

Pazzani [1988] suggests another content-based approach: deciding between explanations by comparing their predictions to observed states in the world. His strategies include avoiding explanations that predict events that were not observed, and preferring explanations that account for more of the observed features of the situation. However, these strategies are only usable if relevant effects are observable, and if observed features are restricted to relevant effects. Neither condition can be counted on in the real world. First, real-world situations often require explaining in situations for which important effects cannot be verified directly: Any signs of burn damage on Challenger's seals were destroyed when the seals were destroyed by the explosion. Although it is possible to seek evidence in the form of less direct effects, this is a costly and unconstrained inference problem.

Second, in attempting to favor explanations accounting for more of the observed features of a situation, it may be hard to decide which features of a situation actually need to be accounted for. For example, if a guest is late, and the radio news has reported some drug-related arrests, the delay could be explained by the guest's being arrested or by heavy traffic. Although the arrest accounts for two features of the situation (the news report and the delay), for most guests we would consider the news report irrelevant and favor the latter explanation.

Our approach judges plausibility primarily by explanations' content, but using internal information: It evaluates consistency between new explanations and prior knowledge. ACCEPTER judges explanations' reasonableness by checking whether the assumptions they contain conflict with prior beliefs, expectations, or stereotyped patterns. Structural criteria are only used to decide between explanations whose content is considered equally reasonable. The ability to judge plausibility of explanations in themselves, rather than only comparative plausibility, allows ACCEPTER to reject explanations that are insufficiently plausible regardless of how much more plausible they are than competing alternatives.

2.3.7   Evaluating Usefulness

Methods for explanation evaluation often consider only the validity of explanations, without considering their usefulness [Charniak, 1986; Granger, 1980; Hobbs et al., 1990; Kautz & Allen, 1986; McDermott, 1974; Ng & Mooney, 1990; Norvig, 1989; Peng & Reggia, 1990; Thagard, 1989; Wilensky, 1978]. However, as we have previously argued, different explainer questions and goals require different explanations of the same event; it is impossible to pick the best explanation without taking into account how a candidate explanation fits its intended use. One AI area in which usefulness has been studied is explanation-based learning, and the following sections discuss how our perspective relates to some points in that work.

EBL can be characterized as a knowledge transformation process [Keller, 1988]: It starts with a concept definition that is correct, but hard to use, and produces an operational concept description, i.e., one that can be used efficiently by the performance element that will apply it.[7]

---

[7]The idea of operationality was introduced (in slightly different form) by Mostow [1983].

To illustrate the role of operationality in explanation-based learning, we sketch an example modeled on work by Winston et al. [1983]. Suppose a vision system were given an initial concept definition for "cup" that described cups in functional terms: cups are objects that are liftable and can hold liquid. Neither property is likely to be directly recognizable by the vision system, which is more likely to be designed to recognize the shapes of objects. Consequently, the initial concept definition is not operational for the vision system: It cannot directly apply the definition to recognize a cup. However, given the original definition and a sample cup, the explanation-based learning process can formulate an operational description. It builds an explanation deriving the sample cup's concept membership from observable features, and then generalizes that explanation to form a description of cups in terms of observable features. For example, an EBL system might explain that the sample cup satisfies the "cup" concept definition—is liftable and holds liquid—because of two features that the vision system can recognize: it has a handle and has a convex shape. The explanation can be generalized to form a new description for future use: convex objects with handles are cups.

How to decide whether a description is operational, given system knowledge, is generally a difficult question. Mitchell et al. [1986] suggest annotating the predicates used to identify features according to their operationality for the performance system, but that approach may fail to capture the actual difficulty of recognition, especially as system knowledge changes [DeJong & Mooney, 1986]. In response to this problem, more dynamic models that reflect current knowledge have been proposed [DeJong & Mooney, 1986; Keller, 1988; Minton, 1988].

In the cup example, the operationality of a set of features is judged by whether each feature individually satisfies the same operationality criterion— the goal is to describe a cup entirely in terms of observable features. EBL traditionally assumes that the operationality criterion is a single test that must be satisfied by all antecedents of an explanation [Mitchell et al., 1986]. Although that assumption is appropriate for certain tasks, it prevents describing requirements for which not all antecedents need to have the same properties—for example, in order to use an explanation to find how to block an event, the explanation needs only to identify a single necessary antecedent that can be blocked. In Chapter 9 we show that for everyday tasks, usefulness requirements must often depend on antecedents having a mix of properties.

Our view also differs in considering explanations themselves strongly goal-dependent. Although EBL applies usefulness tests to the antecedents of explanations, it is commonly assumed that all valid explanations involving operational antecedents are equivalent. The basic view is that given "multiple, but equally-valid, explanations ... [a]ny selection results in a different, but correct, generalization. For multiple valid explanations, the selection of an arbitrary explanation will not have major implications" [Rajamoney & De-Jong, 1988]. We claim that for many purposes, the choice between valid explanations is crucial; the usefulness of even explanations with identical antecedents and consequents may be quite different. For example, it would be possible to learn to recognize medical problems from lab results by explaining the connection either with correlational rules or causal ones. However, the correlational explanation would not be useful for other purposes, while the factors cited in the causal explanation might suggest a treatment or a way to alleviate symptoms.

A final difference in our treatment of usefulness is the breadth of goals we consider. As the previous discussion shows, explanations may serve many different purposes, but EBL operationality research concentrates on operationality for the single fixed purpose of concept recognition—either in independent recognition systems or to facilitate object recognition for overarching tasks such as selecting appropriate role-fillers for plans [Kedar-Cabelli, 1987]. (See Keller [1988] for a sampling of some of this work.) However, there is a wide range of other tasks for which explanations may be used [Keller, 1988; Leake, 1988b]. To capture the idea of operationality in this wider context, Keller proposes a definition of operationality that makes explicit reference to the performance system being used and to current performance objectives. Likewise, Hirsh [1990] presents a general framework for reasoning about operationality according to a user-supplied theory of operationality. Neither of these proposals, however, attempts to determine the possible uses for explanations and the operationality requirements for those uses. In Chapter 9, we address these questions, categorizing the range of possible purposes for explanation and identifying their information requirements for those purposes.

2.3.8 Ramifications for Using Partial Explanations

As mentioned previously, the explanations in EBL are deductive proofs that demonstrate the sufficiency of certain conditions for concept membership. This limits the applicability of EBL: When it is impossible to construct a complete deductive proof according to the domain theory, the EBL approach does not apply. Because processing cost or lack of information will sometimes prevent construction of complete explanations, this is a serious limitation. Suggestions have been made to alleviate the problem by using an approximate domain theory or making simplifying assumptions (see section 2.3.5), but two problems remain. First, even using the simplified theory it may be impossible to build complete proofs; second, explanations based on a simplified domain theory are less reliable than those based on the full theory.

We propose an alternative way to extend the applicability of explanation-based methods. Rather than making general simplifying assumptions, our method uses knowledge of what information is needed to decide which specific simplifications can be made safely in a given situation. The result is that partial explanations can be used without sacrificing reliability for current goals, and that no effort is expended on elaborating unimportant parts of the explanation.

Our approach reflects the intuition that people often concentrate on the features of a situation that are important to their goals, even if those features are not a full explanation. For example, if we try to explain what caused the Challenger explosion and can determine only that the explosion was enabled by its booster seal design, we can fix the seals, even though safe previous shuttle flights with the same seal design showed that the design is not sufficient to cause an explosion.

In order to accept partial explanations when they provide sufficient information, new standards are needed for deciding whether explanations are acceptable. Our theory of goal-based evaluation gives criteria for when an AI system can accept a partial explanation, and for extracting needed information from that explanation.

2.3.9   Relationship to Expert System Explanation

Whereas explanation-based learning systems generate explanations for internal use, expert system explanation concentrates on generating explanations for communication with a human user. For example, the explanation components of expert systems might be designed to educate the user about a task domain, or to justify system decision making [Shortliffe, 1976]. A long line of expert system explanation facilities has been developed, including systems that show both their decision paths and the underlying reasoning [Swartout, 1983]; systems whose explanations are sensitive to the user's prior knowledge level [Paris, 1987]; and systems in which the explanation process is a continuing dialogue between system and user, allowing clarifications and elaborations to be offered in response to follow-up questions [Moore & Swartout, 1989].

Although ACCEPTER's explanations are built for the system's own use, the spirit of research on expert system explanation is like ours in stressing that explanations must provide the information needed for the tasks they serve. However, ACCEPTER's view is closer to that of the *user* of such explanation systems than the systems themselves: Our work models how an understander with particular knowledge and goals can decide whether it needs an explanation, whether a given explanation is sufficient, and what additional information is needed.

2.4   Comparison to Views from Psychology

Explanation has long been recognized as a crucial part of human understanding: It allows people to give meaning to the events they encounter, and by virtue of that meaning to predict and control their environments [Heider, 1958, p. 123]. Experiments have supported the psychological validity of explanation-based processing in a number of areas, including how juries select important features in a situation and judge evidence [Pennington & Hastie, 1988], schema acquisition [Ahn et al., 1987], and prediction of outcomes [Pazzani, 1990, pp. 174–177].

Likewise, much psychological research supports that human processing is need-based. In a survey, Zukier [1986] concludes that "a person will structure and process information quite differently, depending on the future use he or she intends to make of it." Nevertheless, psychological studies of explanation evaluation generally consider it outside of any context of how the explanations will be used. We discuss next the main current of early work and then compare our view to more recent context-dependent approaches.

Attribution theory: Seminal work by Heider [1958] initiated psychological research into how people decide to favor certain explanations. Heider originated attribution theory, which investigates how people decide whether to explain an action in terms of features of its actor, or features of the actor's environment. (Most work in attribution theory assumes that either personal or situational factors will apply, but not both.)

Kelley's [1967] *covariation principle* gives a hypothesis for how people make the decision between attributing an outcome to personal or situational factors. It suggests that people look at covariation across different people, time, and entities other than the actor in order to decide which type of factor applies. For example, if John dislikes a movie, but most other viewers are enthusiastic, Kelley's covariation principle suggests that John's dislike should be explained by aspects of John, rather than aspects of the movie.

Although attribution theory gives criteria for deciding which *class* of factors to implicate, it does not suggest how to decide which particular personal or environmental factors are important. In the example of the movie, it says that a good explanation must involve *some* aspect of John, but deciding *which* is beyond its scope. However, as Lalljee and Abelson [1983] point out, people would usually try to find a more specific reason for the dislike. For example, suppose Mary invites John to a movie, expecting him to like it. When it turns out that he dislikes it, she will probably try to find out *why*, in order to anticipate his reaction better next time.

Traditional attribution theory is neutral to the influence explainer goals and processing context have on evaluation. However, Lalljee et al. [1982]

showed that the explanations people seek, rather than being determined by abstract criteria, vary with circumstances: Unexpected behavior requires more complex explanations than expected behavior and is likely to require more of *both* situational and personal elements. This is consistent with AC-CEPTER's model: Routine events receive simple explanations, but more complex explanations are required for unusual events, because those events need to be reconciled with failed expectations as well as understood in themselves.

A knowledge structure approach: Lalljee and Abelson [1983] respond to the preceding problems of attribution theory by suggesting a knowledge structure approach to attribution. The knowledge structure approach involves two types of explanation: *constructive* and *contrastive*. In constructive explanation, people explain events in terms of knowledge structures such as scripts and plans [Schank & Abelson, 1977]—for example, someone locking a bicycle might be explained in terms of the standard plan to protect it from theft. Contrastive explanation explains surprising events by showing why the events deviated from the expectations provided by knowledge structures. If someone left his bicycle unlocked, that choice might be explained in terms of *goal reversal:* Rather than having the normal goal of wanting to protect it, on which the expectation was based, he might actually have wanted to get rid of it.

Our theory follows the basic lines of Lalljee and Abelson's approach. Our evaluation criteria require that the explanation of an anomaly provide both a constructive explanation (to understand the surprising information) and a contrastive one (accounting for the failure in previous expectations or beliefs). We go beyond this, however, in looking at how preference for explanations is affected by goals beyond the general desire to resolve anomalies.

Excuse theory: The influence of one class of goal has been extensively studied in psychology: Research in excuse theory examines how explanation is influenced by the goal to absolve the explainer from blame. This work shows that the desire to form excuses makes people manipulate the types of factors to use in attribution, attributing their bad performance to external influences [Snyder et al., 1983].

2.5 Comparison to Views from Philosophy

Explanation has been studied extensively in philosophy, with particular attention directed towards analysis of scientific explanation. Rather than attempting to give an exhaustive survey, we simply highlight a few approaches that are particularly relevant to our work.

Philosophical accounts of scientific explanation have been strongly influenced by Hempel's Deductive-Nomological model [Hempel, 1966], which views explanations as deductive arguments that start with a set of true premises and derive that the explained event had to occur. Deductive EBL models can be viewed as following in this tradition.

An alternative philosophical view considers explanation an abductive process rather than a deductive one. The phrase abductive reasoning was originated by Pierce, who considered abduction the inference process involved in forming and accepting explanatory hypothesis. Pierce [1948, p. 151] characterizes the pattern of abductive inference as follows:

> The surprising fact, C, is observed;
> But if A were true, C would be a matter of course,
> Hence, there is reason to suspect that A is true.

When abductive inference is attempted, it will often be possible to hypothesize multiple possibilities accounting for the observed fact, making it necessary to compare the alternatives in a process of "inference to the best explanation" [Harman, 1965].[8]

Our view of explanation is abductive rather than deductive: We view explanation as primarily a process of hypothesizing causes of events and expectation failures, rather than deriving them from known factors. This is consistent with a growing current of abduction research in AI, a sampling of which can be found in O'Rorke [1990] and Dasigi [1991].

Goals and explanation: Philosophers have noted that a rich range of explanations exists for any event. This view is well expressed by Hanson [1961, p. 54], who observes:

> There are as many causes of *x* as there are explanations of *x*. Consider how the cause of death might have been set out by a physician as 'multiple haemorrhage', by the barrister as 'negligence on the part of the driver', by a carriage-builder as 'a defect in the brakeblock construction', by a civic planner as 'the presence of tall shrubbery at that turning'.

However, Hanson does not attempt to analyze the possible purposes for explanation, or how those purposes translate into the requirements that explanations must satisfy; our theory addresses these questions.

Mackie [1965] stresses the context-dependence of explanations, describing explanation as a process of making a distinction between some current situation and another class of situations. The background is the *causal field* of

---

[8]For a detailed discussion of the abductive reasoning process, see Josephson [1991].

situations to be distinguished by the explanation.[9] The causal field consists of the situation leading to the outcome to explain, and some class of situations in which the event being explained did not occur. The causal field determines the focus of explanation: An explanation shows causes that led to the outcome being explained but were not present in the other situations in the causal field. For example, the explanation of "why did the car crash going around the turn?" would be different if the causal field were other turns, in which case the explanation might be the turn's sharpness, or if the causal field were other instances of the car going around the same turn, in which case the explanation might be that the driver was sleepy.

Van Fraassen [1980] argues in favor of Hanson's view of dynamic explanation and accounts for the choice of causes with an idea very similar to the causal field. To Van Fraassen, an explanation shows why something occurs instead of a *contrast class* of other alternatives. For example, if we were asked why a car cost $10,000, the answer would be different if the contrast class were cars costing $20,000, or costing $5,000. In the first case, an explanation would show reasons why it is less expensive, such as its defects; in the second, it would show why the car cost more, such as being a rare model sought by collectors.

In section 2.3.1 we argued that explanations must focus on anomalies rather than events. Our arguments there can be viewed as claims about the proper contrast class for explanations of anomalous events: The contrast class for explanations of anomalous events is the set of beliefs that are consistent with prior knowledge and expectations.

2.6   Summary

There is no point in explaining unless the explanation fills a need for information. When a system has reasons to explain, it seems obvious that those reasons should guide the explanation process, to generate an explanation that fills the system's needs. Previous AI work on explanation has relied on approaches that are context neutral, or that have very limited models of how explanations can be used, and has judged explanations more by their structure than by the information they provide. This book argues for the opposite view: that explanations' goodness can *only* be judged in terms of what the explainer knows and what it needs to find out.

The importance of contextual factors and explainer needs has been advanced by some theories of explanation outside of AI, such as Hanson and Van Fraassen's abstract work, and Lalljee and Abelson's work on a knowledge-structure approach to attribution. However, that work has not examined

---

[9]The idea of the causal field as background for explanation was introduced by John Anderson [1938].

how those needs guide the explanation construction process, or how purpose translates into concrete requirements for explanation evaluation. Our theory addresses these points, examining how needs can be detected, showing how explanation can be guided towards providing useful information, and delineating the information requirements that different purposes impose.

Constructing useful explanations depends on a theory of the content of explanations and anomalies, and of the goals that explanations can serve. The following chapters develop this theory and trace its implementation in ACCEPTER. They begin by examining what reveals the need for explanation: how anomalies signal gaps in a system's understanding.

3 Anomalies and Routine Understanding

Anomalousness is context-dependent: What is anomalous depends on what was previously expected. Consequently, any anomaly detection system reflects the theory of understanding that guides its routine understanding process. ACCEPTER uses schema-based understanding to make sense of routine events, with an actor-centered schema selection process that may simultaneously apply multiple schemas to a single situation. New information is considered anomalous when it is judged to refer to prior beliefs or schema-based expectations but conflicts with them.

3.1 The Nature of Anomalies

Intuitively, an anomaly is something surprising. When we ask people to say why an event is anomalous, they tell us which aspects of the event surprised them. Their response reflects a commonplace view: that anomalousness is a property of the event itself. However, this view has a basic flaw: No aspect of an event is anomalous unless it differs from what was previously expected or believed. Thus anomalousness results from interactions between events and the understanding context.

For example, if a driver has a blowout on the highway, the driver's prior beliefs determine what (if anything) is anomalous about the blowout. If the blowout conflicts with the driver's expectation that tires last longer, the anomaly is their early failure; if the tires have been bald for months and were expected to fail long before, the anomaly is that the blowout happened

71

so late; if the driver noticed broken glass on the road moments before the blowout and expected the tires to be punctured, the blowout might not be anomalous at all.

New anomalies may be triggered or old ones resolved by activating new knowledge. For example, the anomaly of the blowout might be resolved by the information that tires of the brand in question tend to fail early, but that information might prompt another anomaly: why a trusted mechanic put them on the car.

> Information is anomalous if it conflicts with our active beliefs and expectations.

Because the anomalousness of new information depends on the system knowledge that is currently active, the expectations activated during routine understanding have a strong effect on anomaly detection. Consequently, we begin this chapter by discussing how expectations arise in the schema-based process used for ACCEPTER's routine understanding. We next describe how ACCEPTER detects conflicts with schema-based expectations and specific prior beliefs. Detecting such conflicts depends on deciding whether partially matching expectations are relevant to new information, and we present simple heuristics for that purpose.

Consistency with schema-based expectations is only one of ACCEPTER's criteria for judging the reasonableness of new information, and Chapter 4 discusses ACCEPTER's use of pattern-based checks to detect a wider range of anomalies.

3.2   ACCEPTER's Routine Understanding

ACCEPTER's basic understanding process is quite standard for language understanding systems: ACCEPTER makes sense of new information by placing it in schemas that connect it to other relevant information and provide expectations for future events [Charniak, 1978; Cullingford, 1978; DeJong, 1979; Minsky, 1975; Schank & Abelson, 1977]. The program's memory is organized following the dynamic memory theory of Schank [1982], with schemas organized in an abstraction network and with shared substructures. Accepted information is stored in the program's memory, organized by the schemas used to process it [Kolodner, 1984; Lebowitz, 1980; Schank, 1982]. For example, ACCEPTER understands the launch of Challenger by recognizing it as part of the standard sequence of events in a space mission and stores the launch in memory under the knowledge structure for space missions.

3.2.1   Schema Representation

The schemas in ACCEPTER's memory are represented as MOPs (Memory Organization Packages, [Schank, 1982]). MOPs represent stereotyped sequences of events that take place in particular contexts, such as the fact that a space launch includes a launch, a space walk, and re-entry. (In the following discussion of MOP representation, we illustrate MOPs' structure with examples from the space shuttle domain.) In familiar situations, an understander can rely on MOPs to provide expectations without having to build inference chains from scratch, allowing precise expectations to be generated efficiently—for example, although it might be hard for an average person to predict by reasoning from scratch that a space shuttle launched in Florida will land in California, that expectation is provided by knowledge of standard practice for shuttle missions.

The basic events described in a MOP are called scenes. MOP scenes normally describe events that take place in a single location, with a single purpose, and in a single time interval. Cross-contextual learning is allowed by having different MOPs share the same structures for their scenes. For example, some preparations for a space launch, such as final briefings, are common to other military flights. In the MOP model, the shuttle pilot's MOP for shuttle flights would refer to the same briefing scene as the pilot's MOP for jet flights. If a shuttle pilot learns something about briefing procedure during a prelaunch briefing for a jet flight—for example, that the military has decided to require that questions be held until the end of the briefing— the briefing scene is changed accordingly, and the new knowledge becomes available to provide expectations in any other MOP that uses that scene. In addition, MOPs are organized hierarchically in memory, allowing portions of MOPs (such as the scenes involved) to be inherited from their abstractions.[1]

In ACCEPTER's memory, each definition of a MOP includes three kinds of information. First, it includes links to the abstractions and specifications of the MOP. Second, it includes the scenes of the MOP, and the roles that actors and objects fill in them. Third, it includes stereotyped information about fillers of the MOPs' roles; ACCEPTER uses these stereotypes as the basis for its pattern-based anomaly detection.

Abstraction and Specification Information

ACCEPTER uses information about MOPs' abstractions and specifications to guide inheritance of default features. A single memory node may have

---

[1]Problems involving the choice between competing alternatives to inherit have not been addressed here; ACCEPTER simply searches breadth-first in its MOP network for a MOP with the needed type of information and stops search as soon as it finds the information in any MOP.

multiple abstractions; this reflects the fact that a single object or event may be categorized in different ways, depending on the viewer's perspective. For example, a space mission can be viewed in many ways, such as a military operation, a scientific one, or a dangerous activity.

Because most MOPs involve multiple actors in multiple roles, there may be many different ways to map a MOP to a particular abstraction. For example, a space launch may be considered a dangerous activity for the astronauts, or for the ground workers who fuel the rocket. These multiple abstraction relationships are also recorded in ACCEPTER's memory net.

MOP Scenes and MOP Prohibitions

ACCEPTER's MOPs include information both about the standard events expected in a situation, and about the events the situation should preclude. Descriptions of events that are expected *not* to happen, as a result of the MOP being in effect, are called prohibitions. An example of a MOP prohibition is that, during the course of the MOP for athletic training, the athlete is expected not to break training—to refrain from drug use and excessive parties.

The scenes and prohibitions of ACCEPTER's MOPs are represented in terms of a limited number of belief types, which are also used to represent inputs to the program, and to represent beliefs in its memory. ACCEPTER's belief types represent the following classes of facts:

- **Object/actor definition**: The fact that an object of a given type exists. For example, one of the facts in ACCEPTER's representation of the Challenger disaster is that the story involves a particular instance of spacecraft.

- **Object/actor description**: The fact that an object has a given feature. For example, that the name of a space shuttle is "Challenger."

- **Action or MOP definition**: The fact that an instance of a Conceptual Dependency Theory primitive action [Schank, 1972] or a MOP occurred. For example, Challenger's launch is represented as an instance of space-launch, ACCEPTER's MOP for spacecraft launches.

- **Packaging description**: The fact that an object or event fills a role in an action or MOP. For example, that Challenger fills the spacecraft role in the MOP for a spacecraft's launch.

The scenes in ACCEPTER's MOPs are annotated with information on the temporal separations between them—for example, that a space walk usually takes place a day or so after the spacecraft is launched. ACCEPTER's temporal representation is coarse-grained; temporal relationships between MOP scenes are expressed as displacements of none, minutes, hours, days, weeks, or years.

Role-filler Stereotypes

ACCEPTER's MOPs also represent information about basic stereotypes concerning the actors and objects that fill roles in the MOP. ACCEPTER uses this information to judge reasonableness of particular instantiations of the MOP. For example, the system's MOP for space missions includes the information that the sponsor of the launch is usually a superpower, and that those flying in the spacecraft are usually astronauts. ACCEPTER's stereotypes are discussed in detail in Chapter 4.

Another Example: The Air-Raid MOP

In July of 1988, the American warship Vincennes was patrolling the Persian Gulf. Tension was high; an American warship had previously been hit by an Iraqi missile, and the Vincennes had recently skirmished with Iranian boats. The Vincennes' radar detected an Iranian plane taking off from a nearby airport but was unable to definitively establish its type. When the plane was reported to descend towards the Vincennes, as a fighter would in preparation for an attack, the Vincennes fired missiles and shot it down—only to discover later that it had shot down Iran Air flight 655 .

A key factor in the Vincennes' decision was the report that the Iranian plane was descending towards the Vincennes—that maneuver was a standard step in preparations for an air attack. When ACCEPTER processes a simple version of the information available to the Vincennes, it generates similar expectations, based on its MOP representing air-raids.[2]

ACCEPTER's MOP for air raids is shown in Figure 3.1. Initial information in the definition describes four ways that the MOP can be abstracted: as a military action on the part of either the attacker or defender, and as a violent action on the part of either one. The MOP then describes the roles and scenes that it involves. The scenes are the approach of an attack plane, attempts to defend the target, and bombing. (Although the Vincennes story does not specify the type of the plane, after activating the air-raid MOP ACCEPTER infers that the plane is an attack plane, because that is the normal type of plane involved.) The roles include the attacker, defender, and target. (MOP definitions may specify a permanent filler for any role—for example, that a certain class of space launches always takes place at a Kennedy Space Center. The asterisks after each role in our MOP definition indicate that no role-filler is prespecified.)

---

[2]The MOP is activated when a plane from one hostile nation descends towards a military resource of the other.

```
(define-node air-raid
    a military-action ((actor attacker))
    a military-action ((actor defender))
    a violent-action  ((attacker attacker)
                       (victim target))
    a violent-action  ((attacker defender)
                       (victim attacker))
    with-role attacker *
    with-role defender *
    with-role target   *
    with scenes
        ((flight-path      ((plane attacker)
                           (to target))
                           minutes)
        (air-raid-defense ((defender defender)
                           (attacker attacker))
                           minutes)
        (bombing          ((attacker attacker)
                           (target target))))
    with norm-fillers
        ((attacker (type attack-plane))
        (defender (type military-unit)
        (target   (type military-resource)))))
```

FIG. 3.1.   ACCEPTER's definition of the MOP for air-raids.

Each scene in the air-raid MOP is defined by a reference to another MOP
in ACCEPTER's memory. For example, the air-raid MOP refers to air-raid
defense, which is a MOP that includes moving people to shelters, concealing
targets, and trying to shoot the attacker down. Scene definitions also describe
how role-fillers in the scene's constituent MOPs correspond to role-fillers in
the MOP being defined. For example, the filler of the **plane** role in the **flight-
path** MOP for approaching the target is the same as the filler of the **attacker**
role in the air-raid MOP. Finally, the MOP definition gives information on
stereotypes for the MOP's role-fillers: The approaching plane is an attack
plane, the defender is some kind of military group, and the target is a military
resource.

3.2.2   MOP Activation

When ACCEPTER processes an input fact, the first step in its understanding
process is to try to recognize the fact as something previously believed or
expected. If that fails, it tries to find a MOP that will account for the new

fact. If it finds an applicable MOP, it infers that previous events in the MOP have taken place (e.g., given an input about a space walk, it would infer that a launch had preceded it) and generates expectations for following events in the MOP (e.g., a re-entry from space). Subsequent inputs are understood in terms of these expectations whenever possible; those that are irrelevant to the MOP are understood by activating a new MOP. This process is modeled on the script application process of SAM [Cullingford, 1978].

For example, recall the Challenger trace presented in Chapter 2. When ACCEPTER processes the first line, "Challenger was an American space-craft," it checks whether that information is accounted for by prior beliefs or by expectations from an already active MOP. Because it is the start of a new story, the information is not accounted for, so ACCEPTER attempts to find a MOP to package it. ACCEPTER finds **space-mission**, which is indexed as the default MOP to package objects of type **spacecraft**, and activates expectations from that MOP.

```
Processing:  There is a SPACECRAFT with USA as its SPONSOR, and
             CHALLENGER as its NAME.
          :
   Checking if a packaging MOP can be instantiated for "CHALLENGER".

   A possible package for CHALLENGER is "SPACE-MISSION".

   Verifying whether SPACE-MISSION is a reasonable package.

   Applying routine understanding process to USA'S
   SPACE-MISSION ...
   :

      Activating expectations/prohibitions from USA'S
      SPACE-MISSION.

         Expectations:
           CHALLENGER'S SPACE-LAUNCH.
           ASTRONAUT-26'S SPACE-WALK.
           CHALLENGER'S RE-ENTRY.
         :

   Accepting "There is a SPACE-MISSION with ASTRONAUT-26
   as its ASTRONAUT, CHALLENGER as its SPACECRAFT, and
   USA as its SPONSOR" to package "CHALLENGER".
```

The next line of the story, "Challenger was launched at Kennedy Space Center," satisfies expectations from **space-mission**, so no additional processing needs to be done—it is simply merged with the expectation for a launch and stored in memory under the accepting MOP.

```
Processing:   There is a SPACE-LAUNCH with KENNEDY-SPACE-CENTER
              as its LOCATION, and CHALLENGER as its SPACECRAFT.

Applying routine understanding process to
CHALLENGER'S SPACE-LAUNCH ...

   Phase 1:  Trying to recognize fact as known or expected.

      Checking if "CHALLENGER'S SPACE-LAUNCH" is already known,
      or conflicts with facts in memory.

      ... No relevant belief found.

      Checking if "CHALLENGER'S SPACE-LAUNCH" is expected from
      (or prohibited by) active MOPs.

         The fact "CHALLENGER'S SPACE-LAUNCH" satisfies the
         expectation for CHALLENGER'S SPACE-LAUNCH from USA'S
         SPACE-MISSION.

         The fact "CHALLENGER'S SPACE-LAUNCH" has been installed
         in the expectation for CHALLENGER'S SPACE-LAUNCH from
         USA'S SPACE-MISSION.
```

Aspects of the new situation that are specified in the input, but not specifically expected—the location of the launch and when it took place—are checked for reasonableness. No problems are found, so ACCEPTER accepts the information.

```
The values for LOCATION, and TIME of CHALLENGER'S SPACE-LAUNCH
are not accounted for by the expectation, and will be
checked for reasonableness.

The information about CHALLENGER'S SPACE-LAUNCH has been accepted
in context BELIEF-SET-6.
```

There are two main differences between ACCEPTER's schema application and that of previous systems. First, it is hierarchical. Rather than activating a single MOP that accounts for the immediate context of an event,

ACCEPTER tries to account for facts in terms of a succession of higher contexts. For example, if someone buys a subway token, SAM assumes that he is taking a subway but does not attempt to activate scripts to provide a larger context. ACCEPTER recursively tries to generate higher level MOPs accounting for each MOP it activates, until no MOP can be found or until the newly activated MOP matches a previous belief or expectation. In this respect, ACCEPTER's approach is similar to that of plan recognition systems such as PAM [Wilensky, 1978], which first find the immediate goal that accounts for the action and then recursively account for the hypothesized goal, until finally reaching a known or expected goal.

The second difference is how ACCEPTER decides which MOP to apply. Standard approaches to frame selection, such as those used by SAM, assume that frame selection depends entirely on the situation—a given type of event is always interpreted the same way. For example, when SAM processes a restaurant story, it always focuses on the customer's role. However, people take other information into account when they generate expectations: Context changes the focus they use.

Consider the story: "Last week John moved here. Yesterday I walked past McDonald's, and he was serving someone a hamburger." Although the situation in the second line involves a restaurant, in this context, it seems unlikely that a person would apply the restaurant schema at all. That schema focuses on the customer, whereas the story focuses on John, making it likely that expectations about him (rather than the customer) will be more useful in future processing—for example, we might wonder why he has taken a dead-end job and expect him to move to another job as soon as he can find a better alternative. We consider this type of flexible focus desirable in programs' schema selection process as well.

Deciding on Prospective Packages

The previous example shows that situation-based schema selection may not focus on the right parts of a situation. One way to dynamically direct focus is to concentrate on needed information: We have already argued that when anomalies arise they should be the focus of explanation, and Ram [1989] argues that processing should be focused on information relevant to prior questions.

However, much of the information we receive is related neither to prior expectations nor unanswered questions. In these cases, we need ways to increase the likelihood of focusing on important information. Activating *all* applicable schemas would be overwhelming, because any complex event involves the intersection of many different factors (for example, in principle we could view the Challenger launch in terms of countless schemas likely to be irrelevant, such as the life of each person involved, and in terms of the life cycle of each machine involved).[3] We need criteria for focusing on information likely to facilitate future processing.

In general, the level of explanation needed for actions depends on three factors: how well the understander knows the actor, how unusual the action is, and how specifically known patterns match the situation. There are four cases that affect the decision of whether to try to elaborate motivation. They are as follows:

1. **The action is confirmed by actor's behavior patterns.**

   Here activation of the schema is probably sufficient. For example, if we know that John is an avid bowler, we will not question his going bowling.

2. **Actor participation is not predicted by specific behavior patterns, but action is a common one for members of the actor's group.**

   - **For role-fillers that we know or that are worth a lot to us, elaborate.** For example, if John is a high school student working at McDonald's, and also he's a friend of ours, we may ask why he chooses to work there.

   - **For role-fillers that we know little about, or that are distant from us, no elaboration is needed.** For example, we won't usually ask why a high school student we have never met is working at McDonald's.

3. **No behavior pattern applies, but there are no conflicts.**

   Here the understander's other goals determine whether to elaborate. For example, if we are detectives trailing someone, we'll try to explain his every turn, in order to guess his destination. But if we are walking down the street and we see a friend drive by, it is less likely that we'll wonder—unless we're worried about whether he will get back in time to give us the ride he promised.

4. **Stereotypes conflict with the action.**

   Conflicts need to be elaborated. For example, if we see someone middle-aged working as a McDonald's counterperson, we'll probably try to explain it. We examine this case further when we discuss pattern-based anomaly detection in Chapter 4.

---

[3]We can imagine how any of these might become relevant—for example, metal fatigue might make the life cycle of the spacecraft a crucial concern. However, such schemas are probably not considered by casual observers until an anomaly (such as a device failure) shows that they should have been taken into account.

When processing actions, ACCEPTER's main focusing heuristic is to concentrate on the involvement of known actors. If an actor has been encountered previously, it is reasonable to concentrate on a situation's ramifications for that actor, to try to connect the old and new incidents. For example, if a racing fan has been reading about Swale in the newspapers and already has a model of him, reading about Swale's Belmont win can add to that model—it is reasonable for him to form further expectations about Swale's career. However, if the fan has not been following Swale but does recognize the jockey riding him, the main interest in the story is its effects on the jockey, rather than on aspects of the situation that are unconnected to prior knowledge. ACCEPTER's schema selection is actor-centered: Rather than always using the same schemas to package for a routine situation, ACCEPTER tries to track the actors it knows about.

> ACCEPTER's schema selection is actor-centered.

Actor-centered schema selection provides the flexible focus we described in the previous example of John working at McDonald's.

If ACCEPTER knows more than one actor in a situation, it will form expectations for the ramifications on each one, just as someone knowing both a horse and his jockey might consider the effects of a racing victory on both of their futures. If no known actors are involved, ACCEPTER selects MOPs providing expectations for each nonstereotyped actor. Schema selection efforts are often concerned with finding the single "best" schema to account for a situation; in our view, multiple schemas are frequently needed.

> ACCEPTER may activate multiple schemas to understand a single routine situation.

In the sentence "John served the customer a hamburger," the customer is a stereotype (has no features beyond the standard ones for its category), so ACCEPTER will generate expectations about what John will do next, rather than what the customer will. If all the actors in an event are stereotyped, the system falls back on SAM's event-based approach to schema selection and activates the default MOP for packaging the given situation.

For example, consider how ACCEPTER processes two alternative versions of a story about a Kentucky Derby loss by the horse Total Disaster, ridden by a jockey named Mark.

```
Processing:  There is a M-HORSE-RACE with LOSE as its OUTCOME,
             KENTUCKY-DERBY as its NAME, TOTAL-DISASTER as its
             HORSE, and MARK as its JOCKEY.
```

When ACCEPTER tries to generate a packaging structure for the input, there is no way to decide the best focus: Both Total Disaster and Mark are new to the system, so either could be important. Consequently, it generates expectations for the ramifications on each:

```
Checking if a packaging MOP can be instantiated for
"KENTUCKY-DERBY".

    Identifying important roles to package.

    No known actors fill roles in KENTUCKY-DERBY

    The role(s) HORSE, and JOCKEY of KENTUCKY-DERBY are filled by
    nonstereotyped actors.

        Checking for packages focusing on the JOCKEY role of
        "KENTUCKY-DERBY".

        A possible package for KENTUCKY-DERBY is "There is a
        M-JOCKEY-LIFE with MARK as its ACTOR."
        ⋮

        Checking for packages focusing on the HORSE role of
        "KENTUCKY-DERBY".

        A possible package for KENTUCKY-DERBY is "There is a
        M-RACEHORSE-LIFE with TOTAL-DISASTER as its ACTOR."
        ⋮
```

In the following example, however, ACCEPTER processes a version of the story that does not specify which horse Mark rode. In this story, ACCEPTER assumes that the ramifications for the horse are unimportant, and only activates a MOP to generate expectations for Mark:

```
Processing:  There is a M-HORSE-RACE with WIN as its OUTCOME,
             KENTUCKY-DERBY as its NAME, MARK as its JOCKEY,
             and RACEHORSE-575 as its HORSE.
             ⋮

    Checking if a packaging MOP can be instantiated for
    "KENTUCKY-DERBY".
```

```
Identifying important roles to package.

No known actors fill roles in KENTUCKY-DERBY

The role(s) JOCKEY of KENTUCKY-DERBY are filled by nonstereotyped
actors.

    Checking for packages focusing on the JOCKEY role of
    "KENTUCKY-DERBY".

    A possible package for KENTUCKY-DERBY is "There is a
    M-JOCKEY-LIFE with MARK as its ACTOR".
```

Finally, if Mark is already known to the system, ACCEPTER concentrates on him, even if the horse is mentioned by name. This is shown by the processing of the story "Mark was a 17-year-old jockey. Total Disaster lost the Belmont Stakes with Mark as his jockey." ACCEPTER's processing of the first line places Mark in memory:

```
Processing:   There is a HUMAN with 17 as its AGE, and MARK as
              its NAME.
                 ⋮
The information about MARK has been accepted in context
BELIEF-SET-561.
```

When ACCEPTER processes the next line, Mark is the only known actor, so it focuses on aspects of the event that are relevant to him, even though the horse is specified.

```
Checking if a packaging MOP can be instantiated for
"BELMONT-STAKES".

Identifying important roles to package.

The role(s) JOCKEY of BELMONT-STAKES are filled by known actors.

    Checking for packages focusing on the JOCKEY role of
    "BELMONT-STAKES".
```

A possible package for BELMONT-STAKES is "There is a
M-JOCKEY-LIFE with MARK as its ACTOR".

In this case, ACCEPTER does not activate its schema for a racehorse's life.
However, it might activate that schema later, if it were given another input
concentrating on the horse.

3.3   Overview of ACCEPTER's Anomaly Detection

The previous sections show how ACCEPTER generates the beliefs and expectations that make up its routine understanding; we now turn to how it
notices flaws in that understanding.

Conceptually, ACCEPTER'S anomaly detection has three main parts.
First, as it processes new information, it compares that information to specific prior beliefs and expectations. Second, when no specific information is
applicable, it judges the reasonableness of new information by comparing it
to patterns and known causal restrictions. Third, when problems are found,
it applies additional checks to identify the problems as precisely as possible.
Figure 3.2 sketches the components of this process.

In the remainder of this chapter, we concentrate on the first phase of
ACCEPTER's processing: detecting conflicts with beliefs and expectations
concerning specific events. In Chapter 4 we discuss the latter phases, pattern-
based anomaly detection and finer grained checks.

3.4   Conflicts with Specific Prior Expectations

The most basic reason to accept new information is to recognize it as an
instance of something we already knew or expected. If the new information
refers to a previous belief and simply reiterates what we thought, no further
verification is necessary. On the other hand, if new information conflicts with
what we knew or expected, it is anomalous and needs to be explained—both
to revise our erroneous view of the world, and to prevent future errors. For
example, when the crew of the Vincennes shot down the plane that they
expected to attack the ship and then learned that they had shot down an
airliner, they mounted an enormous effort to explain the error and avoid
repetitions in the future.

Detecting expectation failures, or conflicts with existing beliefs, depends
on three steps:

1. **Recognition** of the most closely related beliefs or expectations in memory.

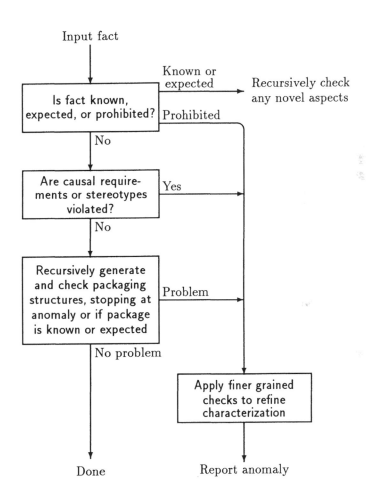

FIG. 3.2.   ACCEPTER's anomaly detection algorithm.

2. **Evaluation of similarity** between prior knowledge and new information, to determine if the most similar beliefs or expectations are actually relevant.

3. **Identification of differences** between relevant prior knowledge and the new information; these differences are anomalies.

The process of recognition—retrieving from memory the most similar expectation or belief—has not been seriously addressed by ACCEPTER. Because of the form of ACCEPTER's input, the third step—identification of differences—is comparatively straightforward: Input information specifies only limited numbers of features, and ACCEPTER controls comparison cost by doing no inference to derive features that are unspecified. The second step—evaluation of similarity—is a difficult problem for any anomaly detection system, and we next discuss some of the issues involved.

3.4.1   Partial Matching

Detecting anomalies requires matching events that are only partially consistent: noticing that new information and prior knowledge refer to the same situation, despite conflicts between them. Although prior understanding systems and case-based reasoning systems have addressed the problem of matching events, their needs have been different from those of an understander that can learn from anomalies, leading them not to consider the problem of when disparate references refer to the same thing.

Matching in story understanding: Partial matching was recognized early on as a difficult problem in story understanding [Charniak, 1978]. However, most expectation-based story understanding systems assume that different descriptions of a single event or object will not conflict, so that inputs always match relevant expectations without any conflicts. Even for the well-circumscribed domains that SAM processed, this approach severely limited the stories that could be processed. For example, if SAM processed a story in which one waitress brought John his menu, and another brought him his food, the scene of delivering food would not be recognized as satisfying the expectation for John to be served.[4] By definition, SAM's expectations never fail—when SAM matches inputs to stereotyped expectations, its requirements for matching prevent it from ever finding a problem.

---

[4]Some flexibility was added by having alternate tracks for problems: For example, the system could recognize that a hamburger that arrived burnt was a substitution for the normal hamburger that was expected. However, alternatives like this had to be explicitly anticipated in a script.

> A system that requires perfect matches cannot detect anomalies.

CBR matching—always accepting the closest match: In order to apply knowledge from the closest old case, CBR systems must find the closest old case to a new situation, despite their differences. Although it is assumed that the current situation is new, whether or not it is new is actually irrelevant to the system's processing: All that is important is that the closest possible prior reasoning be applied.

Partial Matching for Anomaly Detection

The problem faced by an anomaly detection system is more subtle: It must not only find the most similar case in memory but must decide whether that (possibly conflicting) case describes the same situation (in which case the conflicts are anomalies) or simply another similar one (in which case the conflicts are unimportant). An anomaly detector must decide whether the conflicts mean that system knowledge is flawed or are evidence that the two descriptions do not refer to the same thing. To choose between these possibilities, it needs heuristics for deciding when feature conflicts suggest distinct objects, and when they do not.

> An anomaly detector must distinguish between (1) conflicting descriptions of a single object or event, and (2) similar but distinct situations.

For example, when the American warship Vincennes shot down the Iranian airliner, early reports said that the plane was diving. However, later newspaper reports described an Iranian airliner that was climbing before being shot down. Readers recognized that the two descriptions referred to the same event, rather than referring to two distinct episodes, and noticed the conflict between reports as an anomaly to explain.

ACCEPTER's Approach to Matching Specific Objects and Events

When an event is expected, and a similar (but different) event occurs, in general there is no way to be certain of whether the new event occurs *instead of* the expected one. However, in many cases we can make reasonable hypotheses about whether one event substitutes for another. ACCEPTER has four simple rules for deciding when to merge two pieces of information, despite possible conflicts, and when to consider them unrelated.

Matching Two Objects or Events

If someone says that Iran Air flight 655 was shot down in 1986 over Iran, we recognize that the episode referred to is the Vincennes shootdown, even though the date and location are wrong. ACCEPTER merges objects or events if they belong to compatible categories, and they share *identifying features*—features that are uniquely associated with a given object or event, such as a flight number or name.

For example, one of the stories ACCEPTER processes involves an airline's change of departure gate for a flight: The first line of the story gives the check-in information that John is traveling to New York on flight 207, leaving from gate 5 at 7:00. ACCEPTER accepts the information and generates expectations for John's boarding, for his plane's take-off, flight, landing, and for his deplaning after the flight. ACCEPTER is next given the boarding announcement, which is that flight 207 is boarding at gate 7. Because the flight number is the same in both cases, it assumes the conflicting information refers to a single flight, so the conflict of gate numbers is anomalous. Noticing and explaining the conflict, either as a gate change or an erroneous announcement, would make it possible to go to the correct gate.

This method could be extended to use additional identifying features, such as lasting, highly unusual features—either physical features, or unusual behavior patterns or mannerisms. A New Haven teenager kept up with punk fashion by piercing her ears and nose, and wearing a chain connecting them. When people mentioned seeing someone's ears and nose connected by a chain, people always assumed she was the same person, despite wild variations in clothing and hair color. Another identifying feature is filling a particular role, if that role has fixed, unchanging fillers over a long time span. For example, we might assume that the owner of a given store is the person it was previously, even if a friend's description of her is not quite what we remembered.

However, to account for the flexibility of some partial matches, context-dependent criteria are needed. One context-dependent criterion is causal substitution [Schank, 1982]: When trying to match an event to an expectation, we can consider them to match if they satisfy the same goals. For example, if we expect an airline to deploy a jetway to allow passengers to board a plane, and the airline uses stairs instead, both serve the expected purpose, so we recognize that the stairs substitute for the jetway. Having noticed the anomalous substitution, we can go on to explain why one is used instead of the other.

Matching Two Descriptions of a Feature

In the preceding examples, it was necessary to decide whether an object or event substituted for expected ones. Anomalies can also arise when it is already known that a single object or event is being described, but there is a conflict between different descriptions of some of its features. There are two possibilities for how feature descriptions for a single object or event may conflict:

Value of feature differs, but times overlap: This situation is a straightforward conflict; for example, it occurs if someone states that Iran Air flight 655 was descending moments before being shot down, and someone else claims it was climbing at that time.

Times conflict, but feature has the same value: This case is more subtle, because the conflict may not actually indicate a problem. The given feature value may have held at both the expected time and the new time, making the new feature description irrelevant to the prior expectation or belief. For example, if we expected Sue to be in New York next week, and we find that she was there today, it might be because she took an additional trip. In that case, the new information is unrelated to our expectation, and is not anomalous. However, it might also be the case that the feature value holds the expected value at the new time instead of at the expected time, requiring an explanation of the change. This would be the case if Sue changed the date of her expected trip, in which case the timing change is an anomaly.

ACCEPTER has only a simple heuristic for deciding between these cases. If an event happening in a story at time t_1 causes ACCEPTER to generate an expectation for a feature to have a value at some time t_2, and an input feature description states that the feature had the value at some time t_3, ACCEPTER assumes that the input description is relevant to the expectation whenever time t_3 is later than t_1. For example, in one of ACCEPTER's stories, ACCEPTER is given an input that someone sets out on a subway trip, and arrives a few hours later. ACCEPTER assumes that the late arrival replaces the expected one that was supposed to be much earlier, and considers the late arrival anomalous. However, if a story describes someone starting a subway trip to station X at noon, and the story also includes the information that the person was at station X at 9:00 AM that day, the arrival would be assumed to be part of a previous trip.

Note that the preceding criteria apply only when ACCEPTER matches inputs against prior beliefs and expectations. When ACCEPTER matches inputs against prohibitions, it assumes that any difference between the input and the prohibited fact makes the prohibition inapplicable. For example, if a child was told not to buy candy and bought fruit instead, ACCEPTER would not consider that the prohibition applied, because the object purchased was different. This differs from how relevance would be judged if an expectation were involved, instead of a prohibition: If the child were expected to buy candy and bought fruit instead, it would note the partial match between the expectation and the input and report an anomaly.

3.5   The Need for Additional Tests

The previous sections show how ACCEPTER uses MOPs to guide its routine understanding, and how it matches new inputs against specific beliefs and the explicit expectations from active MOPs. When an expectation or belief partially matches new inputs, any conflicts are anomalous, and ACCEPTER requests explanation in order to update its world model.

However, many of the inputs an understander encounters are novel ones that match no prior beliefs, and that do not fit into any previously active schemas. To determine the consistency of prior knowledge with these inputs, a mechanism is needed for finding less explicit conflicts.

One alternative would be to do exhaustive inference chaining to try to connect the new inputs to prior beliefs, noting conflicts as they arise. However, as we have discussed in section 2.3.2, the cost of such inferencing is prohibitive.

The next chapter addresses the problem of detecting implicit problems. To control verification cost, it proposes an alternative approach to inference chaining: pattern-based verification. Pattern-based verification replaces inference by table lookup through stereotyped patterns that are associated with actors, primitive actions and MOPs, and signals anomalies when those patterns conflict with new information.

4 Pattern-Based Anomaly Detection

Perfect detection of belief conflicts would require inferring all the ramifications of the new information to compare them to prior knowledge—an overwhelming inference task. We propose avoiding this cost by an alternative method: basing anomaly detection on table lookup. In this approach, new information is compared to standard patterns stored in memory. Information that conflicts is judged anomalous, and nonconflicting information is accepted. We develop a theory of the content of the needed tables, describe their organization in memory, and argue that the tables' coverage is sufficient to detect a wide range of anomalies.

When new information conflicts directly with specific prior beliefs and expectations, as described in the previous chapter, anomaly detection is relatively straightforward. However, new information and old beliefs may be incompatible even if there is no direct conflict. For example, there is no direct conflict between being an impoverished student and flying first class, but the thought of a poor student flying first class still seems anomalous. We need a process for detecting these more subtle problems.

One method for detecting them is to build inference chains deriving the ramifications of new information, to compare those ramifications with prior knowledge. In the flying example, we could infer that flying first class is probably enabled by possessing a ticket, that possessing a ticket is probably achieved by buying one, and that buying a first class ticket is enabled by possessing a large amount of money—which conflicts with the belief of the student's poverty. However, because of the combinatorial explosion of possibilities as we build the inference chains, this method would be overwhelmingly expensive to apply [Rieger, 1975].

We propose an alternative method for anomaly detection. Rather than being based on inference chaining, our method is based on table lookup of stereotyped patterns. When the new information matches no prior expectations or beliefs and conflicts with patterns, it is anomalous; otherwise it is accepted without further verification.

> ACCEPTER decides the reasonableness of new information by using table lookup to retrieve stereotype-based patterns, and checking the information for conflicts with them.

The anomaly of the student flying first class can be noticed because of a pattern conflict: People who fly first class are usually business people. After pattern-based checks detect this anomaly, finer grained checks can be used to decide the seriousness of the problem, and to characterize the problem more precisely, in order to guide search for explanations (e.g., to direct explanation towards the problematic aspect of the flight: how the student could afford it). However, such processing is done *only* if pattern conflicts are found: Pattern-based checks provide a low-cost mechanism for focusing further processing.

In this chapter we present a theory of what tables of patterns are needed, how they are organized, and how pattern conflicts can be analyzed by finer grained checks. Finally, we consider the coverage of the pattern-based approach. The goal of pattern-based anomaly detection is not to detect all anomalies, but to achieve a reasonable tradeoff between the efficiency and coverage of anomaly detection—to detect a reasonable proportion of anomalies that people notice in everyday situations. We survey the types of anomalies that this method can and cannot detect and substantiate its coverage of a wide range of everyday anomalies.

4.1   Overview of ACCEPTER's Pattern Types

Human understanding is shaped by stereotypes about what to expect. For example, schemas allow us to fill in the details of standard situations (e.g., [Bower et al., 1979; Schank & Abelson, 1977]). Stereotypes also seem important in deciding which beliefs to accept: Kahneman et al. [1982] show that when subjects are asked to decide the *probability* of a person having a given occupation on a list, the subjects' rankings are the same as when they are asked to judge the person's *similarity* to the stereotypes for people in that occupation.

As Kahneman et al. point out, similarity-based judgments can be poor estimators of likelihood because of ignoring factors that affect probability but not similarity, such as the prior probability of having a particular occupation. However, as they also point out, such heuristics are often helpful. First, similarity-based judgments frequently *do* give useful answers. Second, they are efficient to use, and rely only on information that is likely to be available, whereas probabilistic approaches rely on information that may be hard to obtain and hard to update accurately, and on many interrelated factors whose influences may be hard to assess.

When ACCEPTER's prior beliefs and expectations are irrelevant to new information, ACCEPTER judges the new information's reasonableness by checking how well it fits stereotyped patterns [Leake, 1989]. Selection of patterns to check is based primarily on the current understanding context: ACCEPTER judges how reasonable inputs are by evaluating both the reasonableness of the inputs in themselves, and how well they fit the MOPs activated to accept them.

Each of ACCEPTER's patterns focuses on a single aspect of a situation and is stored separately in ACCEPTER's memory. ACCEPTER evaluates multiple aspects of complex events by retrieving and applying the most specifically applicable pattern of each applicable pattern type.

> The reasonableness of novel, complex events can be judged in terms of combinations of standard patterns.

ACCEPTER uses six types of patterns:

- **Causal patterns**, which express standard causal requirements for filling an event.

  For example, anything that performs the primitive action GRASP from Conceptual Dependency Theory, be it a person or a space shuttle's robot arm, must have some kind of hand to do the grasping.

- **Normative event sequence patterns**, which express the normal order of events and their temporal separation in a given context.

  For example, that a space mission usually includes a launch, a spacewalk within a few days, and re-entry within a few days of that.

- **Object feature patterns**, which represent the standard attributes of objects in a given category.

  For example, that space suits are usually white.

- **Stereotypes for events' role-fillers**, which represent the usual types of actors or objects expected for each role of an event. Stereotypes for role-fillers are divided into two subtypes:

  - **Normative role-fillers**, which contain information on the standard types of objects that fill roles in an event.

    For example, that those who fly on space missions are usually astronauts.

  - **Predisposing features for a role**, which represent the features that make an object likely to fill a specific type of role.

    For example, that top military test pilots are likely to become astronauts.

- **Feature-based functional limitations**, which suggest that certain object features cause deficiencies for filling a role.

  For example, that space suits made of a particular material are less flexible than normal.

- **Actor's behavior patterns**, which reflect the types of actions in which an actor often participates.

  For example, that some astronauts are known for performing practical jokes.

The following sections discuss the content and structure of each of these stereotypes, and their organization in ACCEPTER's memory.

4.2   ACCEPTER's Patterns and their Structure

4.2.1   Causal Patterns

One criterion for judging the reasonableness of simple events is to consider whether they are consistent with causal knowledge. For example, people can only walk if they have functional legs. If we gave money to a beggar who claimed to have no legs and later saw him walking, the conflict would be anomalous. An explanation pointing to fraud could help us avoid being taken advantage of in the future.

Organization and representation of causal patterns: Causal patterns are stored in memory under the events they describe, indexed by the event and the name of the role being described. They are represented in terms of four components: the package (act or MOP) for which causal restrictions are being described, the role being described, the required type of object to

TABLE 4.1
Components of Causal Patterns

Component	Example
Package	GRASP
Role	Actor
Required object type	No requirement
Required features	Opposable moving parts

fill the role (if any), and a list of any required slot values. Table 4.1 shows the causal pattern for being able to perform the Conceptual Dependency primitive action GRASP, which specifies that the actor must have movable parts that can apply pressure on opposite sides of an object in order to do the grasping.

Despite the usefulness of causal patterns, it is impractical to use them to check complex events: There may be too many causal requirements to enumerate, or it may be too hard to delineate the attributes involved. For example, a task like car repair has intellectual and physical requirements such as quantitative and qualitative reasoning skills, knowledge, experience, strength and dexterity, and so on—we could not hope to describe and quantify all of them. For this reason, ACCEPTER relies primarily on normative patterns that leave many causal connections implicit; we begin our discussion of them next.

4.2.2   Normative Event Sequences

ACCEPTER's information about routine event sequences is contained in its MOPs, which are organized in an abstraction net in the system's memory. As discussed in section 3.2.1, MOPs represent the standard sequence of events expected in routine situations, and the timing between events. Contradictions of these expectations are anomalous. For example, Swale's death partially matches the expectation for a racehorse's death but conflicts with the expectation that the death will be a few years after his racing days, making it anomalously premature.

4.2.3   Object Feature Patterns

Object feature patterns describe normal features expected in members of a category—for example, the fact that successful racehorses tend to be in good physical condition. ACCEPTER's categories are not defined in terms of a set of necessary and sufficient features for category membership, but in terms of conditions for recognizing members of the category, and inferences that can be drawn once a category instance has been recognized [Schank et al., 1986]. Consequently, any of the "normal" features may or may not be present in a particular concept instance. However, deviations from normal features are still surprising if not already expected—it is anomalous for a racehorse to be broken down, even though some racehorses are.

When input describes an object feature that differs from category norms, ACCEPTER considers the conflict anomalous and requests an explanation.[1] Explaining the conflict may help to refine object categories: perhaps only racehorses running in the very best races are in top condition, or all racehorses are in bad condition from the rigors of training, so the generalization should be corrected.

The following output shows ACCEPTER detecting the conflict between normative expectations for racehorses' condition, and input of a conjecture that Swale's death resulted from him being in bad physical condition.

```
Checking if "SWALE'S LOW PHYSICAL-CONDITION" is already
known, or conflicts with facts in memory.

    "SWALE'S LOW PHYSICAL-CONDITION" conflicts with inherited
    feature.  SUCCESSFUL-RACEHORSEs usually have HIGH as
    PHYSICAL-CONDITION.

    ... Conflict with prior beliefs--- anomalous unless expected.

    Checking if "SWALE'S LOW PHYSICAL-CONDITION" is expected
    from (or prohibited by) active MOPs.

    ... Expectations don't account for the conflicting feature(s).

Anomaly detected!
```

Organization and representation of feature patterns: ACCEPTER's categories are organized in its memory in the same abstraction net used for specific objects and for its MOPs. Object feature patterns are stored under the categories, indexed by the name of the feature being described. They contain the category, the feature being described, and its usual value for category members, as shown in Table 4.2.

---

[1] Although ACCEPTER does not model differences in the strengths of expectations for normative features, people find some deviations more anomalous than others: Even though most lawyers are rich, people may not be surprised to see a lawyer with a modest income; but people are always surprised when they see blue corn for the first time.

TABLE 4.2
Components of Object Feature Patterns

Component	Example
Category	Successful racehorse
Feature	Physical condition
Normative value	High

4.2.4 Normative Role-Fillers

Just as people have stereotypes for situations and objects, they have stereotypes for the types of actors that perform certain acts, and the types of objects that are appropriate to use in those acts. Noticing an unusual actor or object, and explaining why it can fill the role, may give us useful information: If we always thought that changing a car's oil required a mechanic, but we see someone changing the oil for himself, we can learn that it is simple enough for us to do as well.

ACCEPTER's descriptions of normative role-fillers have two components. The first is the category in memory that most closely fits the usual role-fillers. For example, the actor of surgery is normally a member of the class of doctors. Referring to the category avoids individual checks for all causally needed category features, replacing them with single check for category membership.

The check for category membership is inexpensive for ACCEPTER to apply. Its representation of objects and events includes a link to the most specific categories to which they belong, and it decides whether these are specifications of the desired category by following their abstraction links. No effort is made to infer category membership from object or event features, because it would potentially be very costly.

The second component of normative role-filler descriptions is a list of features that cannot be assumed for category members. For example, a doctor might only be qualified to perform a particular procedure if he or she had received additional certification. In that case, the role-filler pattern for the actor of the procedure would be (doctor) + (certified in the procedure).

In the preceding example, the special features hold in addition to the usual features of members of the normative category. However, special features can also be exceptions to usual features for category members. For example, if we believed that most doctors are skillful, but that malpractice suits involve incompetent doctors, we might expect the defendants in malpractice suits to satisfy (doctor) + (low professional skill).

ACCEPTER represents role-filler stereotype patterns as:
(category of normal filler) + (special features)

To judge whether an input matches a role-filler pattern, ACCEPTER first checks the role-filler's category and matches explicit role-filler features against the special features in the pattern. When the input does not specify values for the relevant features, ACCEPTER uses the values inherited from the abstractions of the input's category. When deciding whether the features hold, ACCEPTER again controls inference by using only explicit information, rather than chaining to attempt to derive the desired features from others.

Output from the Challenger example in Chapter 2 contains an example of ACCEPTER's use of normative role-filler patterns. Because ACCEPTER starts with no expectations about Challenger, it applies normative role-filler information to the input "Challenger was an American spacecraft," to verify whether the spacecraft's sponsor is reasonable (the name "Challenger" is assumed reasonable, because the system has no patterns describing which names are likely). The usual sponsor of space missions is one of the superpowers, so it accepts the input as reasonable:

```
Phase 2:  Judging plausibility by comparing to patterns.

   Checking if the role-fillers of "CHALLENGER" are reasonable.

      Checking if action/actor combination makes sense.

         ... CHALLENGER CONFIRMS expectations from the role-filling
         pattern "SUPERPOWERs routinely fill role SPONSOR
         in SPACECRAFT".
```

In the story of the Vincennes' shootdown, a conflict with normative role-filler patterns reveals an anomaly to be explained. Soon after the Vincennes shot down the Iranian airliner, and before the story had reached the United States through Navy channels, Iranian news reports claimed that the United States had shot down an airliner—something that American readers rejected as implausible. Likewise, when ACCEPTER processes the Iranian statement without any prior information about the incident, it considers the airliner an unlikely target:

```
Phase 2:  Judging plausibility by comparing to patterns.

   Checking if the role-fillers of "VINCENNES'S SHOOTDOWN"
   are reasonable.
      .
```

```
Checking if action/actor combination makes sense.
⋮
Checking if nonactor slot-fillers make sense.

    Checking whether IRANAIR'S AIRLINER is a normal type
    of filler for role TARGET of SHOOTDOWN.

    Retrieving stereotypes for TARGET of SHOOTDOWN.
    Stereotyped TARGET is a MILITARY-PLANE.

Anomaly detected!

 IRANAIR'S AIRLINER AS TARGET OF VINCENNES'S SHOOTDOWN
 has the problem NON-NORMATIVE-ROLE-FILLER.
```

Organization of normative role-filler patterns: ACCEPTER's normative role-filler patterns are indexed under the MOP whose roles they describe, and the names of the roles they describe. When no information is available for a given role under the input MOP type, ACCEPTER searches its abstraction net breadth-first to find a MOP for which normative filler information is specified and applies that information to the more specific MOP. For example, if no specific information were available about the normal types of planes used in a particular type of attack, it would be possible to move to air attacks in general and inherit the normative role-filler pattern for the planes used in them.

Representation of normative role-filler patterns: The patterns are represented in memory structures with four components: The package (act, MOP, or object) to which the pattern applies, the role for which the pattern describes normative fillers, the usual category of fillers, and special features with respect to that category. For example, for a drug overdose to be believable, the drug taken must be a strong drug. Table 4.3 summarizes ACCEPTER'S representation for normative role-filler information for the drug taken in its MOP M-drug-overdose. When ACCEPTER considers the explanation that Swale might have been killed by performance-enhancing drugs administered by his trainer, the conflict between this pattern and knowledge that performance-enhancing drugs are administered in low doses prompts an anomaly: that the dose should not have been high enough to be fatal.

Normative role-filler information is useful for detecting role-fillers that are implausible. However, it gives no information about whether a plausible role-filler is particularly likely. The following section discusses patterns

TABLE 4.3

Components of Normative Role-Filler Patterns

Component	Example
Package	Drug overdose
Role	Drug taken
Usual filler type	Drug
Special filler features	High medicinal-strength

that complement normative role-filler patterns by supporting the likelihood of certain role-fillers.

4.2.5 Predisposing Features for a Role

ACCEPTER considers that an object or event is likely to fill a role, instead of simply possible, if it has certain features in addition to those associated with the normative role-filler type. For example, a predisposing feature for being a jogger is being health conscious; we are more likely to believe that someone went jogging if we believe he is health conscious.

Predisposing feature patterns are used when ACCEPTER checks the reasonableness of Swale dying of a heart attack. The normative victim of heart attack is an animal—only animals have heart attacks, and any animal might be susceptible—but not all animals are actually likely to have them. If a particular animal is high-strung, however, the likelihood of heart attack is increased. Thus a predisposing feature for filling the victim role of a heart attack is being high-strung. When ACCEPTER evaluates the plausibility of Swale having had a heart attack, it retrieves the predisposing feature pattern, indexed under instances of heart attacks, stating that high excitability is a predisposing feature for heart attacks. Because Swale is a racehorse, and racehorses are high-strung, Swale inherits the feature of being high-strung, and the pattern applies to him. This makes ACCEPTER consider the heart attack plausible.

To avoid excessive inferencing, ACCEPTER's search for predisposing features is once again limited to features that are already explicitly known for the object, or that can be inherited from its abstractions.

Organization of predisposing features: Predisposing feature information is indexed and inherited in the same way as normative role-filler information.

Representation of predisposing features: Predisposing feature patterns describe features that make objects likely to fill a particular role in

TABLE 4.4
Components of Predisposing Feature Patterns

Component	Example
Package	Heart attack
Role	Victim
Predisposing features	High excitability

a MOP, so they include the MOP, the role in that MOP, and a list of pre-disposing features for filling the role.[2] Table 4.4 shows the components of ACCEPTER's predisposing feature pattern for heart attacks.

4.2.6   Feature-Based Functional Limitations

Consistency with normative filler types does not assure that the action is reasonable. For example, not all racehorses are reasonable candidates for running in races: An injured horse will be kept out of races until he heals.

Checking for such problems raises two questions: which object features to consider, and how to check the features' importance. Given the right context, any of an object's individual features might cause problems for an action, yet for complex objects the number of features to check can be extremely high. Furthermore, most of the attributes we might know about are likely to be irrelevant—features such as horse's lineage, monetary value, or press coverage are very likely to be irrelevant to deciding whether it is reasonable for the horse to run in a race.

When ACCEPTER checks for limitations that are relevant to a current action, it does not search under all object features: it only checks features that conflict with standard features for the normal type of filler for the role. By only checking these features, ACCEPTER focuses its verification by context.

> When checking for problems, ACCEPTER focuses on features that are unusual compared to stereotypes for the normal role-filler.

ACCEPTER's restricted comparison identifies features like a racehorse's injured hoof, but not features related to other abstractions, even if the horse is also unusual compared to those abstractions. For example, the particular horse might be a celebrity in its own right after a number of TV specials, but differences between the horse and other celebrities would not be checked—the

---

[2]It would be reasonable for predisposing feature patterns to include information about the types of objects likely to fill the role, as do normative role-filler patterns. However, this information is not included in ACCEPTER's representation of predisposing features.

fact that the horse had never been interviewed, though unusual for celebrities, is unlikely to be important to his racing performance.

The following output gives an example of this process. The system is processing the fictitious story of Last Chance Louie, a lame racehorse, winning the Kentucky Derby. When evaluating Louie's racing, the program looks for unusual features of Louie compared to other racehorses and identifies a problem because he is lame:

```
Checking if the role-fillers of "KENTUCKY-DERBY" are reasonable.

Checking if action/actor combination makes sense.

Searching up the abstraction net for limitations

... LOUIE AS HORSE OF KENTUCKY-DERBY has the problem
PHYSICAL-DISABILITY.
```

Anomaly detected!

```
PHYSICAL-DISABILITY problem:  LOUIE AS HORSE OF KENTUCKY-DERBY
CONFLICTS-WITH the prohibition of KENTUCKY-DERBY due to
LAME-ANIMALs are unable to fill the role ACTOR of MOVE-BODY-PART.
```

When ACCEPTER finds a possibly relevant feature that is unusual, it analyzes the importance of the feature in terms of underlying problems. The mechanism it uses is decomposition of an action into its constituent actions, which we describe in section 4.5.1.

Organization of functional limitations: Functional limitations are indexed under the features that prompt the limitations, and the behavior that is impeded by the limitations.

Representation of functional limitations: ACCEPTER's object limitation patterns include information about the object (or category of objects) with the deficiency, and the package and role for which the deficiency arises. In addition, they include a summary of the reason for the deficiency (currently implemented as a keyword describing a problem class). Table 4.5 shows the object limitation pattern for a lame animal.

4.2.7   Actor's Behavior Patterns

The tests just described do not consider the effect of an actor's preferences and habits on its actions. However, this information can be important: Although

TABLE 4.5
Components of Object Limitation Patterns

Component	Example
Object with limitation	Lame animal
Package that limitation affects	Move body part
Role affected	Actor
Problem description	Physical-disability

ACCEPTER's normative role-filler information about fast food restaurants tells us that any human might eat in them, we expect gourmets to prefer to avoid them. ACCEPTER represents this type of knowledge in *actor's behavior patterns*, which represent the actor's tendencies to favor or avoid participating in particular actions and plans.[3]

Actor's behavior patterns are a form of the expectations and prohibitions already described; they represent information about the classes of actions that an actor favors or avoids. This kind of information often comes from role themes, which represent stereotyped knowledge about the plans and goals associated with actors in certain societal roles [Schank & Abelson, 1977]; for example, we expect that a policeman will direct traffic and investigate crimes. The patterns may also be built up from experience with particular actors (if we often see John at some restaurant we may generalize that he follows a pattern of going there) or from group stereotypes (such as the French liking wine). Similar patterns exist for avoided actions, as in the expectation that a policeman will avoid drinking when on duty. Additional prohibitions may arise from social norms (it is anomalous to make noise in a library), or legal requirements that people usually respect (unlicensed people seldom drive).

ACCEPTER's actor's behavior patterns allow it to detect an anomaly when processing the story of Len Bias. Len Bias was a college basketball forward, the highest scorer ever at the University of Maryland. In 1986, when he was 22, he became eligible for the professional basketball draft and was ecstatic to be chosen as the Boston Celtics' first pick. However, the day after being chosen, as he chatted with his friends, he collapsed on the floor. His heart had stopped beating, and all efforts to revive him failed.

ACCEPTER is given a version of Len Bias' story that begins with the information that Bias was selected in the basketball draft. Applying its routine understanding process, it instantiates a MOP to package that event: the

---

[3]Note that ACCEPTER's routine understanding process does not seriously address the problem of hypothesizing an actor's plans. For some approaches to that problem, see Charniak [1986], Kautz and Allen [1986], Norvig [1989], Schank and Abelson [1977] and Wilensky [1983]. Our attention is restricted to the problems of how to decide whether the hypothesized plan is reasonable (examined in the present section) and how to guide search for explanations if it is not (examined in section 6.2).

MOP for an athlete's active career, which includes scenes for initial training, the athletic draft, and athletic competition. Because athletes are prohibited from breaking training, the MOP also includes a prohibition for drug use during the career.

```
Checking if a packaging MOP can be instantiated for
"BIAS'S M-ATHLETIC-DRAFT".

    Identifying important roles to package.

    The role(s) ATHLETE of BIAS'S M-ATHLETIC-DRAFT are filled
    by known actors.

    Checking for packages focusing on the ATHLETE role of
    "BIAS'S M-ATHLETIC-DRAFT".

    A possible package for BIAS'S M-ATHLETIC-DRAFT is "There
    is a M-ACTIVE-PLAY with BIAS as its ACTOR".

    Verifying whether BIAS'S M-ACTIVE-PLAY is a reasonable
    package.

    Doing routine understanding of the input ...
    ⋮

    Activating expectations/prohibitions from BIAS'S M-ACTIVE-PLAY.

        Expectations:
            BIAS'S M-ATHLETIC-TRAINING.
            BIAS'S M-ATHLETIC-DRAFT.
            BIAS'S M-ATHLETIC-COMPETITION.

        Prohibitions:
            BIAS'S M-RECREATIONAL-DRUGS.
```

The next fact in ACCEPTER's story is that Bias is dead. ACCEPTER considers the death anomalous because it is premature, and it asks for explanations.

Bias' death reminded one Yale student of Janis Joplin's, prompting the hypothesis that Bias was taking drugs to relieve the pressure of fame and died of an accidental overdose. When this hypothesis is evaluated by AC-CEPTER, it considers it anomalous because Bias should have been avoiding drugs because of training.

```
Checking if "BIAS'S M-RECREATIONAL-DRUGS" is already known,
or conflicts with facts in memory.

... No relevant belief found.

Checking if "BIAS'S M-RECREATIONAL-DRUGS" is expected
from (or prohibited by) active MOPs.

Problem detected installing "BIAS'S M-RECREATIONAL-DRUGS" in memory:
the prohibition of BIAS'S M-RECREATIONAL-DRUGS to BIAS'S
M-ACTIVE-PLAY.
```

ACCEPTER's question matches the hesitation of many people who found it implausible that Bias, who was upstanding in all respects, would have used drugs. In this case, the final explanation contradicted stereotypes: The death was eventually attributed to the effects of cocaine.

Actor's behavior patterns can give information beyond the mere fact that an actor tends to avoid or participate in a certain class of action: They can specify other details of that action, by including other role-fillers that are commonly expected when the actor performs the action. For example, we might know not just that someone often takes vacations, but that he takes them in Europe.

Behavior patterns do not represent the rational decision-making process that underlies the action, or the goals for which the actor uses the action. They say what a class of actor tends to do, but not why the actor does it. People often rely on this type of incomplete knowledge: For example, although many people know that those who were abused as children tend to abuse their own children, few know the mechanism underlying that pattern. ACCEPTER does not attempt to do detailed analysis of the motivations underlying its patterns, but section 4.5 discusses some heuristics for finding anomalies in the decision making underlying unusual actions.

Organization of actor's behavior patterns: Behavior patterns are indexed under the action, the actor, and the role being considered for the actor.

Because preferences reflect the relationship of an actor to an action, both the actor involved, and the actions the actor performs, may need to be abstracted in order to find an applicable pattern. To retrieve behavior patterns, ACCEPTER first searches patterns indexed under the specific action, for the specific actor, and then for abstractions of the actor. When that fails, it repeats the process for increasingly abstract characterizations of the action.

For example, to find whether Mary likes to play softball, this process

TABLE 4.6
Components of Avoidance Patterns

Component	Example
Package	M-restaurant at restaurant Y
Avoided role	Diner
Actor who avoids role	Person X

would first check whether Mary is known to be a frequent player, or whether she belongs to groups that play often—perhaps she belongs to a club that is proud of its softball team. If the search fails to retrieve information specifically applicable to baseball, it would investigate her preferences concerning abstractions of the game—perhaps team sports, or simply exercise. If we find that she is an exercise fanatic, it is reasonable to think of her as a softball player.

Representation of actor behavior patterns: ACCEPTER's patterns for what actors tend to do, and what they tend to avoid, include three components: the actor (or class of actor) whose behavior the pattern describes, and the type of action and role in that action that the actor participates in or avoids. Specifying the particular role is important because a given actor may avoid some parts of an action and favor others. For example, when X moved to New Haven, she got a job as a waitress in a restaurant Y, a very popular restaurant. When she saw conditions in the kitchen, she resolved never to eat there herself; nevertheless, she continued to be a waitress. These behaviors could be characterized by two patterns: the tendency to fill the **server** role in instantiations of the MOP **M-restaurant** at that restaurant, and the tendency to avoid filling the role of **diner** in **M-restaurant** there. Table 4.6 summarizes the components for her avoidance of the restaurant.

4.3   Pattern Retrieval

Each of ACCEPTER's stereotypes is installed in its memory net. For normative event sequence patterns, normative role-fillers, and predisposing features for a role, the primary index is the most specific MOP to which the pattern applies. For object feature patterns and behavior patterns, the primary index is the most specific class of objects or actors to which they apply.

When ACCEPTER tries to retrieve a pattern to use to check a fact, it first computes indices based on the fact and the pattern type. If these fail, it climbs the abstraction net, abstracting the primary index breadth-first until it can retrieve an applicable pattern. If nothing is found, it repeats the process, while abstracting the secondary index breadth-first through the memory

TABLE 4.7
ACCEPTER's Patterns and the Indices Used to Retrieve Them.

Pattern type	Used to Judge	Primary Index	Secondary Index
Normative event sequence	MOP scenes	MOP	Scene
Object feature	Object features	Object type	Feature
Normative role-filler	MOP role-fillers or obj. attributes	MOP or object	Role or feature
Predisposing feature	MOP role-fillers	MOP	Role
Functional limitation	MOP role-fillers	Object	MOP + role
Actor's behavior	MOP participation	Actor	MOP + role

hierarchy. Table 4.7 summarizes the indices for retrieving the knowledge AC-CEPTER uses for stereotype checks.

4.3.1   Choosing between Conflicting Stereotypes

ACCEPTER always applies the patterns most specifically applicable to the object or event being evaluated. However, sometimes two equally specific patterns will apply, and those patterns will conflict. For example, if we think of someone as both an athlete and a *bon vivant*, we might have trouble deciding if he is likely to party long into the night: Both the expectation for partying, and for refusing it, are associated with equally specific abstractions. ACCEPTER arbitrarily gives precedence to the first stereotype encountered in its breadth-first search of abstraction. A better method would be to identify the conflicting stereotypes and then use case-based reasoning to see which of those factors was stronger in similar situations in the past.

4.4   The Need to Identify Underlying Problems

If pattern conflicts arise, the understander needs to account for the discrepancy by explaining them. However, pattern conflicts give little information about the focus needed for explanation: pattern-based checks only identify unusual situations, rather than stating why the unusual features might be important. Consequently, when pattern conflicts are detected, it can be useful to apply finer grained tests to generate a more specific problem characterization before explaining. That characterization facilitates explanation construction by providing additional focus for explanation search.

For example, if someone tries to bake a casserole in a plastic dish, the type of dish is anomalous: People usually use ceramic ones. However, if the problem is described as "using a plastic dish rather than ceramic," and that description is used to retrieve explanations, *any* reasons to favor plastic over ceramic might be retrieved, including:

> *Buying plastic is more affordable than buying ceramic.*
>
> *Plastic is unbreakable, so it's safer when there are small children around the house.*
>
> *Plastic is lighter weight, so it's easier for the elderly to handle.*
>
> *Plastic containers are often made in brighter colors, so they're more cheerful to have around the house.*

All these explanations fail to address the real issue in the anomaly, which is that using a plastic dish for a casserole is anomalous because of a bad effect: The dish will melt.

Not only does the general characterization of plastic versus ceramic allow retrieval of the wrong explanations; it fails to allow retrieval of some relevant explanations that do not consider the relevant goodness of the materials:

> *This plastic is a special kind that can take high heat.*
>
> *People who usually cook in microwave ovens forget that most plastic containers can't take high heat.*

To avoid retrieving the explanations in the first set, and to be able to retrieve the explanations in the second, we need to know what causal properties make ceramic the usual choice. To be a good index for retrieving explanations, the anomaly description must state not only that plastic is unusual, but also that plastic does not satisfy the requirement that casseroles be cooked in heatproof containers.

> Pattern-based checks are a low-cost mechanism for finding problems; additional processing of pattern conflicts may be needed to give a useful problem description.

After ACCEPTER detects a conflict with patterns, it uses finer grained checks in an effort to recharacterize it in terms of *why* it should be surprising, in order to guide search towards explanations that address the underlying source of the conflict.

> For effective explanation retrieval, descriptions of pattern conflicts should be recharacterized in terms of specific causal problems.

4.5   Finer Grained Checks

ACCEPTER supplements its pattern checks with three types of finer grained checks that recharacterize pattern conflicts. The checks are *basic action decomposition*, which evaluates a role-filler's suitability for a role, and two motivational checks: *examination of direct effects*, which is used to check whether an action is consistent with actor goals, and *plan choice checks*, which see if the actor's observed plan choice conflicts with our model of the actor's decision making preferences. Although these checks are more expensive to apply than pattern-based checks, the inferencing they involve is still limited.

4.5.1   Basic Action Decomposition

People who fly first class are usually business people. But although it is unusual for a nonbusiness person to fly first class, the characterization "a nonbusiness person flying first class" is not very helpful in finding an explanation. By looking at the problems that the nonbusiness person might have with flying first class, we can generate more useful indices. For example, one requirement is being wealthy enough to pay for an expensive ticket. If we find that the person flying did not have much money, and the anomaly is characterized as "how could he do something he could not afford?," we might be able to use that to retrieve relevant explanations (such as winning a prize in a travel contest).

By looking at the restrictions on constituent parts of a complex event, we can generate a specific characterization of what might go wrong with an unusual role-filler. Basic action decomposition takes a MOP, decomposes it into its scenes, and checks any restrictions associated with those scenes that are relevant to the unusual role-filler. For example, if we heard that someone nonathletic had become a professional wrestler, we would be surprised, because usually wrestlers are athletes. If we checked what was involved in being a wrestler, we might find that most of the wrestler's activities are publicity appearances that anyone could handle, but that our candidate would be too frail to be successful in actual wrestling. This gives a precise aspect of the situation to explain: how someone weak can perform in wrestling matches. An explanation for this might be that the wrestling matches are faked.

In the following output, ACCEPTER applies basic-action decomposition to a fanciful explanation of Swale's death: that Swale, like Janis Joplin, felt the pressure of stardom and died of an overdose of the drugs taken to escape. Normally, only people take recreational drugs, so ACCEPTER's normative role-filler checks detect a problem. To characterize the problem more precisely, ACCEPTER does basic-action decomposition. ACCEPTER's MOP for injecting drugs has the steps of someone grasping the syringe, moving it to his arm, and taking the drugs into his body. Because Swale does not have hands, administering the drugs would have been impossible for him.

```
... SWALE AS DRUGGEE OF M-INJECT-RECREATIONAL-DRUGS-1880 has the
problem NON-NORMATIVE-ROLE-FILLER.

Doing basic action decomposition to check SWALE as DRUGGEE of
M-INJECT-RECREATIONAL-DRUGS-1880.

    The following roles in scenes of M-INJECT-RECREATIONAL-DRUGS-1880
    involve its DRUGGEE, and will be checked for problems:

    The role ACTOR of the scene SWALE'S GRASP.

    The role ACTOR of the scene SWALE'S PTRANS.

    The role ACTOR of the scene SWALE'S INGEST.

    ... SWALE AS ACTOR OF SWALE'S GRASP has the problem
    ILLEGAL-ROLE-FILLER.
```

This problem must be repaired by adaptation of the explanation. One alternative is to repair the explanation by deciding that, although Swale could not have administered the drugs, someone else might have—leading to the suggestion that perhaps his trainer administered drugs to him instead. Because trainers sometimes administer performance-enhancing drugs, this leads to a more plausible explanation: that his trainer might have given him an overdose of performance-enhancing drugs.[4]

4.5.2   Motivational Checks

ACCEPTER has two types of finer grained motivational checks, both intentionally limited to reduce processing cost. *Examination of direct effects* compares the immediate effects of an action to the actor's active goals, and stereotyped goals for the actor's group, to see if the action conflicts with them. For example, if someone wants to go to New York, we might ask why he took the bus to Boston, because taking that bus presumably has the standard effect of his arriving in Boston. Plan choice checks see if the actor's choice of a standard plan conflicts with our model of his decision making. For example, even if a friend has the goal of getting money, we would be surprised if he robbed a bank, because it is a risky way of getting cash.

---

[4]However, ACCEPTER also notices an anomalous assumption in this explanation that will have to be resolved before it can be accepted: that the trainer administered the wrong dose.

Examination of Direct Effects

Actors try to avoid actions that have bad effects on them. Although such actions are anomalous, we cannot hope to detect all possible bad effects of an action: For any action, there would be infinitely many effects to check. However, simply checking an action's direct effects can give an indication of whether the action undermines the actor's goals. For example, direct effects of buying a car are having possession of the car, and having less money. If we know someone is avoiding buying a car, and he buys it anyway, we can compare his goals to the direct effects of buying the car. If he is trying to save money, we can reformulate the anomaly as spending money on the car, which conflicts with his goal to save money.

ACCEPTER identifies goal problems by checking actions that conflict with actor's behavior patterns, to see if their direct effects undermine the actor's goals (either goals specifically known for the actor, or inherited from abstractions).[5] For example, when the system evaluates the explanation that Swale was poisoned by his owner, it detects a problem: The poisoning would have been illegal, and one of ACCEPTER's patterns is that people generally avoid illegal acts. This prompts it to look for the underlying motivation, to see whether the action satisfies an important goal. However, the only direct effect it finds is that the owner's property is destroyed, which conflicts with the goal of increasing wealth that is inherited from ACCEPTER's category for business people. Consequently, it rejects the explanation:

```
Checking if the role DRUGGER in M-POISON is a normal role for
BUSINESSMAN-2393 (or abstractions).

... BUSINESSMAN-2393'S M-POISON has the problem
CONTRADICTS-ROLE-AVOIDANCE-PATTERN.

No patterns of BUSINESSMAN-2393's behavior account for the role
DRUGGER in BUSINESSMAN-2393'S M-POISON.

Trying to infer possible motivations by checking effects of
BUSINESSMAN-2393'S M-POISON against BUSINESSMAN-2393's goals.

M-POISON-480 ==>
(by the link M-POISON-SCENE.17085)

    DEAD-AS-HEALTH-OF-SWALE ==>
```

---

[5]ACCEPTER's characterization of direct effects is quite arbitrary: It considers direct effects to be the effects that are reached by short inference chains (in the current implementation, chains of length 4 or less).

```
(by the link DEATH-OF-OWNED-ANIMAL ==> DESTRUCTION-OF-PROPERTY)

    DESTRUCTION-OF-PROPERTY-481 ==>
    (by the link DESTRUCTION-OF-PROPERTY ==> REDUCTION-OF-WEALTH)

    DECREASED-AS-WEALTH-OF-BUSINESSMAN-2393

... BUSINESSMAN-2393'S M-POISON has the problem GOAL-THREATENED.
```

Plan Choice Checks

To accept an action, we need to look not just at the goals it serves but also at whether it is a reasonable plan for those goals. In general, this is very hard to decide for a novel plan—doing so would require projecting all its ramifications, which involves both issues of controlling inference and of anticipating the changing world. However, when an actor uses a standard plan, the judgment is easier, and standard plans account for a large part of people's behavior.

Case-based planning has been advocated to avoid the effort of having to generate each plan from scratch, as well as to improve planning effectiveness by learning to anticipate and avoid problems [Hammond, 1989a]. There is, in addition, another advantage to acquiring a library of standard plans. By using standard plans ourselves, and observing others' use of them, we gather comparative information about ways of accomplishing a goal. We can learn the likely cost of a plan, whether the plan is likely to fail, and how efficient it is compared to plans we have used before. We can use this knowledge to choose between plans based on our current priorities. For example, if we know that the local bus service is an inexpensive but unreliable way to travel, and taxis are more expensive but more reliable as well, we can use the bus when punctuality is unimportant and use taxis otherwise.

Knowledge of plan characteristics also helps us predict the actions of others. If we know the goal orderings of different actors, we can anticipate their priorities and predict that they will favor plans that reflect them [Carbonell, 1979]. For example, an impatient executive on an expense account might put a low priority on saving money, but a high priority on saving time. From this, we might expect him to fly on the Concorde whenever possible.

To reason about plan selection, we need to be able to characterize plans along the dimensions that affect people's plan choices. One way to identify these dimensions is to look at stereotypes about the concerns of different people, and to translate them into parameters for characterizing plans. For example, the stereotype of a miser directs the choice of the lowest cost plans possible. To know which plans a miser is likely to pick, we need to have an estimate of their relative monetary costs. People who are impatient give saving time a high priority; thus relative speed of a plan is important. Cautious people avoid risk; thus risk must be represented also. Using these dimensions, we can represent both people's general preferences, and those that only apply in particular domains (e.g., someone might be timid in personal matters, but bold in finance.) Some central differences between plans can be characterized along the following dimensions:

- **Reliability** of a plan for accomplishing goal.

  Reliability can be either absolute (e.g., this plan always works) and relative to other plans for the goal (e.g., this cancer treatment has only a 50% success rate, but is still the best available.)

- **Risk level** of using the plan.

  Again, this can be measured both relative to other plans, and on an absolute scale, according to the likelihood of bad side effects.

- **Cost** compared to other plans for the same goal.

  Cost can be characterized along standard dimensions, such as those described in [Wilensky, 1978]: time, consumable functional objects (like money), nonconsumable functional objects (like a stove), and abilities.

- **Yield** compared to other plans for the same goal.

  If the effects of a plan can be measured along a scale, yield can be used to compare the effectiveness of the plan. For example, having a paper route and being a lawyer are both plans for making money, but the yield of the paper route is low, while the yield of law is high.

  Yield can also be balanced against costs, to determine a plan's efficiency.

Note that although the actual value for any of these features depends on many contextual factors, examining those factors would enormously increase the processing cost and might not be possible at all: The information might not be available. However, it is easy to give a commonsense characterization of many plans along these dimensions, assuming an average context, and to use that to judge actors' plans. Table 4.8 shows two examples of such characterizations, of bank robbery and medical school as plans for the goal to achieve wealth.

Actors' plan choices can be predicted by looking at candidate plans in terms of the values the actors favor for each dimension. Different actors will have very different priorities: For example, someone who had recently become rich might actually prefer doing things in an expensive way, or a

TABLE 4.8
Plan Dimensions of Two Plans

Bank robbery as a plan for wealth

Dimension	Value
Reliability	LOW
Risks	HIGH
Cost	LOW costs on all dimensions
Yield	HIGH

Medical school as a plan for wealth

Dimension	Value
Reliability	NORMAL
Risks	LOW
Cost	HIGH cost in time and money
Yield	HIGH

teenager might favor risky plans to maintain his or her image. Someone who has been rich for a longer time might simply disregard the cost when choosing between standard plans.

A program example: Next is an example of ACCEPTER's use of plan choice checks. In it, the system evaluates the explanation that Russia sabotaged Challenger to gain an advantage in space exploration, by destroying an important tool used in the American space program.

ACCEPTER's evaluation depends on two pieces of background information. First, it relies on the information that there was international hostility between Russia and the United States at the time of the launch. This information generates the expectation that the two countries will engage in hostile action towards each other. Second, it depends on basic knowledge that, unless there is information to the contrary, an actor probably avoids risky plans.

Given its prior expectations, ACCEPTER considers the sabotage plausible: it is a form of the expected hostile action. However, the expectation did not specify that sabotage would be the specific hostile action used. Because the specific form of the hostility was not predicted, ACCEPTER checks how reasonable the sabotage is as a particular hostile act by Russia. To do this, it checks only those features the sabotage that are not inherited from the already expected category of hostile actions in general.

Not all hostile actions are violent, but the particular form of sabotage, destroying the tool used in another's plan, is a specification of the category for violent actions in ACCEPTER's memory net. Indexed under the node for violent actions is a procedure to estimate the relative risk of performing a violent action. The risk value depends on comparative strength of the attacker and victim: If the victim is weaker, there is little risk, but the risk is high if both have the same strength, or the attacker is stronger. By applying this procedure, the risk of the sabotage is judged to be high. Consequently, ACCEPTER decides that it is unlikely Russia would have chosen that plan, despite the expectation for Russia to perform hostile actions against the United States:

```
Checking if "RUSSIA'S DESTROY-TOOL-PLAN" satisfies expectations.

The fact "There was a DESTROY-TOOL-PLAN with CHALLENGER as its TOOL,
USA'S SPACE-MISSION as its PLAN-REQUIRING-OBJECT, USA as its VICTIM,
and RUSSIA as its ACTOR" satisfies the expectation for RUSSIA'S
HOSTILE-ACTION from INTERNATIONAL-HOSTILITY-2437.
  .
  .
  .

Retrieving plan dimension generators for RUSSIA'S DESTROY-TOOL-PLAN.

Plan dimension generator procedure for RUSSIA'S DESTROY-TOOL-PLAN
inherited from VIOLENT-ACTION.

Applying procedure to check RISK of RUSSIA'S DESTROY-TOOL-PLAN.

Applying RISK-GENERATOR:  Checking risk of retaliation.

Comparing the power of RUSSIA and USA.

   For countries, power depends on military strength.  Comparing....

   RUSSIA inherits HIGH as its MILITARY-STRENGTH, from its
   abstraction INDUSTRIALIZED-COUNTRY.

   USA inherits HIGH as its MILITARY-STRENGTH, from its abstraction
   INDUSTRIALIZED-COUNTRY.

   ... Strength is the same.

... Risk is HIGH.
```

To decide the significance of the risk, ACCEPTER then looks for information in memory that applies to Russia's way of selecting plans. It searches up abstractions from Russia to retrieve the most specific information possible. However, the only relevant information it has is the rule that generalized actors favor plans whose risk is low or normal. It assumes this holds for Russia and considers the explanation unlikely, because of the risk that sabotage would involve:

```
Comparing to planning tendencies for RUSSIA.

  Looking under RUSSIA for PLAN-TENDENCIES ... none found.

  Plan tendencies for RUSSIA inherited from ACTOR.

  Tendencies found:
    ACTORs usually accept plans with RISK being LOW, or NORMAL.
    ACTORs usually accept plans with COST being LOW, or NORMAL.
    ACTORs usually accept plans with RELIABILITY being NORMAL, or
      HIGH.
    ACTORs usually accept plans with YIELD being NORMAL, or HIGH.

Anomaly detected!

PLAN-SELECTION problem:  "RUSSIA'S DESTROY-TOOL-PLAN" CONFLICTS-WITH
planning tendencies for RUSSIA, due to HIGH RISK.
```

Libya also has a hostile relationship to the United States and has repeatedly shown willingness to take high risks to accomplish its aims. Because ACCEPTER has knowledge of Libya's acceptance of risk-taking, it considers sabotage by Libya a more plausible explanation than sabotage by Russia:

```
Checking if "LIBYA'S DESTROY-TOOL-PLAN" satisfies expectations.

The fact "There was a DESTROY-TOOL-PLAN with CHALLENGER as its TOOL,
USA'S SPACE-MISSION as its PLAN-REQUIRING-OBJECT, USA as its VICTIM,
and LIBYA as its ACTOR" satisfies the expectation for LIBYA'S
HOSTILE-ACTION from INTERNATIONAL-HOSTILITY-2429.
  .
  .
  .

Applying procedure to check RISK of LIBYA'S DESTROY-TOOL-PLAN.
```

Applying RISK-GENERATOR: Checking risk of retaliation.

Comparing the power of LIBYA and USA.

    For countries, power depends on military strength. Comparing ...

    LIBYA inherits LOW as its MILITARY-STRENGTH, from its abstraction
    THIRD-WORLD-COUNTRY.

    USA inherits HIGH as its MILITARY-STRENGTH, from its abstraction
    INDUSTRIALIZED-COUNTRY.

    ... Strength is lower.

... Risk is HIGH.

Comparing to planning tendencies for LIBYA.

    Looking under LIBYA for PLAN-TENDENCIES.

    Tendencies found:
      LIBYAs usually accept plans with RISK being LOW, NORMAL, or
      HIGH.

HIGH RISK plans are acceptable to LIBYA.

... No decision problems found.

Checking Magnitude of Effects and Need for Action

Two additional checks, concentrating on the triggering of actions, would be
useful as an extension to ACCEPTER's motivational checks. Even if a plan
has desirable effects and is a reasonable way to achieve the goal, it may not
be worthwhile to put the plan into effect. To be sure a plan is reasonable, it
would be necessary to ask two more questions:

- **Is the direct effect significant?**

  Even if an effect is desirable in the abstract, it may not be large enough
  to be worth achieving. For example, even though rich people may have
  the goal to increase their wealth and may have considerable spare time,
  we would not expect them to send in box tops to get a rebate check
  from their breakfast cereal: 25 or 50 cents will not make a difference to
  them.

TABLE 4.9

Finer Grained Checks Triggered by Pattern Failures.

Problem Type	Checks to Apply When Pattern Fails
Normative role-filler conflict	Basic-action decomposition
Unusual features vs. norm	Basic-action decomposition (if it finds no problems, the feature is unimportant)
Actor behavior conflict	Examination of direct effects, and Plan choice checks.

- **Is the action actually needed to achieve the effect?**

    If the effect is expected anyway, there's no need for an actor to act. For example, if we expect someone to give us a car for Christmas, we would not buy one ourselves.

4.5.3   Summary of Triggering for Finer Grained Checks

ACCEPTER's finer grained checks are triggered by conflicts with object feature patterns, normative role-filler patterns, and behavior patterns. Depending on which pattern conflicts were found, ACCEPTER applies different finer grained checks, as summarized in Table 4.9. In addition, plan choice checks are applied to judge the reasonableness of particular specifications of expected plans, to determine whether an actor's manner of carrying out an expected plan is reasonable.

4.6   What ACCEPTER's Checks Miss

By looking for conflicts with the patterns described previously, and applying finer grained checks in response to pattern problems, an understander can detect a wide range of anomalies. However, there are classes of problems that are in principle beyond the scope of ACCEPTER's strategies. ACCEPTER's procedure—search for conflicts with a packaging structure—is not designed to identify the classes of anomalies that we describe next.

4.6.1   Anomalous Trends and Feature Correlations

ACCEPTER cannot detect anomalous trends or correlations. When something happens more frequently than generalizations predict, people find it anomalous, even when no individual instance conflicts with expectations. For example, anomalies noticed by students at the Yale AI lab included the questions "why do so many cars in New Haven have a headlight burned out?," and "why are so many teenagers turning to drugs?." Detecting these anomalies can be important: A school principal needs to notice the drug problem in order to combat it.

ACCEPTER would notice problems when a car has nonfunctional lights, or when a wholesome teenager turns to drugs. However, it has no mechanism for noticing that a series of anomalies forms a trend.

4.6.2   Beliefs of Others

Sometimes people make moral judgments that conflict with others' values or make claims about particular facts that conflict with others' knowledge. When they do, both the things they believe, and the fact that they believe them, are anomalies.

One prime example of the difference between different actors' beliefs is the conflict of beliefs across the generation gap. Adults often have strict moral rules they believe teenagers should follow. Teenagers, who do not share their attitudes, question their view of morality. When the two views conflict, the teenagers ask why they should believe adults. Following are a few examples of the types of questions that arise, as reported in an article in a New Haven newspaper about teenagers' questions:

Why shouldn't teenagers drink?
Why shouldn't girls have sex?
Why shouldn't kids have kids?

Judgments based on moral values, and on others' knowledge, are outside the scope of ACCEPTER's theory.

4.6.3   Gaps in Understander Knowledge

Our final class of anomaly, anomalous gaps in system knowledge, was not represented in the anomaly data we collected but nevertheless seems important for judging hypotheses about events that are significant to the explainer. People are aware of what they are likely to know, and they sometimes draw conclusions about the reasonableness of events based on that self-knowledge: If people think they would remember an event but fail to do so, they consider the event unlikely. For example, if we are asked if a space mission went to Mars last year, we know it did not, because we would remember the mission if it had occurred. Likewise, an expert on a particular subject may discount as untrue any facts in that subject of which he or she is unaware. (For a discussion of the phenomenon of drawing conclusions from lack of knowledge, see Gentner and Collins [1981].)

When the unknown information is in fact correct, despite our inability to retrieve it, the anomaly is the conflict between how well informed we think we are and how well informed we actually turn out to be. Noticing such conflicts is important because they may signal deficiencies in our ways of acquiring information in areas particularly important to our goals.

In order for a system to know when retrieval failures are significant, it must know which types of facts it would normally know about, if they did occur. Although this is highly idiosyncratic, there are some basic categories of incidents that people tend to remember. These incidents either conflict with fundamental beliefs (e.g., we would certainly remember if there had been no gravity one morning) or involve major goals or commitments. Rare anomalies provide a good index into events, making them more likely to be retrieved from memory; major goals or commitments are connected to many aspects of our lives, so that we would expect to be able to elaborate indices to confirm them, if they existed. Thus failure to retrieve either type of incident can be expected to be significant, suggesting that the following are some of the types of memorable facts:

- **Anomalous**: Situations that would have caused anomalies when they were first encountered.

  People would remember if McDonald's served *nouvelle cuisine* the last time they ate there.

- **Vital**: Situations that threaten a high-priority state that the agent wishes to preserve but does not always pursue actively (such goals are instances of important *preservation goals* [Schank & Abelson, 1977]).

  For example, people would remember being threatened by an armed gunman.

- **Obligational**: Initiations and terminations of long-term commitments.

  People remember if they are married, or if they are divorced.

- **Social**: Rites of passage; events that society designates as landmarks along your life.

  People remember their first communion, or their senior prom. This category also includes events that the press presents as strongly affecting society, such as an assassination of a president.

- **Personal**: Knowledge in a domain that's focused on especially by an idiosyncratic understander.

  For example, a car buff might know all the engines used by a given manufacturer and know that his list was exhaustive.

Of course, whether an individual fact is memorable depends on the understander. Any event that is normally a landmark fact can become routine if it is repeated enough; a policeman might not remember a particular encounter with an armed gunman. However, he would have generalized his encounters with armed gunmen and could retrieve this generalization, which is itself enough to confirm the likelihood of the fact.

4.7   Judging ACCEPTER's Anomaly Detection

Given the types of anomalies that ACCEPTER does and does not detect, how can we evaluate its performance? At this point, there is no way to do a controlled evaluation of any theory of everyday anomaly detection: Anomaly detection is too idiosyncratic and experience based. However, we can still consider what makes a good theory of anomaly detection and present informal support of our methods.

There are two criteria by which anomaly detection schemes must be measured: *efficiency* and *sensitivity*. Efficiency depends on the added cost to a system of doing anomaly detection, compared to the cost of routine understanding. As previous sections show, the effort necessary for ACCEPTER's anomaly detection scheme is strongly limited.

> ACCEPTER's anomaly detection is efficient because it applies a limited set of checks to new information, and the checks require minimal inference.

Sensitivity reflects the proportion of anomalies detected. Perfect sensitivity is impossible: It is obvious that only exhaustive checking can hope to find all conflicts with the system's knowledge, and we have already argued that exhaustive checking would be impossible in any but the most trivial domains. However, the relative thoroughness of these checks, given the system's task, is an important criterion for a categorization's usefulness.

ACCEPTER's initial set of anomaly categories was suggested by anomalies that arose in stories the system processed, and in the (sometimes fanciful) explanations offered to account for them. Thus ACCEPTER attempts to test both for anomalies that people might notice in the world (such as the death of Swale) and for anomalies that appear in wild hypotheses rather than real life (for example, the idea that Swale might have been using drugs because he was overwhelmed by the pressure of being a star, and that he died of a self-inflicted drug overdose).

Although the categories were developed in response to very limited data, the categories described spanned problems from many explanations that students hypothesized for Swale's death. After the categories were developed, we very informally tested their generality by collecting anomalies that people reported in real-world events, to see if the checks would also account for those anomalies. To do so, we collected a list of about 180 anomalies and explanations from students in the Yale AI lab (most of which are contained in Kass and Leake [1987]). The data were not gathered in a controlled way and may leave out some important anomaly classes, but they nevertheless provide an extensive range of anomalies that must be accounted for by any general purpose anomaly-detection system.

After a plausible context was hypothesized for each of the anomalies, they were grouped according to the problems they involved. The basic initial set of patterns spanned many of the anomalies, though the data suggested adding the category of functional limitations and finer grained motivational checks. The data also helped identify the limitations of the categories: For example, approximately 20% of the anomalies that people reported involved feature correlations (e.g., "Why are baseball pitchers lousy hitters?") and trends (e.g., "why are insurance rates skyrocketing?"), which are beyond the scope of ACCEPTER's anomaly detection tests. However, conflicts with patterns account for a majority of the remaining anomalies.

> Pattern-based checks can account for a significant proportion
> of our anomaly data.

Nevertheless, comparison with additional and more systematically collected data would be desirable to give further indications of the categories' coverage.

4.8   Summary

No fact is intrinsically anomalous; what we find anomalous depends on our active knowledge. Because an understander cannot afford to check for *all* possible conflicts between its world model and reality, it must have standards for knowing what kinds of problems are probably worth noticing. The preceding sections outline an anomaly detection procedure that is efficient enough to be done as part of the routine understanding process, and that accounts for many of the anomalies that people notice.

Our central claim is how to control verification inference: We argue for avoiding inference by substituting table lookup. ACCEPTER's pattern-based checks look for confirming or conflicting information in a series of tables in memory. These tables explicitly store patterns for likely events and behaviors, organized hierarchically. ACCEPTER judges plausibility by searching the tables for confirming or disconfirming information; it accepts or rejects inputs on the basis of this partial verification, avoiding costly inference.

The effectiveness of this approach depends on a related content theory: which tables are needed, and what information they contain. This chapter presents such a theory. ACCEPTER's tables include causal patterns, normative event sequence patterns, stereotypes for events' role-fillers, feature-based functional limitation patterns, and actor's behavior patterns. These tables allow ACCEPTER to detect a wide range of anomalies, with low verification cost.

The patterns defined here are designed for detecting anomalies, not for guiding their resolution. In many cases, additional description is needed before the anomaly descriptions give sufficient focus to aim explanation. Thus in an understander, noticing that a problem exists is only the beginning of a larger process of explanation and belief revision. In the following chapter we turn to the next phase of that process: characterizing anomalies to guide search for explanations.

5 Anomaly Characterization

Anomaly detection directs an understander's attention towards defects in its world model; repairing those defects depends on being able to explain the anomaly. We discuss how to facilitate the search for explanations by characterizing anomalies in a uniform way, and using the characterizations to index into stored explanatory knowledge. We also develop design criteria for an effective anomaly characterization scheme, laying the groundwork for the theory of characterization presented in Chapters 6 and 7.

5.1 From Detection to Characterization

The preceding chapters argue that anomalies are conflicts and present strategies that an understander can use to detect them. Of course, detecting anomalies is not an end in itself: The real reason for systems to detect anomalies is to improve their performance. The conflicts found by anomaly detection reflect flaws in system understanding, and explaining and correcting them makes it possible to avoid the problems the flaws might have caused.

As we have previously discussed, constructing explanations by standard methods can be prohibitively expensive. Instead, we advocate a case-based approach. However, that approach involves difficult questions in its own right, one of which is how to efficiently retrieve relevant cases. If retrieval is expensive, or if the cases retrieved are inappropriate, retrieval and adaptation costs will nullify the efficiency advantages of reasoning from prior experience rather than from scratch.

This chapter lays the groundwork for our theory of how to guide the search for explanations. It discusses how explanatory knowledge can be organized in memory to facilitate effective retrieval, and how to generate the right indices to access that knowledge. Our basic approach is to develop a characterization scheme for expressing what needs to be explained, and to use it to organize explanations in memory. When a new anomaly is encountered, the anomaly is characterized in the same vocabulary used to describe explanations, and the retriever searches for stored explanations with similar characterizations.

The principle behind this approach is simple: If problems are described in the right way, similar problems will have similar solutions. If anomaly characterizations capture the significant aspects of the situation to explain, anomalies with similar characterizations will have similar explanations, so explanatory knowledge can be organized by the anomalies it explains.

> Anomaly characterizations both describe anomalies and organize their explanations.

In this chapter we discuss the general requirements that an anomaly characterization scheme must satisfy in order to facilitate explanation. We look at the information anomaly characterizations must include, how that information is structured, how it can be used to guide search for explanations, and how the characterizations are generated when anomalies are detected. In Chapters 6 and 7 we take a more concrete approach, demonstrating that a useful anomaly characterization vocabulary exists by defining a set of anomaly categories and describing the explanatory knowledge they organize.

5.2   The Information Characterizations Include

Prior explanation systems construct their explanations out of context: They always explain the same event in the same way, regardless of why it is being explained. We argue instead that explanations must take into account the context of an explanation, explaining both why the surprising event occurred, and for why prior beliefs or expectations went wrong. For example, different circumstances make people explain a car recall in very different ways. If the recall were mentioned during a conversation about greedy companies refusing to admit to problems (in order to save the costs of dealing with them), a relevant explanation might be that the company thought lawsuits would cost more than the repairs. If the recall were mentioned during a discussion of the company's excellent quality control, an explanation might address how the defect slipped through the company's checks or might show that, contrary to prior beliefs, the company actually did not do adequate quality control, so defects should have been expected. The explanation that addresses the company's apparent altruism is irrelevant to the company's quality control, and vice versa, even though both explain the same surprising fact.

The preceding example shows that for two situations to have similar explanations, the situations must be similar along three dimensions. First, the situations must involve similar events. Second, similar aspects of those events must be surprising. Third, the reasons that those aspects are surprising must be similar.

Because our goal in characterizing anomalies is to group them by what needs to be explained, useful anomaly characterizations must include precisely the information that is relevant to similarity of explanations. Consequently, the aforementioned requirements apply to anomaly characterizations as well: characterizations must include the events in the anomalous situations, the surprising aspects of those events, and why the aspects are surprising. Because other aspects of the situation do not affect the explanations, we can abstract away from them by leaving them out of the characterizations. The resultant characterizations provide the guidance needed to focus explanation: An explanation retriever can judge whether two anomalous situations are likely to have similar explanations, simply by seeing if their anomaly characterizations are similar.

Our anomaly characterizations have two basic components. First, they include a pointer to an anomaly category. The category groups explanations in which reasoning based on a particular type of knowledge fails in a particular way. For example, one of our categories is SURPRISING-PLAN-CHOICE, which describes instances in which an actor chooses a plan that conflicts with our expectations. Here the reasoning that fails is based on our model of actors' decision making, and the way it fails is in the outcome of the plan selection process. Subcategories of SURPRISING-PLAN-CHOICE describe more specifically why expectations are violated. For example, BLOCKED-PLAN describes the anomaly of someone picking a plan that we expect to fail because of some known blockage.

The second component of anomaly characterizations is a structure whose slots are filled in to reflect specifics of the instance being described. In the case of SURPRISING-PLAN-CHOICE, the structure includes slots for who the actor was, the actor's assumed goal, the plan that was surprising, and which plan was expected. With the combination of the anomaly category and its associated structure, each anomaly characterization includes the event, the surprising aspects of the situation, why they were surprising, and the relationship between the important constituent parts.

5.3   How Characterization Guides Search

Anomaly characterization facilitates explanation retrieval in two ways. First, because the characterization structures identify the classes of features of the situation that are likely to be relevant to its explanation, they aid the explainer in deciding which known features of an anomalous situation are important, which unknown features are worth investigating, and which known features may safely be ignored. Second, after the characterization structures have been filled in with information from the current situation, they aid the explanation search process by directing it towards hypotheses appropriate to the anomaly.[1]

5.3.1   Selecting Important Features

In order to retrieve cases that are similar to an anomalous situation, we must be able to decide what constitutes an important similarity—which features of the anomalous situation are causally relevant and consequently will be important to the explanation. If we can retrieve a similar case that shares those features, its explanation should apply. Unfortunately, determining the features seems impossible: to know which features are causally relevant, we must already know the explanation.

One of the functions of anomaly categories is to help overcome this problem, by giving a priori suggestions about which features are likely to be important. The knowledge structure associated with each anomaly category highlights certain aspects of the situation: Each characterization structure has slots for features that are usually important for explaining the type of failure it describes. An explainer can use the characterization structure to suggest what types of features are likely to be relevant to the failure and can assume that other information may be ignored.

> The slots of anomaly characterization structures guide description of anomalies.

For example, consider the anomaly category REDUNDANT-PLAN, which describes the anomaly of an actor making a plan that is unnecessary because the goal will already be satisfied without additional action. This category would characterize the anomaly of John buying an airplane ticket to Florida on Pan Am when he already has a ticket on Eastern.

---

[1]Anomaly descriptions are also useful for indexing two types of information beyond the scope of this book: *adaptation strategies*, to guide repair of candidate explanations involving anomalous beliefs or connections, and *recovery strategies*, to guide a planner's response to anomalous situations. Kass [1990] examines the former use; Owens [1991] presents a vocabulary of plan failures designed for the latter purpose.

TABLE 5.1
REDUNDANT-PLAN Characterization

Slot	Filler
Actor	John
Goal	Be in Florida
Plan	Fly on Pan Am
Existing goal satisfier	Fly on Eastern

The characterization structure for REDUNDANT-PLAN has four slots: the actor, the goal, the plan, and the plan (or event) already expected to satisfy the goal. Thus the structure suggests that in order to explain it may be useful to consider who made the decision, what the goal was, what the redundant plan was, and how we originally thought the goal would be satisfied. Table 5.1 shows the characterization for this example.

5.3.2 Organizing Explanatory Information

Characterizations can organize both explanation patterns and more abstract explanatory structures in memory, helping to suggest relevant hypotheses.

Organizing XPs: One of the claims of case-based explanation is that when domain knowledge is uncertain, explanations based closely on experience are more likely to be correct than those that are not. If anomaly characterization structures reflect the important aspects of a situation, the way to remain close to experience is by favoring those explanations with the most specifically matching characterization structures—we can simply search for past cases with as many identical corresponding slot-fillers as possible. (When the same number of slots match, criteria are needed for deciding their relative importance, but we have not addressed that question.)

If we search for REDUNDANT-PLAN descriptions with slot-fillers similar to those describing the anomaly of John's extra ticket, we may find a REDUNDANT-PLAN XP in memory with a similar characterization. For example, the XP *buying two tickets to be safe when the airline is strike-prone* could have been built to account for someone who planned to take the Eastern shuttle but decided to buy back-up tickets on Pan Am. The characterization for that anomaly matches the new anomaly in two components:

Plan	Fly on Pan Am
Existing goal satisfier	Fly on Eastern

If no XPs are indexed under any of the specific features used in the anomaly characterization, an explainer could also abstract individual role-fillers of the characterization, to match a wider range of characterizations.

For example, suppose we are taking a trip on an airline, and we see that the airline is using a propeller plane. This is anomalous and could be described as SURPRISING-PROP-CHOICE on the part of the airline. One XP indexed under an airline's surprising choice of plane might be *airlines cut costs by using small planes for short hops.*

If we cannot find any XPs that apply to the substitution of airplanes, we can abstract to see if there are any more general explanations. SURPRISING-PROP-CHOICE characterization structures include slots for both the plan with the unusual prop and the role the prop fills in that plan. Both need to be abstracted simultaneously to make a reasonable description. For example, we could abstract **airline travel** to **travel** in general, and **airliner** to the **vehicle** associated with travel. At this level, the anomaly description would correspond to "a strange travel vehicle," which could suggest an XP built for a bad experience with an ancient rental car, such as *when there's little competition, companies use old equipment to keep costs down.*

If we cannot retrieve XPs even at that level of generality, we can abstract **travel** to a generalized **plan**, and **vehicle** to a generalized **prop** filling a role in that plan. Some possibilities are that the normal prop was unavailable—perhaps the scheduled plane had mechanical difficulties, and this was a backup—or that the actor's ability to use the standard one was impaired—all their jet-certified pilots were on strike, so they were falling back on propeller planes. This abstraction path for the package and role is shown in Figure 5.1. Note that there are many aspects of a characterization that might be abstracted independently of each other, and different combinations of abstractions can suggest different XPs. However, we have not addressed the question of the order in which they should be abstracted.

This example shows that explanations can be retrieved at many levels of abstraction. Each of the explanations we considered is a plausible explanation in the abstract and is relevant to the anomaly being explained. However, the search for explanations is intended only to give relevant alternatives at low cost; additional evaluation is needed to decide if any of the explanations is actually acceptable.

A library of XPs is implemented in ACCEPTER, with XPs indexed by the characterization structures for the anomalies they explain. XPs are stored under the most specific anomaly categories or subcategories that apply and then organized in an abstraction net according to the role-fillers in their characterization structures. Once the most specifically applicable candidate has been retrieved, ACCEPTER verifies its plausibility, using a process we describe in Chapter 8.

Organizing Abstract Explanatory Knowledge: In addition to organizing XPs, anomaly categories can organize another kind of explanatory

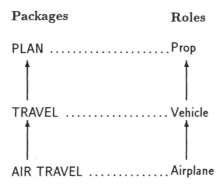

Packages   **Roles**

PLAN .... Prop

TRAVEL .... Vehicle

AIR TRAVEL .... Airplane

FIG. 5.1. Some abstractions of the air travel plan and its role for the airplane used.

information: explanation strategies [Hammond, 1987]. Explanation strategies can be viewed as abstracting the information in XPs; they represent
general information about factors likely to be implicated in an explanation.[2]
Even if no relevant XP is indexed under an anomaly, explanation strategies
can focus the search for explanations.

For example, suppose someone's hair turns prematurely gray. The change
is anomalous because it conflicts with knowledge of the normal aging process;
this anomaly falls into the anomaly category PROCESS-SPEEDUP. If no XP
is found indexed under the anomaly characterization structure for this particular type of PROCESS-SPEEDUP, the explainer can try to apply explanation
strategies stored under the PROCESS-SPEEDUP anomaly category. One
such explanation strategy is "look for presence of catalysts associated with
the process." Under the process of graying might be stored the information
that its catalysts include stress, suggesting checking whether the victim is under stress. If the victim's job is stressful, this would suggest the explanation
of prematurely graying because of a high-pressure job. Explanation strategies themselves give domain-independent advice—a strategy such as "look
for presence of catalysts associated with the process" could equally well be
applied to many other domains, such as explaining why bread rises quickly
(e.g., there is extra sugar in the dough) or why a car rusts rapidly (e.g., there
is salt in the air because of being near the sea). The purpose of explanation
strategies is to suggest the classes of information that an explainer should
look for in memory; the combination of the strategy's general advice with

---

[2]Explanation strategies are not implemented in ACCEPTER.

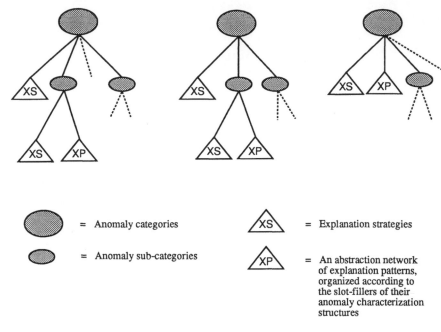

FIG. 5.2.   Organization of explanatory information by anomaly categories.

information about the specific situation provides guidance towards relevant domain-specific information.

Figure 5.2 illustrates how anomaly categories and subcategories organize explanation strategies and explanation patterns.

5.4   Mapping Conflicts to Characterizations

Anomaly characterization is the bridge between anomaly detection and case-based explanation. It takes a conflict, noticed by the anomaly detection process of Chapters 3 and 4, and puts it in a form that summarizes what a relevant explanation must address. That characterization is then used as an index for retrieving explanations from memory.

5.4.1   Transforming Conflicts to Characterizations

When ACCEPTER detects a conflict with expectations or beliefs, it passes three things to its anomaly characterizer: the memory structure for the expectation or belief, the conflicting information, and any available information on how it conflicted. Because the anomaly category depends on the source of the expectation, the characterizer first tries to trace back from the expectation to find its source.

For explicit expectations, such as those generated during MOP application, ACCEPTER's representation of the expectation includes a pointer to the expectation source, so the system can simply follow that pointer. For conflicts with implicit expectations, such as normative expectations for features of the members of some category, the process that detects the conflict passes both expectation source and the conflict to the anomaly characterizer. (In general, expectations could be the result of long inference chains, but the characterizer considers only prior beliefs leading immediately to the expectation.)

After the characterizer identifies the expectation source, it selects the anomaly category associated with that type of source and the current conflict. For example, if the conflict is that a goal was expected to be satisfied in one way but new information states that it will be satisfied in another, the source of the expectation is a goal-plan link, and the conflict is a differing plan. This combination of type of source and conflict is mapped to the anomaly category REDUNDANT-PLAN.

Once ACCEPTER has decided on the anomaly category, it uses category-specific rules to fill the slots of the characterization structure. If possible, the category is also specified to a more specific subcategory by a concept refinement process [Lytinen, 1984].

As an example, we return to the Audi recall described in Chapter 1. In that example, the conflict ACCEPTER detected was that it inferred from the recall that the car was defective, when it had been expected to be in good mechanical condition. We call this conflict the raw conflict description: It simply describes what was expected and what was observed. This is the type of description that systems such as CHEF [Hammond, 1989a] use to focus their explanations.

However, the raw conflict description is inadequate to assure the explanation addresses the underlying problem. In the example from Chapter 1, the defect was surprising because of Audi's quality control, but XP memory might also include XPs accounting for defects that were surprising for other reasons. For example, a defect might have previously been surprising because a mechanic had checked the car and vouched for its good condition, with the explanation that the mechanic was the car salesman's brother. The raw conflict description of "surprising defect" provides no information usable for ruling out the retrieval of that explanation, but that explanation is useless for explaining the quality control problem. Because ACCEPTER knows that the expectation was based on belief in the effectiveness of Audi's quality control plan, it characterizes the anomaly as PLAN-EXECUTION-FAILURE.

```
Processing input:
  There is a M-CAR-RECALL with JOE as its CAR-OWNER,
  AUDI as its MANUFACTURER, and AUDI'S CAR as its CAR.
  ⋮

    Checking expectation for AUDI'S CAR'S LOW MECHANICAL-CONDITION
    from AUDI'S M-CAR-RECALL.
    ⋮

      Checking if "AUDI'S CAR'S LOW MECHANICAL-CONDITION"
      is expected from (or prohibited by) active MOPs.

      Problem detected installing "AUDI'S CAR has
      LOW as its MECHANICAL-CONDITION" in memory:
      the prohibition of MANUFACTURED-OBJECT-199'S
      LOW MECHANICAL-CONDITION due to AUDI'S M-QUALITY-CONTROL.

      Specifying the anomaly characterization:  Since
      a plan to prevent it was in effect, the event
      is a PLAN-EXECUTION-FAILURE problem.
```

Using this characterization, XPs for other quality control failures might be retrieved, such as *products from good brands are sometimes disappointing because they were really built under contract by inferior manufacturers.*[3]

Characterization when Expectation Sources Are Unavailable

The anomaly characterization process depends on being able to identify why a belief or expectation was generated, which in general is a difficult problem. Simply maintaining a trace of all belief derivations [Doyle, 1979] would be infeasible for a large memory, due to the cost to store and maintain it. An appealing alternative is to explain why the expectation was formed, and then to generate an expectation relevant to that derivation [Collins & Birnbaum, 1988]. However, that alternative has the drawback of requiring the system to generate two explanations instead of one, with all the concomitant issues of explanation construction cost and evaluation. When ACCEPTER encounters conflicts with expectations for which it has no justification records, such as its patterns, its finer grained checks use standard criteria for explaining why the failed aspect of the situation might have been important (e.g., by trying to reconstruct causal restrictions underlying normative patterns, or goals underlying behavioral patterns). Sophisticated expectation reconstruc-

---

[3]Note that although this commonly happens in business, it is a fictitious explanation in Audi's case.

tion would allow a much more precise focus and is an interesting area for future study.

5.4.2   From Anomaly Detection to Explanation Retrieval

To summarize the relationship between anomaly detection, characterization, and explanation retrieval, Figure 5.3 shows these steps of ACCEPTER's processing for the Audi recall. First, the routine understanding and anomaly detection procedures from Chapters 3 and 4 are applied. They detect a conflict: the car's bad condition, compared with its expected good condition. The second step involves the characterization process that we have described here and discuss further in the following two chapters: The raw anomaly description is input to the anomaly characterizer, which outputs an anomaly characterization in the anomaly vocabulary. This characterization is input to an explanation retriever, which searches for the XP in memory with the most specifically matching characterization.

5.5   Defining the Content of Anomaly Categories

The benefits of case-based reasoning depend on being able to efficiently select an appropriate case. This in turn requires a way to identify which features in a situation are important, to formulate indices for retrieval, and to search memory for relevant cases. We have argued that for case-based explanation the central index for explanation retrieval is the anomaly to be explained, including the reasons *why* an anomalous fact was anomalous. The preceding sections develop general requirements for characterization of anomalies and show how a vocabulary of anomaly structures can facilitate explanation by guiding the search for explanations in a case-based explanation system.

If situations with similar anomaly characterization structures require similar explanations, the characterizations can be used to organize explanatory information and facilitate the search for explanations. We have discussed two types of information that can be organized by anomaly characterizations: specific XPs, and more general explanation strategies.

However, the real value of these ideas depends on whether they can be applied to a case-based explanation system. They are only worthwhile if we can actually define a set of anomaly categories and anomaly characterization structures that have the properties we need. The following chapters present a constructive argument that we can: They describe a vocabulary of anomaly categories for everyday anomalies and define the characterization structures needed to describe those anomalies.

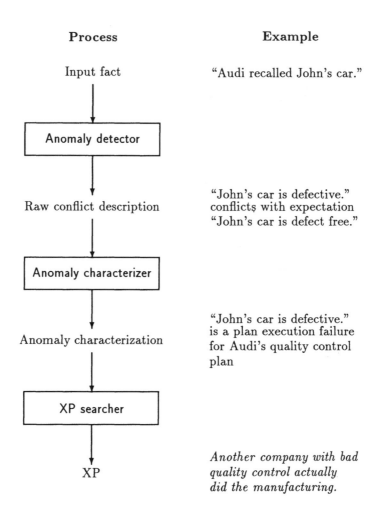

FIG. 5.3.   How anomaly characterization fits into the explanation process.

6 A Vocabulary for Anomalies

In this chapter we introduce a vocabulary for everyday anomalies and illustrate how it can be used to guide search through the space of possible explanations. We describe the portion of our vocabulary that organizes anomalies involving planful behavior, illustrating how the vocabulary is used to characterize anomalies and suggest explanation strategies.

The basic motivation for anomaly characterization is to facilitate explanation. The previous chapter argues for expressing problems in terms of the basic information needed to resolve them—what happened, the reasoning it conflicted with, and how it conflicted. It also argues that anomaly descriptions of this form are useful for indexing and retrieving explanations.

However, the previous arguments are incomplete. Chapter 5 only looks at the abstract requirements for an anomaly characterization scheme; it does not suggest a particular vocabulary for anomalies. In order to demonstrate that anomaly characterization is actually useful, we need to show that there exists a vocabulary of specific anomaly types that facilitates explanation. Facilitating explanation depends on both the practicality of assigning anomalies to the right categories, and the benefit of doing so: The categories must make distinctions that are useful for focusing explanation. In this chapter, we introduce an anomaly vocabulary designed to satisfy these requirements.

We start with an overview of the vocabulary, and of the fundamental importance of grouping anomalies according to the type of knowledge that failed. We then examine a set of anomaly categories involving what we call motivational anomalies—conflicts with expectations from our models about how actors plan for a given goal. For each anomaly category, we discuss how anomaly characterizations are structured and give examples of explanation strategies that can be indexed under them.

Chapter 7 expands further on our anomaly types, defining categories for nonmotivational anomalies—anomalies that arise from conflicts with reasoning other than from explicit consideration of plan choice. The anomalies we consider there concern conflicts with expectations for the effects of an already chosen plan, for the function of devices, for the behavior of physical, chemical and biological processes, and for usual features of objects.

6.1   Overview of the Categories

6.1.1   Relationship to Underlying Reasoning

As we argue in Chapter 5, explanation must be sensitive not just to what was surprising, but why—how the events being explained relate to the reasoning underlying flawed prior expectations.

For example, consider the sentence "John melted through the First National Bank's ATM with a blowtorch at 3:00 this morning and got away with $5,000." There are many different aspects of the sentence that might be anomalous and would consequently need explanation. For example, a burglar reading the sentence might be surprised that the torch *could* penetrate the ATM and need an explanation focusing on the torch's capabilities. On the other hand, if the burglar was a friend of John's and knew that John's *modus operandi* was to use a crowbar, John's choice of a novel plan needs explanation as well. Although the same event is explained in both cases, different aspects are surprising, and require different explanations—in our example, the explanation of the first anomaly might be that the torch was a new design; the explanation of the second might be that John had made an unsuccessful attempt with the crowbar the night before, so decided that a different method was needed.

To focus explanation on the right kinds of information, our anomaly categories are based on the underlying expectations that failed. For example, the anomaly of the torch working is a failure of expectations for the physical effects of heating the ATM (the heating is not expected to melt the ATM material, but it did)—this is an instance of PROCESS-EXECUTION-FAILURE. The anomaly of John picking a plan that differs from his normal tendencies is an instance of SURPRISING-PLAN-CHOICE and can be characterized more specifically as PREFERENCE-FAILURE.

Our vocabulary's top-level categories provide very general information—

for example, that someone's plans deviate from expectations about normal behavior. For each category, specific anomaly characterization structures like those described in Chapter 5 are used to specify details, to guide search towards particular XPs within the category.

The following list summarizes the types of knowledge that underly the reasoning covered by our anomaly categories: knowledge about planning, plan and action execution, physical processes, device behavior, information transmission, inductive feature correlations, and generalizations about object features. Anomaly categories are associated with each of these broad domains of causal knowledge, to organize explanations that are relevant to contradictions of reasoning in those domains. For each type of knowledge, we sketch the anomaly category that applies when reasoning using that type of knowledge fails; we also give an example of an explanation relevant to the particular anomaly category. The example explanations apply to a single event, the ATM robbery just described, and their range reiterates the importance of being able to guide explanation search. Because *all* the example explanations could apply simultaneously to the robbery described, and many other explanations could be hypothesized as well, an explanation system needs a way to find the right ones without exhaustive search.

Knowledge of planning: An understander can anticipate people's actions by deciding which plans they are likely to select, given the understander's view of their goals, preferences, world model, and resources. When their actual plans do not fit the understander's expectations, the actual plans may conflict either with our model of how the actor chooses plans, or how the actor instantiates them. These conflicts lead to two anomaly categories:

- **SURPRISING-PLAN-CHOICE:** An actor chooses a plan that conflicts with the understander's model of the actor's plan-selection process. For example, the robbery would be an instance of SURPRISING-PLAN-CHOICE if we expected John to get money by borrowing from a friend; we would need an explanation accounting for why he chose robbery instead (e.g., the friend was broke).

- **SURPRISING-PROP-CHOICE:** A prop that an actor chooses to use in a plan may conflict with the ones he was expected to pick. For example, we might have expected John to use a crowbar instead of a torch, requiring an explanation for that decision (e.g., crowbars do not work on the brand of ATM involved).

Knowledge of plan and action execution: After a plan has been selected, we often generate expectations about the details of its steps and its likely results. There are two ways that the actual plan may deviate:

- **PLAN-EXECUTION-FAILURE:** When a plan is expected to be successful, deviations from its expected course will be anomalous. For example, details of its steps may differ from expectations, as would be the case if we expected John to do the robbery at 2:00 AM instead of 3:00. An explanation of the deviation from the plan would have to account for the change (e.g., he saw that there were many people out at 2:00, because bars were closing, so he waited until the area was more deserted). Also, the outcome may differ from expectations, as when a plan is expected to work but fails (e.g., the failure of the ATM manufacturer's plan to assure that the ATM was break-in proof).

- **BLOCKAGE-VIOLATION:** When a plan is expected to fail because of an impediment, it is anomalous for it to be successful. For example, if we previously expected John's robbery to fail because the ATM would notify police, who would prevent his escape, the robbery's success would be a BLOCKAGE-VIOLATION anomaly. An explanation would have to account for why the expected blockage had no effect (e.g., John cut the phone line linking the ATM to the police).

Knowledge about physical, chemical, and biological processes: For example, physical processes are descriptions of how states progress in a physical reaction (given the conditions in which it takes place). Expectations based on physical processes would probably have been generated when the ATM manufacturer designed the ATM; they would have been violated if the blowtorch should not have been hot enough melt the ATM but melted it anyway. The category for deviations from models of processes is **PROCESS-EXECUTION-FAILURE**. An explanation of this category of anomaly would have to address the deviations from the model of the process (e.g., heat from the blowtorch was much greater than expected, due to a new torch design).

Knowledge about device behavior: Device models give expectations for the function of a device, without specifying the physical processes underlying it. That the ATM failed to notify police is an instance of **DEVICE-FAILURE** for the ATM alarm system. Device failure may be accounted by deviations of the device from the system's device model (e.g., the phone line being cut).

Knowledge about information transmission: We reason about the reliability of our sources of information, and it is anomalous when information is more reliable or less reliable than expected. For example, if we had previously read in a reliable newspaper that John robbed the bank at 4:00 AM and then discovered that the correct time was 3:00 AM, the newspaper's error would be an **INFORMATION-FAILURE** anomaly. It would have to be explained in terms of the understander's model of how information is collected and transmitted (e.g., reporters take their information from ATM records, and the ATM's clock had not been reset after a recent time change).

Knowledge about feature correlations: Although inductive generalizations are not based on a body of organized causal knowledge, as the previous categories are, they are often the basis of expectations and beliefs. For example, we might think that all ATMs in town are run by another bank, in which case it is anomalous that the owner of the ATM is First National Bank. The category for such anomalies is **UNUSUAL-FEATURE** and is explained by accounting for the flaw in the generalization (e.g., the new First National Bank's ATM was installed very recently).

Knowledge about feature durability: Sometimes we base expectations on generalizations about how long the features of particular objects normally remain fixed. When these expectations are contradicted, the contradictions are anomalous. For example, taking $5,000 from the ATM would be surprising if the machine had been empty the previous evening, and we did not expect it to be refilled until the next day. This anomaly is called **FEATURE-DURATION-FAILURE**. FEATURE-DURATION-FAILURE can be explained by showing why the feature changed earlier than expected (e.g., the manager had been passing by and decided to re-load the ATM so she would not have to do it in the morning).

As discussed in Chapter 2, explanation-based systems construct their explanations by context-neutral methods and accept the first explanation they generate. The range of possible explanations of the ATM break-in shows that different anomalies may require very different explanations, so that it is unlikely an arbitrary explanation would actually address the anomaly needing explanation. Nor can this problem be avoided by having a system explain *all* features of an anomalous situation: The preceding examples show only a few of the many possible perspectives on an event, and for each one the search for explanations can be quite costly. For these reasons, it is essential to be able to guide explanation search towards the right types of explanations. That is the purpose of our anomaly vocabulary.

6.1.2   Our Anomaly Vocabulary

The previous section describes top-level categories that group anomalies based on the type of knowledge underlying the expectations or beliefs that were contradicted. This allows the categories to organize explanations that focus on likely flaws in that type of knowledge, helping to restrict the explanations to consider. However, in order to have the categories actually suggest specific repairs, anomaly categories must correspond not just to *what* failed, but also *how* it failed. We achieve this in our categories by dividing the main anomaly categories into more specific subcategories that reflect the specific ways knowledge can fail. This has led to the following set of anomaly categories and subcategories [Leake, 1991]:

SURPRISING-PLAN-CHOICE
 IRRELEVANT-PLAN
 REDUNDANT-PLAN
 PREFERENCE-FAILURE
 BLOCKED-PLAN
SURPRISING-PROP-CHOICE
PLAN-EXECUTION-FAILURE
 PROP-SUBSTITUTION
 PLAN-DELAY
 PLAN-SPEEDUP
 PLAN-CANCELLATION
 PLAN-OUTCOME-FAILURE

BLOCKAGE-VIOLATION
 INADEQUATE-ROLE-FILLER
 BAD-ACTOR-ABILITY
 BAD-TOOL
 UNAVAILABLE-ROLE-FILLER
PROCESS-EXECUTION-FAILURE
 PROCESS-DELAY
 PROCESS-SPEEDUP
 PROCESS-OUTCOME-FAILURE
DEVICE-FAILURE
INFORMATION-FAILURE
UNUSUAL-FEATURE
FEATURE-DURATION-FAILURE

Our vocabulary includes nine top-level categories which account for a wide range of everyday anomalies. We anticipate that classifying most anomalies in everyday events would involve on the order of 15 top-level categories. Depending on the number of explanations in memory, the subcategories we have described might be further specified to form a hierarchy of categories, in order to provide sufficiently fine-grained guidance to choose efficiently between candidate explanations.

In the remainder of this chapter, and in the following one, we examine individual categories and subcategories in more detail. For each category and subcategory, we first describe the associated characterization structure and then discuss explanation strategies that can be used when no relevant XPs are indexed under the characterization structure. It should be noted that the explanation strategies are included only to illustrate how knowledge of an anomaly's category can suggest general strategies for guiding explanation construction. No claim is made about the strategies' completeness; we expect that more strategies could be generated for any of the categories.

We begin with the categories for motivational anomalies— anomalies that arise when people choose plans different from those we would have expected. Effective interaction with other people depends on having models of how they will act, and flaws in those models can have serious consequences, whether we wish to cooperate or compete. Consequently, it is important to update

TABLE 6.1
SURPRISING-PLAN-CHOICE Characterization

Slot	Filler
Assumed goal	Going to New York
Actor	John
Plan	Bus travel
Conflict description:	Bus travel instead of Commuter train

those models when they fail—when an actor's chosen plan differs from our expectations for the actor's plan choice.

6.2   SURPRISING-PLAN-CHOICE

When we learn that an actor has a goal, we form expectations about how the actor will try to achieve it, based on general planning knowledge and knowledge of the specific actor. SURPRISING-PLAN-CHOICE occurs when the system expects an actor to plan for a given goal, but the plan that the actor selects conflicts with the plan the system would have anticipated. For example, if John wants to go to New York, and commuter train is the usual way to travel there, an understander may predict that he will go by train. If he takes the bus instead, that plan choice is surprising.

Because SURPRISING-PLAN-CHOICE describes conflicts with predictions about plans, SURPRISING-PLAN-CHOICE characterizations must include the information that affects expectations for an actor's planning process: the actor, the goal being pursued, and the expected plan, and the way the chosen plan deviates from it (Table 6.1). When an unusual plan is selected, this structure focuses XP retrieval on similar plan substitutions, by similar actors, and for similar goals. For example, we may have already explained the same plan choice on an occasion when John was passing through New York on his way to New Jersey and took the bus because of better connections. The XP from this episode would be indexed in memory under the same anomaly characterization and could be considered for this case as well.

Explanation strategies for SURPRISING-PLAN-CHOICE: If no applicable XPs can be found, the explainer must turn to more general strategies for building an explanation. Because SURPRISING-PLAN-CHOICE makes no reference to why the plan was surprising, explanation strategies for SURPRISING-PLAN-CHOICE can only give vague guidelines for what an explainer should look for, but they nevertheless allow the explainer to avoid exhaustive search.

The basic idea of most of the strategies we discuss next is to assume that the actor's plan choice was rational, so that we can explain the choice by finding the neglected factors that would have made the choice expected.[1] For example, if someone chooses a tool that is badly suited to his task, reasons might be that he does not know that the tool is bad, or that better tools are unavailable, or that there is a tradeoff involved in the selection process that we have not considered—for example, that the tool he chose costs much less, which is an important advantage if he had to buy it for one-time use or is short on cash.

Assuming that the actor made a rational choice suggests the following strategies for explaining a surprising plan:

- **Link to blockage of expected plan.** We can look for common reasons that the expected plan is blocked and use them to explain the unusual plan. For example, John might have taken the bus instead of the train because the train was on strike.

- **Link to outside control.** If another actor has authority over the actor of the plan, we could see if the strange decision would be expected from knowledge of the controlling actor. For example, if John is being sent to New York by the bus company, it would be natural for him to be sent by bus.

- **Link to lack of information.** The planner could also simply lack information about better alternatives. For example, John may not know that commuter train service exists. In some domains, application of this strategy is facilitated by the existence of XPs for *why* an actor might lack a particular type of information, such as *newcomers to an area take some time to learn about public transit*.

- **Link to plan parameter preferences.** The choice of an unusual plan can often be explained by taking the planner's current goal priorities into account. Chapter 4 introduced the idea of describing planning preferences, and the attributes of plans, in terms of standard dimensions such as reliability, risks, costs, and yield. Normally, actors favor high reliability and yield, and low risks and costs. When an actor selects a surprising plan, we can compare it to the expected plan along the standard dimensions. If it is superior along any dimension, we can try to account for why that dimension would be important. For example, the one dimension in which bus travel is superior to train travel is its cost, which suggests that John might have taken it because of being short on money.

---

[1]The assumption of rational decision making is sometimes violated in people, when behavior is shaped by psychodynamic factors, such as repression or sublimation. The effect of these factors is sketched in Kass and Leake [1987].

When these explanation strategies fail, we can try to account for the choice by a temporary loss of rationality:

- **Link to impaired planner judgment.** Distraction, drugs, or other factors might have impaired the actor's reasoning abilities and made him neglect factors in favor of the expected plan. For example, someone might have taken an unexpected bus simply because of being drunk and waiting at the wrong stop.

6.2.1   Specifying SURPRISING-PLAN-CHOICE

In our anomaly vocabulary, SURPRISING-PLAN-CHOICE can be specified to four more precise anomaly categories, each reflecting a different reason why a plan choice was surprising: IRRELEVANT-PLAN, REDUNDANT-PLAN, PREFERENCE-FAILURE, and BLOCKED-PLAN. These more specific descriptions can index explanation strategies and XPs that apply more precisely. Because they reflect specific types of SURPRISING-PLAN-CHOICE, their characterization structures all include three components of the basic SURPRISING-PLAN-CHOICE description (goal, actor, and plan). In addition, they may include additional components that are relevant to the more specific types of failures.

Given an instance of SURPRISING-PLAN-CHOICE, we can decide which subcategories apply by asking the following questions:

- **Is the problem that the goal is not addressed by the plan?** If so, the anomaly is IRRELEVANT-PLAN.

- **Is the problem that the goal is already expected to be satisfied another way?** If so, the anomaly is REDUNDANT-PLAN.

- **Is the problem that the plan conflicts with the actor's usual plan preferences?** If so, the anomaly is PREFERENCE-FAILURE.

- **Is the problem that the chosen plan will probably fail?** If so, the anomaly is BLOCKED-PLAN.

Note that it is possible for a plan to fall into more than one of these categories. For example, someone might decide to take the Concorde to London, even though she does not have enough money to buy a ticket (BLOCKED-PLAN), and despite the fact that she is already scheduled to go there on a different flight (REDUNDANT-PLAN). If she is trying to save money, the cost of the plan is also anomalous (PREFERENCE-FAILURE). A thorough explanation would have to address each of these problems.

The following sections discuss each of the specifications of SURPRISING-PLAN-CHOICE in more detail.

TABLE 6.2
IRRELEVANT-PLAN Characterization

Slot	Filler
Assumed goal	Going to Las Cruces
Actor	Student X
Chosen plan	Flying to El Paso

6.2.2   IRRELEVANT-PLAN

When an actor chooses a plan for a goal, our most basic expectation is that the plan chosen will be relevant—that success of the plan would actually satisfy the goal. If this does not seem to be true, the plan choice is anomalous, as shown by the following episode at Yale:

> Student X had been to a conference in Las Cruces, New Mexico. When he returned, he submitted a ticket receipt for reimbursement. The request for reimbursement was rejected by Yale: The person processing the claim refused it, pointing out that the ticket was to El Paso, Texas, which was not where the conference was.

In order to retrieve XPs for similar anomalies, we must characterize the problem. The components of IRRELEVANT-PLAN characterizations are simply the assumed goal, the actor, and the chosen plan, giving the characterization shown in Table 6.2 If no XPs are stored under the same characterization, we can search by abstracting the characterization's features as described in section 5.3.2. One abstraction would express "a person going to Texas for the goal of going to New Mexico," which might yield an XP: People often fly to El Paso to reach southern New Mexico, because El Paso is adjacent to New Mexico and air fares to El Paso are less expensive.

Explanation strategies for IRRELEVANT-PLAN: If XP search fails, we can apply explanation strategies. Hammond [1987] suggests using the following strategies to account for an actor performing a plan for an apparently irrelevant goal:

- **Link plan to expected goal.** This suggests looking for ways that going to El Paso serves the goal of going to Las Cruces. It might result in noticing that after flying to El Paso, Las Cruces is an easy drive.

- **Link plan to new goal.** This suggests checking whether the assumed goal is wrong; this strategy would suggest checking whether there was a conference in El Paso as well.

The first of these strategies generates a new picture of the chosen plan; the second, of the goal that it serves.

Even if a plan has the desired effect, it may be anomalous for an actor to use it—either because it is unnecessary, or because it conflicts with the actor's usual way of doing things. The following two categories describe the subcategories for those problems.

6.2.3   REDUNDANT-PLAN

An actor's plan choice may be surprising not because it is a strange plan for the goal, but simply because the actor did not need to pick any plan at all. If a goal is expected to be satisfied soon, there is usually no need for the actor to start another plan to achieve it. We discussed one example of this anomaly type in Chapter 5: John buying a plane ticket on Pan Am, when he already has a ticket for the same trip on Eastern.

For such anomalies, the characterization includes the actor, the actor's goal, the plan, and the existing goal satisfier, as previously shown in Table 5.1, which characterizes the anomaly of someone apparently planning to fly to Florida on Pan Am, when he is already planning to fly there on Eastern. By abstracting to the level of "a person traveling on Eastern arranging to travel to the same place on Pan Am," we might be able to use the characterization to retrieve an XP mentioned on television news: People with Eastern tickets often bought back-up tickets on Pan Am (which was the only competitor on some Eastern routes) to avoid being stranded in case of an Eastern strike or bankruptcy.

Explanation strategies for REDUNDANT-PLAN: When no XPs are found, the following two explanation strategies may be useful:

- **Link to need for fail-safe reliability.** As the explanation for buying multiple tickets shows, actors relying on unreliable plans, or in critical situations, may try to increase the chance for success by starting multiple plans for the same goal.

- **Link to need for combined effect.** Many goals, such as satisfying hunger or achieving wealth, can be satisfied to different degrees, and applying multiple plans for their satisfaction can have a cumulative effect. If an actor chooses two plans for these goals, we can look for needs too great to be satisfied by either of the plans individually. For example, if someone works in two jobs, we may be able to account for it by looking for large expenses or debts.

TABLE 6.3
PREFERENCE-FAILURE Characterization

Slot	Filler
Goal	Satisfying hunger
Actor	John
Chosen plan	Eating in a fancy restaurant
Conflict description	Cost **High** instead of **Low**

6.2.4 PREFERENCE-FAILURE

Even when an actor needs to plan for a goal, and the plan for the goal seems reasonable, the plan may be anomalous because of its manner of pursuing the goal. There are three ways the manner of pursing a goal may be anomalous:

1. The plan may replace a standard plan that the actor usually uses for that goal. This substitution is anomalous even if the new plan seems equally satisfactory in its own right: For example, if someone always buys lunch at McDonald's, it will be anomalous for her to buy lunch at Burger King.

2. Aspects of the plan may conflict with general policies the actor observes in its planning. For example, we expect a miser to choose the most economical plans possible, regardless of the goals being pursued.

3. The effects or side-effects of the chosen plan may interact badly with a goal that is important to the actor. For example, it would be anomalous for someone intent on collecting all the game pieces in a McDonald's contest to eat at Burger King, even if that actor usually had no preference between them.

The characterization structure for PREFERENCE-FAILURE includes the actor, goal, plan, and preference conflict. For example, if John is hungry, and he goes to a more expensive restaurant than he would usually choose, the characterization is as shown in Table 6.3. An XP that might be suggested by this characterization is *people don't worry about what they spend if they're on expense accounts.*

Explanation strategies for PREFERENCE-FAILURE: One general approach to explaining PREFERENCE-FAILURE is to try to show how the surprising plan is actually consistent with expected preferences, by identifying factors outside the immediate situation that influenced plan choice. For example, when a plan conflicts with preferences because it threatens one of the actor's goals, an explainer might use one of the following strategies to explain the plan:

TABLE 6.4
BLOCKED-PLAN Characterization

Slot	Filler
Goal	Being in London
Actor	Mary
Plan	Go to London by Concorde
Blocked step	Buy ticket
Problem	UNAVAILABLE-ROLE-FILLER: Mary has no money

- **Link to higher priority goal that cannot be satisfied otherwise.** If an actor's plan threatens important goals, there may be more important goals at stake. If the goal that is threatened is fairly unimportant, this strategy will give little guidance, but if the threatened goal is an important one, the explainer only needs to examine a limited set of very high-priority goals. For example, if someone desperate for money entertains his boss extravagantly at a restaurant, it might be an attempt to make the boss spare him from impending layoffs.

- **Link to impediments to bad effect.** Another strategy is to look for factors that neutralize the expected problem. The previous XP describes one neutralizing factor: Expense accounts make the price of meals unimportant.

- **Link to circumstances that make bad effect unimportant.** For example, someone might be eating in an unusually expensive restaurant because he just inherited a fortune or won the lottery.

6.2.5 BLOCKED-PLAN

BLOCKED-PLAN, our final category of surprising plan choice, arises when a plan seems an unlikely choice for the simple reason that we do not expect it to work. This plan choice anomaly is characterized in terms of the goal, the plan chosen, the actor, the step of the plan that is blocked, and the reason for the blockage. Table 6.4 shows the BLOCKED-PLAN characterization for someone taking the Concorde to London, despite being bankrupt. In the characterization, the lack of money is described in terms of the characterization UNAVAILABLE-ROLE-FILLER, which describes an actor's lack of a needed resource to carry out a plan. That anomaly type will be examined further in section 7.3.1.

Based on the anomaly characterization, we might be able to retrieve an XP resolving the anomaly. For example, the traveler might be an ex-executive who could continue flying even without money, thanks to frequent flyer miles accumulated in better days.

Explanation strategies for BLOCKED-PLAN: One strategy for explaining an apparently bad plan choice is to see if the choice might actually be reasonable, because the expected blockage does not apply. Note that this strategy, like all the explanation strategies, is only a heuristic: It is possible that the planner misjudged the plan's likelihood of success, or even that the choice reflects *goal reversal* [Lalljee & Abelson, 1983]—the actor wants the plan to fail.

By hypothesizing that the planner selected an effective plan, and trying to find why the plan would work despite the expected blockage, this strategy changes the explainer's focus from a motivational anomaly (why did the planner pick a bad plan?) to a nonmotivational one (why would the plan succeed despite the impediment?). As we describe in section 7.3, success of a plan despite impediments causes a BLOCKAGE-VIOLATION anomaly, which is explained by showing why the blockage failed to apply. Consequently, one way to explain the plan choice is to apply XPs and explanation strategies for BLOCKAGE-VIOLATION of the expected blockage.

In the example of Table 6.4, this strategy suggests asking why Mary's travel plan might be unaffected by one particular sort of blockage: that Mary has no money. The problem corresponds to a specific subtype of BLOCKAGE-VIOLATION: UNAVAILABLE-ROLE-FILLER. An explanation strategy for UNAVAILABLE-ROLE-FILLER is to look for actors who might share the planner's goal and be willing to supply the missing role-filler. If the reason Mary is going to London is to start a new company, a business partner would share the goal of her being there, suggesting the explanation that the partner paid for her ticket.

6.3   SURPRISING-PROP-CHOICE

When a planner chooses an unusual role-filler, the choice raises two questions. The first is "why did the planner make the unusual choice?" Answering this question can give useful information about the planner and also may help the explainer's own planning, by showing how objects can be used in novel roles. The second question is "will the choice change the plan's outcome?"; explaining surprising prop choices can help the explainer update its predictions for the future.

For example, the owner of the local feed store in Ridgewood, New Jersey, discovered a customer was using Bag Balm, a lotion for softening cracked cow udders, as a hand lotion. This reminded him of the previous year, when the teacher of a local pottery class had recommended that students use it

TABLE 6.5
SURPRISING-PROP-CHOICE Characterization

Slot	Filler
Goal	Softening hands
Actor	Pottery class student
Plan	Applying hand lotion
Role	Hand lotion
Conflict description	Bag Balm instead of hand lotion

to keep their hands from becoming dry from handling clay. This allowed him to better model the customers at the store—he realized that the class was starting again, making it worthwhile to stock up on Bag Balm—and suggested that he try Bag Balm for his own hands. Table 6.5 shows the SURPRISING-PROP-CHOICE characterization for the Bag Balm episode.

SURPRISING-PROP-CHOICE can also describe anomalies when planners choose surprising actors to fill roles in their plans: For example, it might be a SURPRISING-PROP-CHOICE anomaly if a town mayor called out the fire department to deal with a flood, when we would have expected the National Guard.

Explanation strategies for SURPRISING-PROP-CHOICE: When no XP is found on the basis of the characterization, the SURPRISING-PROP-CHOICE category suggests explanation strategies including:

- **Link to blocked access.** An actor who cannot access the standard prop will have to make do with a substitute. By looking for standard impediments to accessing an object, it may be possible to find an explanation. For example, for a physical object, common possibilities include *supply shortage* and *insufficient proximity* to the object—if a pottery student preferred Bag Balm to hand lotion but was not using it, these reasons might respectively suggest the explanations *Bag Balm is sold out* or *the student forgot to bring her Bag Balm to class.*

  When unusual actors are chosen to carry out plans, blocked access may arise from *lack of authority* over the desired actors (the mayor of a flood-stricken town cannot call out the National Guard, because only the governor has that authority), or because of *lack of communication with the desired actors*, which would explain the governor's reliance on local groups if telephone lines prevent him from reaching the Guard.

- **Link to competing use.** If a role-filler is available in limited supply, and is needed for multiple plans that cannot share it, some of the plans will have to be run with substitutes. To see if this explains the prop

choice, an explainer can look for other active plans that use the prop
that we expected the actor to use. For example, if the governor fails to
call out the Guard to help one town, it may be because the Guard is
already committed elsewhere.

- **Link to actor's inability to handle standard prop.** An unusual
tool may have been selected because the actor has limitations that make
it impractical to try to use the standard one. To see if this applies, we
can use the functional limitation patterns of section 4.2.6 to determine
whether the actor has any limitations interfering with using the normal
tool. This would suggest an explanation for why someone with a leg
injury would take a car to work, rather than bicycling as usual.

6.4   Conclusion

By explaining motivational anomalies, a system can refine its model of other
actors in order to better predict the plans they are likely to choose. If the
system has a planning component, its explanations may also help it to improve its own decision making: if an explanation reveals important planning
considerations that the system failed to consider, it can learn to take those
factors into account in the future, both when trying to predict plans and
when trying to generate plans for its own use.

The preceding sections describe two categories of motivational anomalies,
SURPRISING-PLAN-CHOICE and SURPRISING-PROP-CHOICE, and discuss how SURPRISING-PLAN-CHOICE can be divided into subcategories
reflecting the specific reasons that a particular plan choice is anomalous. Four
subcategories are identified: IRRELEVANT-PLAN, REDUNDANT-PLAN,
PREFERENCE-FAILURE, and BLOCKED-PLAN. Because those subcate-
gories reflect both *what* was surprising and *why* it was surprising, they reflect
particular classes of conflicts, and can be used to organize XPs and explanation strategies that are relevant to those classes. When a new anomaly is
characterized as belonging to one of those anomaly categories, the characterization can be used to index into relevant explanatory information, strongly
restricting search.

Thus we have illustrated a vocabulary of anomaly categories that enables
an explanation system to focus its search for explanations of motivational
anomalies. The next chapter completes the discussion of our anomaly vocabulary by presenting anomaly categories and explanation strategies for nonmotivational anomalies.

7 Nonmotivational Anomaly Types

We complete the presentation of our anomaly vocabulary by describing categories for nonmotivational anomalies—anomalies involving conflicts with expectations based on factors other than knowledge about actors' decision making during planning. We describe the characterization structures for these anomalies and illustrate the explanation strategies they organize. We end by discussing criteria for judging the anomaly vocabulary's success.

7.1 Overview of Nonmotivational Anomalies

The previous chapter discusses anomalies that arise from conflicts with our predictions about actors' plan choices. However, we also depend on many other types of predictions. In order to anticipate others' actions and their effects, we predict the course of steps in a chosen plan and also predict the plan's final outcome. To guide our behavior and control our environment, we predict the course of chains of events in the physical world and predict the behavior of devices. In order to decide when to believe new information, we predict whether information is likely to accurate. When the world deviates from any of these expectations, we need to explain, to predict better next time. For explanation to be feasible, we need to focus the explanation effort: Our anomaly vocabulary must characterize these types of anomalies as well.

This chapter presents the elements in our anomaly vocabulary that categorize nonmotivational predictions. The anomalies fall into seven main categories: PLAN-EXECUTION-FAILURE and PROCESS-EXECUTION-FAILURE, describing deviations from expectations for the normal course of a plan or process; BLOCKAGE-VIOLATION, which describes the surprising success of an event of action that was expected to fail; DEVICE-FAILURE, which describes conflicts with expectations for a device's function; UNUSUAL-FEATURE, which describes conflicts with inductive generalizations about object or event features; FEATURE-DURATION-FAILURE, which describes conflicts with generalizations about how long particular features of objects and events will remain unchanged; and INFORMATION-FAILURE, which characterizes cases in which an external source's information is not as accurate as expected. These categories do not exhaustively characterize the nonmotivational anomalies in everyday life, but they cover a wide range of situations.

As we did when developing the vocabulary for motivational anomalies, we describe each nonmotivational category's characterization structure and illustrate the explanation strategies it organizes. These categories complete our anomaly vocabulary, and we end the chapter by discussing how to judge whether our vocabulary makes the distinctions necessary to effectively guide search for explanations.

7.2   PLAN-EXECUTION-FAILURE

When an actor begins a plan, we generate expectations about the plan's likely course. These expectations can focus on the props involved (e.g., if John tells us that he plans to rob the First National Bank's ATM, we expect that particular ATM to be the one he breaks open later); the timing of events (e.g., we might expect that driving to the site will take about a half hour, the actual break-in about 5 minutes, and collecting the money a minute more); and the final outcome (e.g., we might expect him to escape with a certain amount of money, or to get caught). When any of these expectations are contradicted, the contradiction is anomalous.

We divide instances of PLAN-EXECUTION-FAILURE into five subcategories, describing deviations from expectations about the plan's individual steps and deviations from its expected final outcome:

- PROP-SUBSTITUTION, which describes a change of prop during execution of a plan.

- PLAN-SPEEDUP, which describes a plan's achieving subgoals or goals more rapidly than expected.

- PLAN-DELAY, which describes a plan taking unusually long to achieve a subgoal or goal.

- PLAN-CANCELLATION, which describes an actor's choice to terminate an active plan before its completion.

TABLE 7.1
PROP-SUBSTITUTION Characterization

Slot	Filler
Package	Leaving car in parking
Role	Car
Conflict description	Car X instead of John's car

- PLAN-OUTCOME-FAILURE, which describes a plan's having a different outcome than normal.

We elaborate on these categories in the following sections.

7.2.1 PROP-SUBSTITUTION

MOPs and other plan schemas include information about the relationships between objects used in their constituent parts. This information sometimes lets us expect that the same object used in one scene of a MOP will be reused in later ones. For example, the MOP for eating out might include expectations for the diner leaving his car in a parking space, going into the restaurant, and then returning to the parking space to pick up his car.

If new information violates the assumption that a given object will be constant across scenes, the replacement of that object is anomalous. For example, if John finds a different car in his space when he returns from the restaurant, he needs to explain the discrepancy in order to regain control of his car.

Table 7.1 shows a characterization for this problem. ("Package" refers to the packaging structure for the prop, which can be either a plan or a MOP.)

The components of the characterization are the packaging structure (a MOP or plan) whose role-filler has changed unexpectedly, the role whose filler has changed, and a description of how it changed. Knowing only the role and package may be enough to suggest XPs: knowing that some other car has been substituted for your car in a parking space suggests the XPs *car missing because it was stolen* and *car missing because it was towed.*

When no XPs are available, three standard explanation strategies may help to account for the substitution. These look for reasons that the actor itself might have chosen to substitute one prop for another in mid-plan, which may be useful for judging the likelihood of the plan's success, or for anticipating changes in the plan:

- **Link to loss of prop control.** We may be able to explain the substitution by showing that the original prop is no longer available. For example, a coach is forced to substitute a new player if the old one quits in mid-game.

TABLE 7.2
PLAN-SPEEDUP Characterization

Slot	Filler
Plan	Car travel
Step	Arrival
Conflict description	A half hour early

- **Link to prop deterioration.** The substitution may have been motivated by the prop being less effective than originally, even though it is still under the planner's control: A coach will substitute a new player for one who is overtired or demoralized.

- **Link to task refinement.** If the task has been refined since the prop was selected, that change may account for the new prop being preferable. For example, a coach who wants to try a particular play will use the players that are best suited to carrying out that play.

7.2.2 PLAN-SPEEDUP

Just as we form expectations for the relationships between objects in plan steps, we form expectations for how the steps will relate to each other—their order and temporal separation. If a plan achieves its goal more quickly than expected, or a step in the plan happens earlier than expected, the change is surprising.

When a plan goes more quickly than usual, it may be useful to explain the change—the explanation may tell us how to speed up our own plans in the future. For example, if we expect it to take 2 hours of driving for a friend to reach us, and she arrives in $1\frac{1}{2}$ hours instead, we may try to find out how she did it, in order both to predict the arrival better next time, and to travel more rapidly ourselves.

To retrieve relevant possibilities, we need to know the plan involved, the step that happened earlier than expected, and the time difference. This leads to the characterization shown in Table 7.2. XPs indexed under this characterization might include traveling at an hour with little traffic.

When no XPs can be retrieved, we may be able to account for the speedup by one of the following strategies:

- **Link to pre-established state.** If some of the normal subgoals in the plan have been achieved before the plan starts, the planner can leave out the unnecessary steps. Consequently, the plan can be completed more quickly. For example, if we usually stop for gas and a snack along the way, and our visitor had done so before setting out, the omission of those steps would explain the time difference.

- **Link to task scale decrease.** The time a plan is expected to take may vary with the goals it achieves. For example, travel time depends on how far the travel is; perhaps our visitor's departure point was closer to us than we thought, so the trip was shorter.

- **Link to actor skills.** If a plan requires particular abilities, the actor's level of skill can speed the plan. For example, if our visitor is good at weaving in and out of heavy traffic, that skill will speed up travel time.

7.2.3 PLAN-DELAY

Plan execution delays are also anomalous and worth explaining: An explanation may allow us to anticipate sources of similar delays in the future, so that we can avoid them or allow more time when they are likely. The characterization structure for PLAN-DELAY is the same as for PLAN-SPEEDUP: the plan, the step that was delayed, and the conflict with the expected time. When no applicable XPs can be retrieved using the anomaly characterization, we might apply explanation strategies looking for unusual conditions affecting the plan's steps, such as:

- **Link to task scale increase.** Just as reducing the intended effects of a plan can make it faster to execute, increasing the intended effects can make it more time consuming. For example, if the car trip starts from farther away than expected, that change can account for the delay.

- **Link to shared resource problem.** Another reason for delay is competition for the resources the plan needs, forcing a wait until other actors relinquish them. For example, it might take a long time to get across a bridge where traffic backs up, or a long time to get through a toll plaza.

- **Link to plan displacement:** At any time, most actors have many pending goals, and many concurrent plans to satisfy them. If one is delayed, we can look for conflict between goals [Wilensky, 1983]: The delay might result from the competing goal being given priority. For example, someone might arrive late because of doing errands before leaving.

- **Link to additional steps to obtain resources.** Plans require certain preconditions to be satisfied before they can begin. As Collins [1987] points out, planners cannot explicitly take all a plan's preconditions into account. Instead, they assume that certain common preconditions will be satisfied. For example, driving depends on having gas. Normally, we assume that a driver will have enough gas in the tank, but if a driver arrives late, we may wonder if he was delayed by stopping to buy some.

TABLE 7.3

PLAN-CANCELLATION Characterization

Slot	Filler
Plan	Engine overhaul
Last step completed	Initial disassembly
Goal of plan	Smoother engine

- **Link to actor skills.** Just as good skills can speed plan execution, bad skills can slow it: An inexperienced driver may take longer to get through rush-hour traffic.

Thus the basic explanation strategy for PLAN-SPEEDUP or PLAN-DELAY involves hypothesizing how individual steps in the plan were likely to be facilitated or hindered. Although it is beyond the scope of this book, heuristics could be developed to suggest which plan steps to examine first when trying to account for speedups and delays. For example, we might want to look first for speedups and delays in the steps that are normally most time consuming, because there is may be more opportunity for unforeseen factors to arise during a time-consuming plan step, and because a given proportionate delay or speedup in an extended plan step has larger effects than in a short one. For example, if someone is late for a meeting he drove 5 hours to attend, we might first suspect a problem during the long drive instead of a problem going up the stairs to the meeting room.

7.2.4   PLAN-CANCELLATION

Once a plan is initiated, we expect its actor to try to carry it through to completion. If the actor does not, it is anomalous. For example, we would be surprised if the mechanic who was supposed to overhaul our car's engine stopped after a few minutes' work.

The components of PLAN-CANCELLATION descriptions include the plan that is cancelled, the step at which it was cancelled, and the goal that the plan was serving. Table 7.3 shows the characterization for the truncated overhaul. For this example, looking at the last step completed suggests an XP: *Mechanics stop work after disassembly because they discover they are missing a part.*

When no XPs are available, explanation strategies can focus on changes in the actor's goals, abilities, or options:

- **Link to plan displacement.** When an actor abandons a plan, we can look for other plans of the actor that require the same resources, forcing him to choose between the plans. For example, the mechanic

TABLE 7.4
PLAN-OUTCOME-FAILURE Characterization

Slot	Filler
Plan	Engine overhaul
Surprising aspect of result	Engine sound
Conflict description	Loud instead of soft

might put a higher priority on fixing his brother-in-law's car than on fixing ours.

- **Link to early goal satisfaction.** For example, he might have realized that a minor repair was all that was really needed to fix the engine.

- **Link to opportunities for better plans for the same goal.** For example, he might have stopped the repair because he had just been offered a low price on a re-built engine, so replacement was less expensive than the overhaul.

- **Link to blocked preconditions for a following scene.** This strategy would suggest the possibility of missing parts, or of missing tools.

7.2.5 PLAN-OUTCOME-FAILURE

The final anomaly subcategory for PLAN-EXECUTION-FAILURE is PLAN-OUTCOME-FAILURE: the anomaly that results when a plan does not have the expected results.

There are two types of plan outcome failures. First, if we expect a plan to cause some situation, we will be surprised if it does not. For example, if a mechanic overhauled our engine and it did not run smoothly, we would want to account for the failure—the explanation might suggest other needed repairs or suggest getting a new mechanic. Second, if we expect a plan to prevent some situation, we will be surprised if it does not. For example, we might expect the overhaul to prevent our car from burning oil and be surprised that it does not.

The characterization structure for PLAN-OUTCOME-FAILURE includes the plan, the aspect of the result that conflicts with expectations, and a conflict description. Table 7.4 shows the characterization for an overhaul that leaves the engine disappointingly loud.

The knowledge needed to diagnose a plan failure is usually quite domain specific, so it is especially valuable to use specific XPs as the starting point for explanation whenever possible. For example, if we know that a particular engine is often noisy because of misadjusted timing, that would be the first thing to look for when explaining the noise.

When no XP is available, the explainer must fall back on very general methods like the one suggested by Collins and Birnbaum [1988] for diagnosing expectation failures: examining each of the beliefs involved in predicting the outcome, until finding one that failed. The following explanation strategy provides some additional focus:

- **Link to failures of difficult steps.** If failures of particular plan steps are common (e.g., there is one part that mechanics seldom adjust properly), failure of that step is a natural hypothesis to take as starting point for explaining the bad outcome.

7.3   BLOCKAGE-VIOLATION

PLAN-EXECUTION-FAILUREs are conflicts with expectations that a plan will proceed as usual, including that it will be completed successfully. We may also have expectations that a plan will *not* be completed successfully, due to something blocking its execution. When the plan that we expect to be blocked is completed successfully, the anomaly is a BLOCKAGE-VIOLATION. For example, it would be a BLOCKAGE-VIOLATION if we expect John to be unable to repair his Edsel for lack of parts, and the repair succeeds.

There are two main reasons we might expect a plan or event to be blocked: Either a needed resource is unavailable, so that some step cannot be initiated, or some resource is inadequate, leading to expectations that the first step using it will fail during the step's execution. The subcategories for these BLOCKAGE-VIOLATIONs are UNAVAILABLE-ROLE-FILLER and INADEQUATE-ROLE-FILLER.

7.3.1   UNAVAILABLE-ROLE-FILLER

UNAVAILABLE-ROLE-FILLER anomalies describe situations in which a needed role-filler is unavailable, but the action using it is successful anyway.

Table 7.5 shows the anomaly characterization for John managing to restore his car when we think that the needed part is unavailable. On the basis of the anomaly characterization, we may be able to retrieve XPs of how similar problems were bypassed—for example, by abstracting to ask how problems with unavailable car parts are usually overcome, we may be able to retrieve an XP about buying a rare part at a collectors' swap meet. If we included the actor in our characterization, to ask how John usually does repairs when parts are unavailable, we might retrieve an XP built for his repairing an Edsel fender: He is an Edsel fanatic with a warehouse full of Edsel parts.

TABLE 7.5
UNAVAILABLE-ROLE-FILLER Characterization

Slot	Filler
Package	Car part replacement
Actor	John
Role with unavailable filler	New part
Needed filler	Edsel hubcap

If no XPs can be retrieved, an explainer can account for the action's success by outside aid in obtaining the role-filler, or possible substitutions of role-fillers that *are* available:

- **Link to aid.** Availability of an object depends on who is trying to obtain it. When one actor obtains unexpected resources, another might have provided them. To narrow the search, we can look at other actors who share the goal of the current plan and see if they could supply the aid. For example, if John is repairing the car to use it in an Edsel club show, another club member with a cache of parts might have helped.

- **Resource substitution.** This strategy looks for an object similar to the missing one that *is* available and satisfies the restrictions for filling the role. For example, if no Edsel hubcaps are available, other hubcaps might work: John might have overcome the lack of an Edsel hubcap by substituting another hubcap of the same size.

7.3.2   INADEQUATE-ROLE-FILLER

If the anomaly is that an event finished successfully despite some role-filler being inadequate, we characterize the problem with four pieces of information: the package whose success was expected to be blocked, the role that was inadequately filled, the deficient role-filler, and a description of why the role-filler was deficient (in terms of the causal patterns of section 4.2.1). For example, unless John is extremely strong, it would be anomalous to learn that John raised the engine out of his car when working on it; Table 7.6 characterizes this anomaly.

Explanations of INADEQUATE-ROLE-FILLER need to reconcile the role filler's deficiencies with the action's success, by showing how the deficiencies were overcome. This suggests two strategies that may help when no XPs are found. The first applies to inadequate actors, and the other applies to inadequate tools.

If the problem can be specified to BAD-ACTOR-ABILITY, a possible strategy is:

TABLE 7.6
INADEQUATE-ROLE-FILLER Characterization

Slot	Filler
Package	Lifting a car engine
Role	Actor
Role-filler	John
Failed restrictions:	High strength

- **Link to tool use.** Using tools makes it possible to overcome some limitations on ability. When an actor performs above his ability, we can ask which tools facilitate the task and see if the actor used them. For example, John might have been able to lift the engine by using a pulley.

If the problem can be specified to BAD-TOOL, a possible strategy is:

- **Link to actor abilities that improve efficacy of tool.** The actor using a tool can often compensate for some of a tool's limitations. We might not expect someone to be able to remove rusted bolts with a hand wrench, because it cannot generate enough leverage. However, a strong actor might succeed anyway. For other tools, skill might be the most important factor: A good driver can overcome many deficiencies in a car's handling.

7.4   PROCESS-EXECUTION-FAILURE

Processes are sequences of events caused by interactions within physical, chemical, or biological systems. For example, the rolling of a ball down a hill, the rusting of a car, and the rising of bread are all processes. When a process is set in motion, we form expectations for its intermediate and final states, based on inputs such as the objects on which it acts and the environment in which it takes place.

Conflicts with expectations from processes can either involve problems with the way the process develops, or with its final outcome; explanations may show conditions we have overlooked, or flaws in our model of the process's function.

7.4.1   PROCESS-SPEEDUP and PROCESS-DELAY

As Table 7.7 shows, the characterizations used for PROCESS-SPEEDUP and PROCESS-DELAY are analogous to those for PLAN-SPEEDUP and PLAN-DELAY. When speed of a process deviates from expectations, the

TABLE 7.7
PROCESS-SPEEDUP Characterization

Slot	Filler
Process	Rusting
Step	Total penetration
Conflict description	Unexpectedly early

TABLE 7.8
PROCESS-OUTCOME-FAILURE Characterization

Slot	Filler
Process	Rising bread
Aspect of result	Volume of bread
Conflict description	Original size instead of doubled

basic explanation strategy is:

- **Link to catalysts.** If our car's body rusts unusually quickly, we might look for catalysts of rusting and find salt. Identifying salt as the explanation for the speedup suggests a way to slow rusting for future cars: Try to reduce their contact with it. For example, we could wash off the underbody after driving on salted roads.

7.4.2   PROCESS-OUTCOME-FAILURE

When a process does not have the expected result, the anomaly is PROCESS-OUTCOME-FAILURE. We may want to explain PROCESS-OUTCOME-FAILURE when the missing outcome was something desirable—for example, if we are trying to make bread but the bread fails to rise. The characterization structure for this anomaly includes the process involved, the effect, and a description of how it conflicted with expectations, as shown in Table 7.8. Once again, we could explain by examining all inputs to the process for deviations from expectations, but that process would be very expensive. We can focus explanation with any of the following three explanation strategies:

- **Link to unusual features in inputs.** Unusual features in inputs, compared to the stereotypes for the inputs to the process, may affect the outcome. For example, substitution of buckwheat for normal wheat may make the bread too heavy to rise.

- **Link to unreached threshold.** Sometimes the value of an input has to reach a specific level for the process to have any effect. For example, yeast must be heated to a certain temperature to be activated; otherwise it will not rise.

TABLE 7.9
DEVICE-FAILURE Characterization

Slot	Filler
Device	Car
Input	Turned key
Conflict description	Engine off instead of engine on

- **Link to precaution failure.** If the process is used by people to accomplish desired effects, its normal success may be facilitated by its users taking precautions to guard against likely impediments. For example, people make sure to keep rising bread away from drafts; our bread might not rise because we failed to take that precaution.

It would also be possible to develop domain-specific strategies for processes in different domains. For example, in the domain of investments, one strategy for accounting for unusually strong effects of a process is to look for leverage: Leverage magnifies effects of market fluctuations on investments.

7.5   DEVICE-FAILURE

Devices can be described by their behavior for given inputs. There are two types of input: *device adjustments*, such as the settings on the controls, and *supplies*, such as the fuel for a motor. Device failures occur when the device's response to either type of input conflicts with expectations. An example of an anomaly involving supply use would be a car getting very bad gas mileage, which we would need to explain in order to repair. Table 7.9 shows the characterization for an anomaly involving device adjustments: A car fails to start when the key is turned. If no applicable XPs are found, some common explanation strategies look for problems in the inputs, assuming that the device is functioning in a normal way:

- **Link to adjustment error.** For example, if a car does not start, perhaps the driver is using the warm engine start procedure, when the cold engine procedure is needed.

- **Link to abnormal input.** For example, there might be water in the gas line, or no gas at all.

If these fail, it may be necessary to use strategies for examining the device itself.

TABLE 7.10
INFORMATION-FAILURE Characterization

Slot	Filler
Information	John was studying in the library
Information source	John's statement
System conclusion	John was studying in the library
Conflicting information	The librarian said he wasn't there

7.6   INFORMATION-FAILURE

When new information conflicts with prior beliefs, the conflict can show that the understander's previous beliefs were incorrect. However, the new information may itself be in error. In order to know whether to believe new information (whether from the understander's own sensors, from other individuals, or from agencies such as news bureaus), an understander needs to estimate the reliability of different information sources. Such estimates help to decide when to revise our beliefs based on new information: We know to be skeptical of state-run newspapers, or to doubt a child with a history of lying about bad behavior.

When information that was expected to be reliable turns out to be wrong, the anomaly is an instance of INFORMATION-FAILURE. Anomalies of unexpectedly false information frequently arise in news reports covering fast-breaking stories—no matter how reliable a news service usually is, deadlines can cause initial reports to be based on unsubstantiated accounts, leading to errors. Later stories often use the correct details without explicitly retracting the old ones, so an understander must notice the conflict and explain it in order to decide which details to believe, and to know whether the source should be trusted less in the future.

INFORMATION-FAILURE anomalies are characterized with four pieces of information: the information in question, the information source, the system's conclusion about it, and what led the system to retrace that conclusion. (Note that when details in information conflict with prior beliefs, it might be necessary to first generate a causal explanation to decide which details are false, before identifying the problem as an INFORMATION-FAILURE anomaly.) Table 7.10 characterizes the INFORMATION-FAILURE anomaly for a child lying about his whereabouts.

This characterization could suggest an XP for a previous episode of pretending to be at the library in order to slip out to play pinball: *John lies to keep from being punished for not studying.*

When no XPs are available, an explainer can guide explanation by using strategies such as:

- **Link to source's own problems obtaining information.** When the source's own information is sketchy, or the source must reconcile conflicting accounts, false information may be transmitted despite good intentions. For example, it is likely that errors in U.S. coverage of the student uprising in China resulted from difficulties of interpretation, rather than from deception.

- **Link to propaganda.** If the false information shows people or objects in a positive light, whereas the true situation does not, and if the sources of information are affiliated with those people, or to people who will take credit or blame for the objects' role, the false report may be propaganda. For example, military contractors are often accused of falsifying test reports on the weapons they build, and people involved in car accidents sometimes lie about the events to show themselves in a better light.[1]

7.7   UNUSUAL-FEATURE

Our final two anomaly categories, UNUSUAL-FEATURE and FEATURE-DURATION-FAILURE, differ from the previous categories. The previous categories describe failures of expectations based on causal knowledge. However, sometimes our expectations are based not on causal knowledge, but on inductive generalizations about what to expect. We often form noncausal generalizations about the possible features of objects: For example, we know that apples are green, yellow, or red. Consequently, we would consider a blue apple anomalous—even if we have no idea of what causes apples to have the colors they do. Likewise, we may expect events to have certain features without knowing why: Although we know that people do not wear shoes inside Japanese restaurants, we might have trouble generating an explanation beyond custom.

UNUSUAL-FEATURE anomalies arise when an object has features that conflict with noncausal generalizations about its category. The basic description of a UNUSUAL-FEATURE has four parts: the object, the abstraction of the object from which the expected feature is expected, the feature name, and a description of how the surprising feature conflicts with the standard one. Table 7.11 shows the UNUSUAL-FEATURE characterization for the anomaly of the stainless steel bodies that were used in the innovative De-Lorean sports car.

---

[1] In general, there is reason to suspect misinformation campaigns whenever the originator of the false information is affiliated with someone who benefits from the false information being believed. However, deciding whether information actually does serve the source's interests could involve substantial inference. Consequently, our explanation strategy is restricted to looking at aspects of the situation that are more readily available.

TABLE 7.11
UNUSUAL-FEATURE Characterization

Slot	Filler
Object	DeLorean car
Category	Automobile
Feature	Body material
Conflict description	Stainless steel instead of regular steel

Because UNUSUAL-FEATURE anomalies are conflicts with inductive generalizations, the category UNUSUAL-FEATURE gives no information about causal factors likely to have resulted in the expectation for the feature. This restricts its ability to suggest explanation strategies, so its primary value is for organizing XPs. Similar unusual features may have similar explanations: For example, the characterization in Table 7.11 might lead to retrieval of XPs for cars made of other unusual materials, such as fiber glass: *cars are made of fiber glass because it doesn't rust.* This explanation applies to the material of DeLoreans as well.

7.8   FEATURE-DURATION-FAILURE

Inductive generalizations may also reflect how long the features of an object or event tend to remain unchanged. For example, we expect people to have the same eye color throughout life, and to live in the same house a few years in a row. When feature changes conflict with such expectations, the resultant anomaly is an instance of FEATURE-DURATION-FAILURE.[2]

Table 7.12 shows the characterization that would be generated if Mary had green eyes last month but has blue eyes now. The problem characterization can be used as an index for retrieving possible XPs for the change, such as *using colored contact lenses.*

Characterizations for FEATURE-DURATION-FAILURE, like the characterizations for UNUSUAL-FEATURE, cannot refer to what should have caused the expected feature value: They reflect inductive generalizations. Consequently, this category too is useful only for organizing XPs, rather than for organizing explanation strategies.

---

[2]This idea of expected feature durations is related to McDermott's [1982] idea of annotating beliefs with their persistences—how long after being asserted they should still be treated as true. However, McDermott's persistences are not expectations in our sense: It is not a failure if an assertion's truth status changes before the end of the persistence, and McDermott's model makes no assumptions that a feature will actually change at the end of its persistence (its value simply becomes unknown).

TABLE 7.12
FEATURE-DURATION-FAILURE Characterization

Slot	Filler
Object or event	Mary
Feature type	Eye color
Difference in duration	Temporary instead of permanent
Change description	From green to blue

7.9   Judging the Vocabulary

In this chapter and the previous one, we have described a vocabulary of anomaly categories to characterize everyday anomalies. We now turn to the question of evaluating this characterization scheme. Although our scheme satisfies the requirement of reflecting the reasoning that failed, and how it failed, this is only a preliminary requirement; whether the characterizations can be used flexibly depends on the specific content of anomaly vocabulary.

If the goal of a case-based explanation system were only to retrieve an XP built to account for an anomaly identical to the present one, the particular characterization scheme used would be comparatively unimportant. Any anomaly vocabulary would allow retrieval of explanations for identical anomalies, provided that the same anomaly was always described the same way and that distinct anomalies always received distinct characterizations. However, the goal of guiding search towards near-miss explanations makes choice of the specific anomaly vocabulary a crucial issue: Retrieving useful near-miss XPs is only possible if similarities in distinct anomalies' characterizations correspond to similarities in the explanations that apply to them.

"Evaluation" in standard terms cannot be used to test this property. In both case-based reasoning systems and people, what is retrieved, like what is considered anomalous, is based on idiosyncratic experience. At this point we cannot generate a representative set of real-world anomalies and XPs on which to test how effectively the characterizations associate new situations with stored explanations. However, we *can* support our vocabulary of anomaly types on other grounds.

The key to our argument is the existence of the explanation strategies we have described for the anomaly categories and subcategories summarized in Tables 7.13 and 7.14. Our anomaly categories and subcategories were developed to group numerous concrete examples,[3] so one way to judge them is to see whether they generalize beyond those examples—whether they actually correspond to general classes of explanations.

This could be demonstrated by showing that we can describe sets of gen-

---

[3]Many of these examples are listed in Kass and Leake [1987].

TABLE 7.13
Focuses of Explanation Strategies for Motivational Anomalies.

SURPRISING-PLAN-CHOICE

1. Blockage of expected plan.
2. Outside control.
3. Lack of information.
4. Planner preferences.
5. Impaired planner judgment.

IRRELEVANT-PLAN
1. Connection to expected goal.
2. Connection to new goal.

REDUNDANT-PLAN
1. Need for fail-safe reliability.
2. Need for combined effect.

PREFERENCE-FAILURE
1. Higher priority goal.
2. Impediments to bad effect.
3. Circumstances making bad
   effect unimportant.

BLOCKED-PLAN
1. Failure of system reasoning
   leading to expectation
   for blockage.

SURPRISING-PROP-CHOICE

1. Blocked access.
2. Competing use.
3. Actor's inability to handle prop.

TABLE 7.14
Focuses of Explanation Strategies for Nonmotivational Anomalies.

PLAN-EXECUTION-FAILURE

PROP-SUBSTITUTION
1. Loss of prop control.
2. Prop deterioration.
3. Task refinement.

PLAN-SPEEDUP
1. Pre-established state.
2. Task scale decrease.
3. Good actor skills.

PLAN-DELAY
1. Task scale increase.
2. Shared resource problem.
3. Plan displacement.
4. Steps to obtain resources.
5. Bad actor skills.

PLAN-CANCELLATION
1. Plan displacement.
2. Early goal satisfaction.
3. Better opportunities.
4. Blocked future preconditions.

PLAN-OUTCOME-FAILURE
1. Failures of difficult steps.

BLOCKAGE-VIOLATION

UNAVAILABLE-ROLE-FILLER
1. Aid.
2. Resource substitution.

INADEQUATE-ROLE-FILLER
1. Tool use.
2. Tool-using abilities.

PROCESS-EXECUTION-FAILURE

PROCESS-SPEEDUP
1. Accelerating catalysts.

PROCESS-DELAY
1. Slowing catalysts.

PROCESS-OUTCOME-FAILURE
1. Unusual features in inputs.
2. Unreached threshold.
3. Precaution failure.

DEVICE-FAILURE
1. Adjustment error.
2. Abnormal input.

INFORMATION-FAILURE
1. Source's lack of information.
2. Propaganda

UNUSUAL-FEATURE
Only organizes XPs

FEATURE-DURATION-FAILURE
Only organizes XPs

eral explanation strategies, associated with elements in our vocabulary, that can be applied to *any* anomaly of that type, and that the strategies are disjoint from each other. If the elements in our vocabulary corresponds to sets of abstract strategies, and those sets are disjoint, the vocabulary partitions the set of anomalies according to abstract causal properties relevant to their explanations. Such a partition would suggest that the vocabulary corresponds to differences that are likely to apply to a wide class of problems, rather than coincidentally working on the specific anomalies and explanations tested.

Because we have argued that explanation depends on the underlying reasoning that failed and how it failed, and this information is represented in our anomaly subcategories, the subcategories become the main testing ground for of our vocabulary's generality: The subcategories should correspond to groups of explanation strategies. In fact, we have shown that for each subcategory, there does exist a distinct set of relevant explanation strategies. (Some of the main anomaly categories also organize their own strategies, disjoint from the strategies for other main categories, and applicable to their subcategories as well.) The existence of these sets of explanation strategies suggests that our vocabulary does in fact make distinctions at the desired level of generality.

7.10   Conclusion

The benefits of case-based reasoning depend on being able to efficiently select an appropriate case. This in turn requires ways to identify which features in a situation are important, to formulate indices based on those features, and to use them to search memory. We have argued that for case-based explanation, the central index for explanation retrieval is a characterization of the anomaly to be explained. However, arguments in favor of anomaly characterization are empty unless we can actually develop an anomaly vocabulary that captures, for our domain, the distinctions that are important to explanation search.

We have developed a vocabulary for describing everyday anomalies. For each element of the vocabulary, we have also defined characterization structures for expressing specifics of the anomalous circumstances, so that those structures can guide choice of explanations within an anomaly category. By showing that the anomaly categories can organize disjoint sets of explanation strategies, we have shown that the elements in our vocabulary make useful abstract distinctions for guiding explanation. These distinctions are relevant even when specifics of the anomalous situations differ, making it possible for our anomaly characterizations to focus explanation towards relevant near-miss alternatives. This allows case-based explanation to suggest useful alternatives even in novel circumstances.

Retrieval is not the end of the process. When no XP applies directly, the retrieved XPs must be evaluated, in order to find their problems. Even explanations with exactly matching characterizations will not always apply, so they require evaluation as well. The following two chapters develop criteria for evaluating candidate explanations and identifying their problems so that they can be repaired.

8   Evaluating Relevance and Plausibility

In real-world explanation, there is no assurance that a candidate explanation will be adequate. Consequently, an explainer must be able to evaluate explanations' goodness. This chapter develops evaluation criteria for the understander's basic task of updating its world model to account for anomalous events. To be useful for this task, an explanation must be relevant to the anomaly—accounting both for what happened and why expectations failed—and its account must be plausible. We describe ACCEPTER's criteria for judging explanations along these two dimensions.

The previous chapters examine what anomalies are, and how anomaly characterizations guide the search for explanations. The remainder of this book concentrates on how to evaluate the candidate explanations that are found.

Much AI research assumes that explanations are context-neutral: that all valid explanations are basically equivalent regardless of context. We take the opposite view, that context is crucial. Deciding explanations' goodness makes sense only in context of what triggered explanation and how the resultant explanation will be used.[1] This chapter examines what makes an explanation useful for an understander's most basic task, reconciling novel information with its prior beliefs and expectations; the following chapter presents a taxonomy of other tasks and considers the requirements they impose on explanations.

---

[1]Sections 2.3.1 and 2.3.7 compare this view to traditional approaches.

We argue in the previous chapters that explanations to resolve anomalous events must be relevant to the anomaly, not just to the event: They must account both for why the surprising features of the situation occurred and why the expected features failed to occur. In the first part of this chapter, we develop criteria for evaluating these properties. We describe the structure of ACCEPTER's explanations, discussing how they account for the occurrence of events and event features; we also discuss how an explanation can account for the failure of expected features, by superseding prior reasoning.

Our relevance criteria do not consider the explanation's validity—they address only whether the explanation would resolve the anomaly if it were valid. Consequently, relevance evaluation must be followed by evaluation of plausibility. The second part of the chapter discusses ACCEPTER's method for judging plausibility, which is different from the structural methods advocated in much research: It judges plausibility primarily by considering the reasonableness of an explanation's content.[2]

Using these criteria, ACCEPTER chooses between competing explanations. First, it rejects irrelevant explanations. Next, it chooses between the relevant explanations according to plausibility, by using its individual plausibility rankings to generate a coarse-grained comparative ranking. If any of the candidates are sufficiently plausible, ACCEPTER accepts the most plausible one. By integrating that explanation into memory, ACCEPTER resolves the anomaly, reconciling its knowledge and expectations with the anomalous event.

Reconciling old and new knowledge is only one of many possible uses for explanations of anomalies. Anomalies reveal aspects of a situation that the understander did not anticipate; those aspects may affect the system's overarching goals, making it important for the system to explain to find the information needed to respond. In the following chapter, we discuss evaluation criteria arising from goals beyond basic understanding.

8.1   Accounting for Surprising Features

In order to make sense of a surprising event, an explanation must show that the surprising features of that event are actually reasonable. This can be done by showing why those features might be expected, based on other factors that are themselves reasonable (either already known, or thought likely). For example, to account for a flat tire, we could note that we drove over glass a few moments before and trace the causal connections between driving over glass and having the tire go flat.

ACCEPTER's derivations of beliefs are packaged in explanation patterns [Schank, 1986]. XPs represent many facets of explanatory episodes, but only

---

[2]See section 2.3.6 for contrasts with previous approaches.

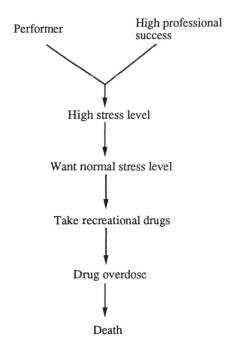

FIG. 8.1.   Belief-support chain for *early death from life in the fast lane.*

one of their components is relevant to explanation evaluation: their belief-support chains. Belief-support chains are belief dependency networks tracing how a belief can be inferred from a set of hypotheses.[3] They make explicit both the inferential links from which the belief is derived, and the intermediate beliefs that arise during the derivation.

For example, the XP *early death from life in the fast lane* traces circumstances leading to the death of stars such as Janis Joplin and John Belushi. Its belief-support chain starts with two antecedents: that the deceased was a performer and was very successful. Because star performers are under considerable stress, we may infer from those antecedents that the star has a high stress level, which makes drugs attractive as an escape. These influences push the performer to use drugs, and the drug use leads to accidental drug overdose and death. Figure 8.1 is a schematic diagram of the belief-support network associated with this reasoning chain.

Although XPs derive a conclusion from a set of antecedents, they simply

---

[3] Although our examples concentrate on causal reasoning, belief-support chains can also express inference chains that provide noncausal support for an fact, such as the chain supporting the belief that we have a flat tire based on someone telling us that we do.

reflect likely tendencies—they are not deductive proofs. For example, one can imagine situations in which any link in the preceding reasoning would fail to hold. Stress does not necessarily lead to taking drugs, nor does recreational drug use necessarily lead to an overdose; the links merely show how their antecedents make their consequents more likely, and how they can be used to account for events after the fact.

> Belief-support chains trace a sequence of plausible inferences leading to a belief, increasing the tendency to accept that belief.

Even though belief-support chains do not establish the necessity of an outcome, some belief-support chains can be used to generate predictions. For example, once we have constructed a belief-support chain leading from glass in the road to having a flat tire, it might be reasonable to use that chain predictively in the future, expecting a flat the next time we drive over broken glass. However, many belief-support chains are unsuitable for predictive use—even though *early death from life in the fast lane* explains some deaths, we do not expect all successful stars to die of drug overdoses.

We might think that a nonpredictive belief-support chain is simply incomplete: that we could require it to include all relevant factors, so that the chain would entail its consequent. (This would turn belief-support chains into the deductive proofs used in EBL.) However, in real-world situations it is impossible to include *all* conditions needed for a rule to hold. Even if we could, we would seldom have all the information needed to apply the rules—even if we knew that a particular rock star used drugs, we would be unlikely to have information about the quality of the drugs the star bought, or how carefully the star measured dosages. Because of their many implicit assumptions, belief-support chains can be used to reason about these complex situations, but they cannot be guaranteed to be valid. Consequently, plausibility evaluation is required, and we describe in section 8.3 ACCEPTER's methods for doing that evaluation.

8.1.1   Representation of Belief-Support Chains

The belief-support chains of ACCEPTER's XPs are divided into four parts: antecedents, internal beliefs, consequent, and links.

Antecedents are the premises on which the belief-support chain depends. In the XP *early death from life in the fast lane*, the antecedents are that the deceased was a performer and was very successful. The internal beliefs include being under high stress, wanting a normal stress level, taking recreational drugs, and accidental overdose; the consequent is the star's death. The links describe the structure of the XP's inference chain, representing how inference rules connect the antecedents, internal beliefs, and consequent. For example, one of the links in *early death from life in the fast lane* represents that being a performer and being professionally successful lead to a high stress level, by the inference rule *being a star performer leads to having a high stress level.*

The inference rules supporting the links may themselves be XPs, or they may be primitive rules along the lines of those suggested in Rieger [1975], Schank and Abelson [1977], and Wilensky [1978]. Table 8.1 lists the types of rules used in ACCEPTER's links.

To illustrate how XPs are represented, Figure 8.2 shows ACCEPTER's definition of the belief-supports and links that were shown schematically in Figure 8.1. In the definition, antecedents, internal beliefs, and the XP's consequent are expressed as variablized templates; when an XP is applied to a new situation, it is instantiated with the particular role-fillers for that situation. For example, the variable ?deceased is bound to the actor whose death is being explained. All the belief templates of the XP are labeled, and the labels are used to refer to them in the section of the definition describing the XP's links.

Link descriptions have three parts: a list of antecedents to the link, a consequent of the link, and a pointer to the inference rule used. For example, want-norm-stress is the label of the internal belief representing the goal of having a normal stress level, take-drugs is the label of the internal belief for recreational drug use, and p-reduce-stress=>m-do-rec-drugs is a pointer to the rule representing that those under stress may take drugs to escape it. (The name for its antecedent, p-reduce-stress, uses Schank and Abelson's [1977] terminology of "P-goals" for preservation goals.) The link connecting them is represented as follows:

```
(want-norm-stress)                take-drugs
p-reduce-stress=>m-do-rec-drugs
```

Additional information on the structure and representation of XPs can be found in Schank [1986] and Schank and Leake [1989].

8.1.2 Deriving the Right Features

A belief-support chain accounts for the surprising features of a situation if its derivation shows why those features arise. ACCEPTER checks this by comparing the surprising features of the anomalous situation (as identified in its anomaly characterization) to the features derived by the chain. If the instantiated chain provides a derivation of those features, it provides an account of why the surprising aspects of the situation occurred.

TABLE 8.1
Link Types in ACCEPTER's XPs

1. **Physical causation**: That an event leads to another by physical or biological effects. Example: Taking certain drugs reduces stress.

2. **Social causation**: That group customs or social patterns lead to a behavior. Example: That a rock star will live a dissolute life.

3. **Economic causation**: That an event leads to another by economic effects. Example: That a reduction in concert tickets available results in higher ticket prices from scalpers.

4. **MOP sequence**: That an event is expected from another because of their relationship in an event sequence pattern. Example: At a concert, lowering of house lights leads to the expectation that performance will start.

5. **Specification**: That because an object or event belongs to a category, and has certain additional features, it belongs to a particular subcategory of that category. Example: A rock performer who is very successful belongs to the category of rock star.

6. **Abstraction**: That because an object or event belongs to a category, it also belongs to some category that abstracts that category. Example: An rock star is also a public figure.

7. **Preservation goal activation**: That something undermining a desirable state may prompt a goal to preserve that state [Schank & Abelson, 1977]. Example: Being under stress makes people to want to keep their stress level under control.

8. **Plan choice**: That having a goal prompts instantiation of a plan to achieve it. Example: Someone who wants wealth will decide to earn more money.

9. **Plan specification**: That once an actor has instantiated a plan, the actor may choose to refine it in a particular way. Example: A rock star might refine the plan to earn money into one to go on tour.

10. **Goal satisfaction**: That a plan will result in its goal. Example: A rock star's tour will make the star wealthy.

```
(antecedents
   performer        (definition (type m-performance)
                       (performer ?deceased))
   star             (description (object ?deceased)
                       (attribute professional-success) (value high)))
(internals
   high-stress      (description (object ?deceased)
                       (attribute stress-level) (value high))
   normal-stress    (description (object ?deceased)
                       (attribute stress-level) (value low))
   want-norm-stress (description (object ?deceased)
                       (attribute goal) (value (ref normal-stress)))
   take-drugs       (definition (type m-recreational-drugs)
                       (druggee ?deceased))
   ingest           (definition (type ingest)
                       (actor ?deceased) (object ?substance))
   overdose         (definition (type m-drug-od)
                       (actor ?deceased) (drugs ?substance)))
(consequent
   death            (description (object ?deceased)
                       (attribute health) (value dead)))
(links
   (star performer)                    high-stress
   star-performer=>high-stress

   (high-stress)                       want-norm-stress
   stress=>p-reduce-stress

   (want-norm-stress)                  take-drugs
   p-reduce-stress=>m-do-rec-drugs

   (take-drugs)                        ingest
   mop-scene

   (ingest)                            overdose
   ingest-drugs=>overdose

   (overdose)                          death
   drug-overdose=>death)
```

FIG. 8.2.   Representation of belief-support chain for *early death from life in the fast lane.*

8.2   Accounting for Why Expectations Failed

Simply accounting for the surprising features of a situation is not enough: Explanations must provide sufficient information to resolve the belief conflicts that made the features surprising. For example, if we are surprised that a star dies young, both *early death from life in the fast lane* and *fatal overdose from change in strength of illegal drugs* account for the early death. However, which explanation we need depends on why the death surprised us. If it surprised us because we did not think the star would consider using drugs, *early death from life in the fast lane* resolves the anomaly—it tells us how the star was driven to use them. If it surprised us because we thought the star was too careful about dosages to risk overdose, *early death from life in the fast lane* is irrelevant, but *fatal overdose from change in strength of illegal drugs* resolves the anomaly—it shows why the star's carefulness could not prevent overdose. Thus for an understander to know which beliefs to revise, an explanation must provide information that shows why the false expectation fails to apply.

> To resolve an anomaly, the information in an explanation must account for why prior reasoning led to false expectations or beliefs.

In order to account for why prior reasoning went astray, an explanation's belief-support chain must not only account for what happened but must also take precedence over the belief-support chain leading to the faulty expectations or beliefs. There are two possibilities: that the expectation was based on false beliefs, or that some relevant factors were not taken into account when generating the expectation.

Explanation shows that the expectation was based on false beliefs: If the failed expectation was based on incorrect beliefs or inference rules, the expectation is invalid. Consequently, if the antecedents or internal beliefs of a valid explanation conflict with the beliefs on which the expectation was based (which shows that those beliefs were false), the explanation takes precedence.

For example, in Chapter 1 we traced ACCEPTER's processing of the sentence "Joe's Audi was recalled." ACCEPTER considered the recall anomalous because it believed that Audi did effective quality control, which should have assured that Joe's car would be defect free. The following factors enter into formation of expectations about Joe's car's mechanical condition:

- Audi makes high-performance products.

- Because high-performance product makers do quality control, Audi does quality control on the products Audi builds.

- Quality control prevents defects of products Audi builds.

- Because the brand of Joe's car is Audi, the car is built by Audi.

- Because the car is built by Audi, and products that Audi builds do not have defects, the car does not have defects.

ACCEPTER determines from the recall that its conclusion fails. A fictitious explanation offered to account for the failure is *products from good brands are sometimes disappointing because they were really built under contract by inferior manufacturers.* We can instantiate this XP to generate the belief-support chain for the following explanation: A company (which we call Acme) built the car, and, because Acme has bad quality control, the car is defective. Although this is not the true explanation of circumstances leading to the recall, we use it to illustrate how explanations resolve anomalies.

The expectation chain and new chain provide two accounts that lead to different conclusions—the first, to the absence of defects; the second, to the car being defective. To reconcile the two accounts, an explanation must show why the new chain's conclusion holds *instead of* what was originally expected. In this case, the reason is that one of the beliefs underlying the expectation was wrong: Joe's Audi was *not* actually built by Audi.

Figure 8.3 shows the complete structure of the resolution of an anomaly: the belief-support chain leading to the prior expectation, the new chain that accounts for the surprising features of the situation, and an account of why the new chain supersedes the old one.

An expectation chain can be invalidated by showing that it depends on false information.

Explanation is based on more specific or complete information: If an expectation was based on vague information, or its reasoning does not take into account some of the factors that the new one does, the new derivation takes precedence.

For example, when ACCEPTER forms the expectation that Swale will live for a few years after the end of his racing career, it bases that expectation only on the fact that Swale is a racehorse, and that the usual life-span of horses extends past racing into old age. When Swale dies young, the death can be explained by showing that additional factors were involved, such as that Swale had a heart defect. This belief was not taken into account by the belief-support chain in the original expectation; the fact that Swale died shows that it should have.

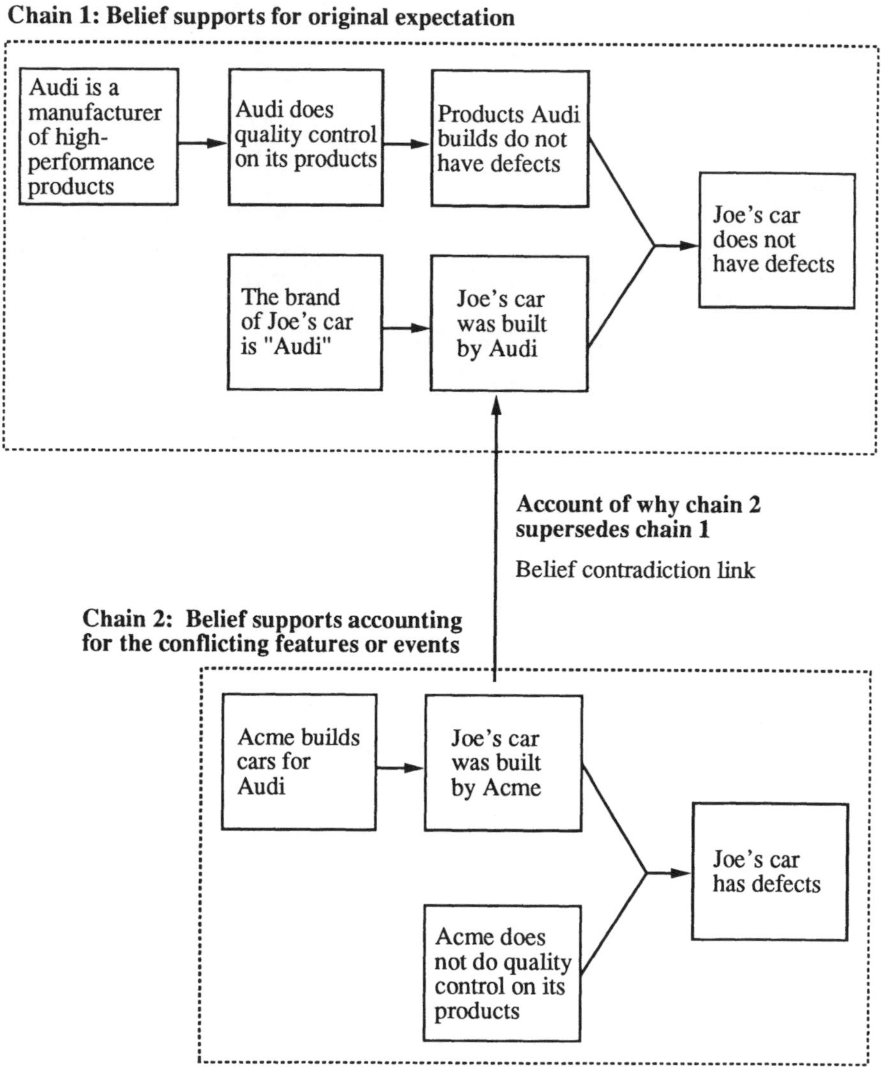

Chain 1: Belief supports for original expectation

FIG. 8.3.   Parts of an explanation resolving an anomaly.

> Expectation chains are superseded by explanations that are
> based on more specific beliefs and inference rules that apply
> more specifically.

8.2.1 ACCEPTER's Approach

If the beliefs in an explanation either contradict the source of prior expectations or show that prior expectations were based on partial information,
ACCEPTER considers that the explanation accounts for why expectations
went wrong.

To test for these conditions, ACCEPTER uses its routine understanding
process. It generates a memory context reflecting only the information that
led to its failed expectation and then integrates the new explanation's beliefs into that context.[4] If its anomaly detection finds conflicts between the
belief-support chain leading to the expectation, and the belief-support chain
of the explanation, those conflicts show the expectation was based on false
beliefs (assuming that the explanation itself is valid, which is judged by the
plausibility evaluation process described in section 8.3 below).

If none of the beliefs in the explanation conflict but some are unexpected,
given the belief-support chain leading to the expectation, the new explanation
takes precedence because it shows factors that previously were not taken into
account, also resolving the anomaly.

Because ACCEPTER does not maintain reasoning traces for all of its expectations, it only has access to limited information about why beliefs are
expected. It does maintain a record of how each MOP-based expectation was
generated; when a MOP-based expectation fails, it checks whether the explanation shows factors of the situation that are not standard for the MOP. If
the explanation does, it suggests a possible reason that the MOP application
failed: The presence of the unusual feature causes the new reasoning chain
to take precedence.

8.2.2 An Example of ACCEPTER's Relevance Evaluation

The following output traces ACCEPTER's evaluation of whether the XP
exertion + heart defect causes fatal heart attack is a relevant explanation for
Swale's death. According to that explanation, Swale's death resulted from
Swale doing physical exertion, which overtaxed a heart defect, leading to
heart attack and resultant death.

Swale's death is anomalous because it occurred earlier than is normally
expected for a racehorse, so a relevant explanation must both account for why
Swale died when he did (which is the surprising feature) and for why normal

---

[4]We describe ACCEPTER's understanding contexts in section 8.3.1.

expectations for a racehorse's life-span were superseded—why, in hindsight, the normal horse's life-span should not have been expected to apply to Swale. The following output traces ACCEPTER's decision that the explanation *exertion + heart defect causes fatal heart attack* does both. In the first phase of the process, ACCEPTER verifies that the explanation accounts for the surprising feature, since a heart attack prompted by current racing would cause immediate death. In the second phase, it verifies that the explanation also accounts for why expectations failed, because it shows a causally relevant factor (Swale's heart defect) that was not considered when forming the original expectation for Swale's life expectancy.

```
Part 1:  Checking if explanation derives surprising event
features.

    Feature(s) important to the anomaly:  TIME.

    Checking if the explanation's consequent accounts for the
    problem that TIME of SWALE'S DEAD HEALTH conflicted with
    expectations.

    Matching SWALE'S DEAD HEALTH and explanation's consequent ...

    The explanation accounts for the surprising feature(s).

Part 2:  Checking if explanation shows why the reasoning underlying
the expectation failed.

    Checking whether explanation shows factors that are unusual
    compared to standard SWALE'S M-RACEHORSE-LIFE.

        Using routine understanding to check whether SWALE'S
        PHYSICAL-EXERTION is standard in context of SWALE'S
        M-RACEHORSE-LIFE.

            Building up new memory context with expectations
            from SWALE'S M-RACEHORSE-LIFE.

            Integrating SWALE'S PHYSICAL-EXERTION into that context.

        SWALE'S PHYSICAL-EXERTION satisfies expectation for
        SWALE'S M-HORSE-RACE from SWALE'S M-RACEHORSE-LIFE,
        so it's routine.
```

```
Using routine understanding to check whether HEART-2169'S
HEREDITARY-DEFECTIVE ORGANIC-STATE is standard in context
of SWALE'S M-RACEHORSE-LIFE.

    Building up new memory context with expectations
    from SWALE'S M-RACEHORSE-LIFE.

    Integrating HEART-2169'S HEREDITARY-DEFECTIVE ORGANIC-STATE
    into that context.

    HEART-2169'S HEREDITARY-DEFECTIVE ORGANIC-STATE isn't
    expected from SWALE'S M-RACEHORSE-LIFE, or from standard
    stereotypes, so it's distinctive.

EXERTION-HEART-ATTACK resolves the anomaly, by accounting
both for the surprising part of the situation happened, and
why predictions went wrong.
```

8.3   Evaluating Plausibility

Plausibility of a belief-support chain depends on whether it adequately accounts for its conclusion—whether it has reasonable antecedents and whether the inferences connecting them to its conclusion are plausible. If so, the chain accounts for why the conclusion makes sense.

We can describe this in another way: Evaluating a belief-support chain means seeing if its antecedents and links show why the state or event in its conclusion *could have been expected* had the beliefs pointed out by the explanation been active before the state or event was encountered. To do this, we can begin with the explanation's antecedents, seeing if they could be expected from background knowledge (specific prior beliefs, expectations, or patterns), and see if the belief-support chain traces a reasonable propagation of expectations, finally leading to an expectation for the consequent.

The mechanism for performing this process already exists in any story understander that detects anomalies: the process we have described is simply the story understanding process, taking the antecedents as the start of a story, and treating links and internal beliefs as additional facts in the story to be understood. If any of the antecedents, links, or internal beliefs are anomalous, the explanation is implausible. Believability of an explanation depends on how understandable the antecedents are, and how understandable the derivation of the consequent is, given the suggested connections in the explanation.

> ACCEPTER finds believability problems in explanations by treating the explanations as stories to be understood, and looking for anomalies.

The output that follows shows ACCEPTER's plausibility evaluation for the explanation *exertion + heart defect causes fatal heart attack* for Swale's death. ACCEPTER starts evaluation by judging the plausibility of each antecedent, given the system's prior knowledge. The following output traces its evaluation of the plausibility of the antecedent that Swale was doing physical exertion.

```
Checking explanation's believability.

  Integrating the antecedent SWALE'S PHYSICAL-EXERTION into memory.

  Applying routine understanding process to SWALE'S
  PHYSICAL-EXERTION ...

    Phase 1:  Trying to recognize fact as known or expected.

      Checking if "SWALE'S PHYSICAL-EXERTION" is already known,
      or conflicts with facts in memory.
      ... No relevant belief found.

      Checking if "SWALE'S PHYSICAL-EXERTION" is expected from
      (or prohibited by) active MOPs.
      ... No relevant expectations found.

    Phase 2:  Judging plausibility by comparing to patterns.

      Checking if the role-fillers of "SWALE'S PHYSICAL-EXERTION"
      are reasonable.

        Checking if action/actor combination makes sense.

          Checking behavior patterns of SWALE and abstractions,
          to see if ACTOR of PHYSICAL-EXERTION is a usual role.

          ... SWALE'S PHYSICAL-EXERTION CONFIRMS expectations
          from the role-filling pattern "RACEHORSEs routinely
          fill role ACTOR in PHYSICAL-EXERTION".
```

In this example, it considers Swale's exertion plausible because exertion fits a stereotyped pattern for racehorses. Consequently, it accepts that antecedent.

After accepting all the antecedents of a link, ACCEPTER integrates the link's inference into memory. To do so, it first verifies that the rule itself is known. It then checks whether the particular rule applies, by testing whether the antecedent satisfies any role-filler requirements of the rule (for example, the rule `ingest-drugs=>overdose` is annotated with the requirement that the rule only applies if the drugs ingested have high medicinal strength). Finally, it checks whether the rule's consequent is reasonable or anomalous given its current beliefs. If no problems are found, ACCEPTER generates an expectation for the rule's consequent to occur.

ACCEPTER then proceeds to the consequents of the link, applying its routine understanding process to them. Normally, those beliefs will satisfy expectations that were generated based on the link's inference rule, but problems may arise (e.g., the beliefs supported may include anomalous features that the link did not account for). The next output shows ACCEPTER's activation of expectations based on an inference link, and its acceptance of the belief the link supports.

```
Activating expectations from EXERTION=>HIGH-EXERTION-LEVEL
after checking their reasonableness.

Integrating the antecedent SWALE'S HIGH EXERTION-LEVEL into
memory.
⋮
The fact "SWALE has HIGH as his EXERTION-LEVEL" satisfies
the expectation for SWALE'S HIGH EXERTION-LEVEL from
EXERTION=>HIGH-EXERTION-LEVEL.
```

ACCEPTER continues to trace through the beliefs and links of this explanation, verifying that each is reasonable. Because no anomalies are found, ACCEPTER concludes that the explanation is reasonable, although it cannot confirm that Swale actually had a heart defect:

```
Plausibility is POSSIBLE.
⋮

Explanation's beliefs have 1 unsupported premise(s)
(SWALE'S HEART'S HEREDITARY-DEFECTIVE ORGANIC-STATE),
and 1 premise(s) supported by patterns (SWALE'S PHYSICAL-EXERTION).
```

8.3.1   Maintaining Competing Hypotheses in Memory

In order to use the understanding process to test plausibility of competing explanations, an evaluator must be able to simultaneously maintain conflicting sets of beliefs. In order to see whether an explanation makes sense of an event, the evaluator must judge whether the explanation would make the explained features reasonable even if it did not know that they had actually happened. Consequently, it must evaluate the explanation separately from those features. In addition, when there are multiple candidate explanations, it needs to be able to evaluate their beliefs separately, so that expectations and beliefs following from beliefs in one explanation do not influence evaluation of another.

> To evaluate competing hypotheses, memory must include a facility for maintaining separate families of beliefs and merging them when necessary.

ACCEPTER maintains conflicting families of beliefs by placing them in hierarchical *understanding contexts*. Understanding contexts are used to maintain a tree of alternative world models [McDermott & Sussman, 1973]; by evaluating competing explanations in different contexts, ACCEPTER avoids interactions between their beliefs. Once one explanation is accepted, the contexts built for evaluating other explanations' beliefs are discarded, and processing continues in the context that includes the new beliefs and expectations that arose from processing the accepted explanation.

When and how new contexts are generated: Before ACCEPTER evaluates a candidate XP, it generates a new context into which to integrate the information asserted by the XP. That context is a subcontext of the understanding context prior to processing of the anomalous fact, which we call the pre-anomaly context. To assure that the pre-anomaly context will be available, ACCEPTER processes each input in a new subcontext of the prior context, and saves the prior context until the new input has been accepted.

For each XP to evaluate, ACCEPTER generates a new subcontext of the pre-anomaly context, and evaluates the XP's plausibility by incrementally integrating beliefs from its belief-support chain into successive subcontexts of the new context. When it accepts one of the candidate explanations, the subcontext reflecting all the XP's beliefs becomes the new understanding context to use for routine understanding. If no XP is accepted, the program reverts to the understanding context in which the anomalous event was originally processed.

The following output shows the points at which ACCEPTER generates new understanding contexts during believability evaluation. First, it generates a new subcontext of the preanomaly context, to use as the main context for evaluating the explanation. Second, during XP evaluation, it generates new subcontexts to reflect the incremental integration of the explanation's beliefs into memory. Finally, once it accepts an XP, it resets the main understanding context to the final context reflecting the explanation's beliefs.

```
Candidate explanation selected:  HORSE-RACING-HEART-ATTACK.

Generating new subcontext BELIEF-SET-2004 of BELIEF-SET-2003
to use as context for evaluating HORSE-RACING-HEART-ATTACK.
⋮
```

Evaluation trace deleted

```
Accepting "HORSE-RACING-HEART-ATTACK" to explain the anomaly
"EVENT-TOO-EARLY problem:  SWALE'S DEAD HEALTH CONFLICTS-WITH
the expectation for SWALE'S DEAD HEALTH from SWALE'S
M-RACEHORSE-LIFE"

BELIEF-SET-2005 is the memory context reflecting the explanation's
premises.

Resetting main understanding context from BELIEF-SET-2001 to
BELIEF-SET-2005.
```

Thus once an explanation has been accepted as believable, the system can simply retain the world view it formed when considering the explanation.

8.3.2   Comparing Explanations' Plausibility

In SWALE, the main purpose for finding XPs' believability problems is for the system to repair them. By adapting explanations with problems, the system can generate more reasonable explanations. However, when the adaptation module has exhausted its repair strategies, it is necessary to choose between the candidates that have been generated and to decide whether any explanation is sufficiently plausible. Consequently, ACCEPTER does a simple scoring of explanations' plausibility.

ACCEPTER bases its scoring mainly on the believability of each explanation's weakest belief or link: An explanation is considered as strong as its weakest part. The system's likelihood estimate for a belief depends on the types of confirmation or problems found for that belief when it integrated the belief into memory during plausibility evaluation. In order of decreasing believability, ACCEPTER's likelihood classes are:

1. **Confirmed** by prior beliefs or active expectations

2. **Supported** by patterns or predisposing circumstances, or by known actor goal

3. **Unsupported**, but without problems

4. **Conflicting** with patterns, beliefs, etc.

For classifying the likelihood of links, only two categories are used:

1. **Confirmed** by the system's causal knowledge (the rule is known, and its restrictions are satisfied)

2. **Conflicting** with the system's causal knowledge (no matching system rule is found, or the restrictions are not satisfied)

ACCEPTER rejects all explanations that include links or beliefs conflicting with memory, even if no other alternatives are available. Explanations that do not conflict are considered possible candidates for being accepted; ACCEPTER accepts the strongest of these candidates.

If the least likely belief in one candidate XP is more believable than the least likely beliefs of the other candidates, ACCEPTER accepts that XP. When two XPs have equally severe problems with their least likely beliefs, ACCEPTER ranks the XPs by the number of hypotheses each has at that likelihood level—it favors the explanation with the fewest problems of that severity. If the explanations have the same number, it chooses between them by looking at how many hypotheses each has in the next most severe category, continuing to compare successively less severe problems until it finds a difference at some level. If no differences are found between the most plausible XPs, ACCEPTER favors the XP whose anomaly characterization most specifically matches the characterization of the current anomaly: In the absence of other information, it assumes that the similarity between old and new anomalies will make it more likely to apply.

This ranking reflects the relative plausibility of explanations' content, except when all the beliefs of two candidate explanations are confirmed, in which case it reduces to a simple structural minimality criterion: The explanation involving the fewest beliefs and links is preferred.

Figure 8.4 shows the result of ACCEPTER's plausibility ranking for the following five explanations of Swale's death:

FIXX-XP: Swale, like Jim Fixx, died because recreational jogging overtaxed a hereditary heart defect.

HEART-DEFECT+HORSE-RACING-HEART-ATTACK: Swale died because running in a horse race overtaxed a hereditary heart defect.

INBRED-HORSE+HORSE-RACING-HEART-ATTACK: Swale died because inbreeding caused him to have a heart defect, which was overtaxed by running in a race.

PERFORMANCE-DRUG-OVERDOSE-BY-TRAINER: Swale died because his trainer administered a fatal dose of performance-enhancing drugs.

POISONING-BY-OWNER-FOR-INSURANCE: Swale's owner poisoned him in order to collect property insurance.

By ACCEPTER's evaluation, INBRED-HORSE+HORSE-RACING-HEART-ATTACK is the most acceptable explanation. Its belief-support chain is reasonable, and both its antecedents are accounted for by prior information: ACCEPTER's background knowledge includes the pattern that racehorses tend to suffer from inbreeding, and Swale was already known to be involved in racing. The second most acceptable is HEART-DEFECT+HORSE-RACING-HEART-ATTACK. It is possible, but does not substantiate why Swale would have had a heart defect, and ACCEPTER has no previous pattern or expectation supporting the belief that Swale had a heart defect.

Each of the other explanations has problems. PERFORMANCE-DRUG-OVER-DOSE-BY-TRAINER is supported by ACCEPTER's belief that trainers often administer performance-enhancing drugs, but conflicts with ACCEPTER's knowledge that dosage of performance enhancing drugs is carefully regulated. The explanation FIXX-XP is unlikely because the hypothesis that Swale was jogging conflicts with the pattern that joggers are human (it also fails to substantiate the heart defect). POISONING-BY-OWNER-FOR-INSURANCE conflicts with the pattern that Swale's owners are law-abiding, although it provides a reasonable motivation (getting money) if they are not. The explanation also depends on Swale being insured, and the program has no reason to believe that he was.

ACCEPTER's plausibility rankings are designed to reflect how well each explanation links the event to factors that are already expected or believed, thus giving an indication of how well the explanations reconcile the anomalous event with prior understanding. Consequently, the resultant ranking may not parallel the explanations' objective probabilities. For example, the explanation INBRED-HORSE+HORSE-RACING-HEART-ATTACK has a lower probability than the explanation HEART-DEFECT+HORSE-RACING-HEART-ATTACK, because the former explanation includes the additional assumption that the heart defect was caused by inbreeding, but it receives a higher ranking because it connects the death to ACCEPTER's belief that inbreeding is common in racehorses.

The ranking of explanations is:

1 INBRED-HORSE+HORSE-RACING-HEART-ATTACK

   Explanation's beliefs have 1 premise(s) supported by patterns
   (SWALE'S INBREEDING), and 1 premise(s) confirmed by prior
   knowledge/expectations (SWALE'S M-HORSE-RACE).

2 HEART-DEFECT+HORSE-RACING-HEART-ATTACK

   Explanation's beliefs have 1 unsupported premise(s) (SWALE'S
   HEART'S HEREDITARY-DEFECTIVE ORGANIC-STATE), and 1 premise(s)
   confirmed by prior knowledge/expectations (SWALE'S
   M-HORSE-RACE).

3 PERFORMANCE-DRUG-OVERDOSE-BY-TRAINER

   Explanation's beliefs have 1 premise(s) or internal belief(s)
   conflicting with beliefs or patterns (DRUGS-5'S HIGH
   MEDICINAL-STRENGTH), and 1 premise(s) supported by patterns
   (ATHLETIC-TRAINER-4'S M-PERFORMANCE-ENHANCEMENT-DRUGS).

4 FIXX-XP

   Explanation's beliefs have 1 premise(s) or internal belief(s)
   conflicting with beliefs or patterns (SWALE'S M-JOG), and
   1 unsupported premise(s) (SWALE'S HEART'S HEREDITARY-DEFECTIVE
   ORGANIC-STATE).

5 POISONING-BY-OWNER-FOR-INSURANCE

   Explanation's beliefs have 1 premise(s) or internal belief(s)
   conflicting with beliefs or patterns (CRIMINAL-7'S M-POISON),
   1 unsupported premise(s) (COMPANY-23'S M-PROPERTY-INSURANCE
   to CRIMINAL-7), and 1 premise(s) confirmed by prior
   knowledge/expectations (CRIMINAL-7'S INCREASED WEALTH AS GOAL
   OF CRIMINAL-7).

FIG. 8.4.   Plausibility rankings for explanations of Swale's death.

8.4   Conclusion

Anomalies reveal problems in an understander's knowledge, and proper repair of those problems depends on having good explanations. Using anomaly characterizations to retrieve explanations can increase the chance of generating good explanations, but retrieval of the right XP is not guaranteed—in truly novel situations, a near-miss XP is all that a case-based explainer can hope for. Consequently, there is no way to explain reliably without evaluating whether candidate explanations are relevant and plausible.

The previous sections develop a theory of how to do this evaluation. Based on that theory, an explanation system can decide whether a candidate explanation is relevant to an anomaly—which determines whether it is worth considering at all—and whether it is plausible—which determines whether it must be adapted and what the focus of any adaptation should be. The theory allows ACCEPTER to judge both the relevance and plausibility of candidate explanations.

If an explanation is relevant and plausible, it provides the information needed to repair the belief problems shown by an anomaly. However, because anomalies show that the world is different from what was expected, they also signal the potential for new threats and opportunities. These threats and opportunities may require a response; choosing or executing that response requires additional information. The next chapter examines how goals beyond simple understanding prompt additional requirements for explanations, demonstrating that explanation evaluation criteria are dynamic, depending on changing system goals.

9 Focusing on Important Factors

Anomalies show differences between the world and the understander's world model. When those differences affect the understander's goals, it must find an explanation that provides the information it needs to respond. We present a wide range of goals that explanation can serve and show the divergent requirements that different types of goals place on good explanations, demonstrating that explanation evaluation must be dynamic and goal-based.[1]

9.1 Each Anomaly Has Many Explanations

The previous chapter considers how to evaluate explanations' usefulness for repairing flaws in an understander's world model. However, maintaining an accurate world model may be done for more than its own sake: The effort to understand is often motivated by the desire to accomplish other goals.

When an understander has goals beyond simple understanding, anomalies affect more than just the understander's world model. Whenever its world model needs to be revised, current goals and plans may need to be revised as well. Selecting and carrying out appropriate responses will often require explaining the new situation to gather additional information, and the type of information needed will depend on the explainer's intended response. Consequently, in order for explanation evaluation to make an accurate assessment

---

[1]Much of this chapter appears in the article "Goal-based Explanation Evaluation," *Cognitive Science*, Volume 15, Number 4, 1991. This material is reprinted with the permission of Ablex Publishing Corporation.

of explanations' goodness, it must reflect the explainer's intentions for using the explanations. In this chapter, we examine the goals that may influence explanation and develop criteria for evaluating whether an explanation provides sufficient information for those goals.

The following sections show how explanation serves a wide range of goals, and how different goals impose quite different requirements on the information an explanation must provide. Our emphasis on the rich range of goal-based influences on explanations differs from other AI research on explanation evaluation, which either ignores goals entirely or takes a limited view of goal-based influences (see section 2.3.7).

Two goals that can drive explanation have been considered in the previous chapter—making an anomalous event reasonable and accounting for why reasoning failed—and we have shown how satisfying those goals requires explanations to include particular types of factors. In this chapter, we discuss eight additional goals that can drive explanation. We illustrate the theory with a detailed discussion of the information requirements for four goals that can be selected to influence ACCEPTER's explanation evaluation: predicting an outcome, repairing an undesirable state, finding how to control recurrence of the surprising state or event in the future, and finding whom to blame for an outcome. We conclude by sketching the information requirements for the remaining goals, and highlighting the effect of goal-based evaluation on explanation adaptation.

9.2   How Goals Affect Explanation

Anomalies indicate an unexpected state of the world, and that state may require a response. To respond appropriately, the system needs information about the current situation. The particular information required depends on the explainer's goals to act in the world, which trigger goals to acquire the type of information required to act successfully.

As an example of the importance of goals in explanation, and the types of information that different goals require, we consider the following story:

> Company X was beleaguered by high taxes, foreign competition, and outdated equipment, despite low labor costs due to being nonunion. Rumors of problems spread, and the company's stock plummeted, but its managers announced their decision not to have layoffs. The next week, it was rumored that they would lay off 20% of their work force.

Because the layoffs violate the managers' pledge, they are anomalous and might prompt explanation. However, different people involved in the layoffs would have different goals, which might make them want to account for the situation in different ways. This desire to highlight certain factors gives each explainer a different *explanation purpose* to guide explanation, as the following examples show:

1. Someone who had believed the managers' pledge, and consequently expected that there would not be layoffs, would want to confirm that the layoffs would really occur. Here the actor's goal is maintaining accurate beliefs, which prompts a plan to substantiate the layoffs. This prompts the explanation purpose of showing that likelihood of the layoffs can be inferred from trusted information, which might be done by the explanation *a newspaper found a secret company memo from the company president, describing the timetable for the layoffs.*

2. The same person might have the goal of avoiding future incorrect predictions in similar situations. One plan to achieve that goal is to explain why the current belief went wrong and repair the source of the problem. Here the purpose of explanation would be accounting for the bad prediction in terms of false prior beliefs. For example, if the explainer had trusted the managers, but the person could explain the conflict between reports by *the managers lied*, that explanation would make it possible to avoid trusting their statements in the future.

3. A worker who expected to be layed off might want to avoid being unemployed in the future, by finding a new job before being layed off next time. For this purpose, a suitable explanation might be *the layoffs were inevitable because of pressure to reduce costs to shore up the company's falling stock:* This explanation makes it possible to predict layoffs from changes in the stock price.

4. A local politician might see the layoffs as bad for the area's economic health, prompting the goal of trying to have the workers recalled. To do this, the politician would have the explanation purpose of finding feasible repair points for the current situation. This would require building an explanation showing how the layoffs are caused or enabled by factors under government control, and whose removal will restore the desired situation. For example, the explanation *the layoffs were forced by high taxes that reduced profitability* suggests repairing the situation by lowering taxes in order to make the factory again profitable, so the workers will be called back.

5. A worker who was still employed might worry about being layed off in the future, prompting the goal of preventing future layoffs. This would prompt the explanation purpose of finding causes of the layoffs that the worker can affect. An explanation might be *lack of unionization enabled*

the layoffs, because the workers had a contract that gave employees no security. The worker could use this explanation to suggest what to do: to try to unionize.

6. The manager who ordered the layoffs might want to avoid negative publicity, and could decide to do so by deflecting blame. One explanation purpose for this goal would be to implicate other actors, perhaps by an explanation such as *an outside expert convinced management that the layoffs were essential.*

7. The owner of another factory might want to improve that factory's profitability. This goal might trigger the plan of analyzing other managers' decisions, to learn better management strategies. This could prompt the explanation purpose of deciding why the other managers chose to have layoffs, as opposed to alternative responses to the company's problems (e.g., increasing advertising to increase demand for products)—a useful explanation might be *the managers chose layoffs instead of advertising because layoffs help win tax concessions from local government.*

8. A worker who wondered whether to look for a new job, or simply wait to be called back, would want to know how long the layoffs were likely to last. This would prompt the explanation purpose of clarifying the situation to help form predictions of the layoffs' duration. This might involve finding if the layoffs resulted primarily from long-term factors or short-term ones. A suitable explanation might be *the layoffs were caused by a decrease in demand because of temporary overstocks.*

9. A business consultant might want to develop a theory of how demographic trends force layoffs in different industries. A plan for that goal is to show how the theory accounts for particular episodes of layoffs, which would prompt the explanation purpose of finding causes of the current layoffs within the framework of that theory.

10. A politician wanting to mitigate negative public opinion of the local economy, in order to be re-elected, might want to show that the layoffs were an unavoidable side-effect of something desirable, perhaps through an explanation such as *layoffs are caused by American industry streamlining operations to become stronger.*

Even though all these explainers could have noticed the same anomaly when the rumor of layoffs began to circulate, each has different goals, prompting a different purpose for explanation. Although we can imagine single explanations that would be usable for multiple purposes, an explanation's usefulness for multiple purposes is not assured: In the previous list, almost all the explanations given for one explainer are inapplicable to the others' purposes.

The wide range of explanations possible for the layoffs suggests how many factors can enter into the explanation of any situation, but our list of explanations for the layoffs itself leaves out countless factors—generating a "complete" explanation of a real-world event is impossible. Good explanations must highlight a few important factors from the many that are involved: the factors that give the explainer the information it needs. In order to make sure that an explanation does highlight the important features, goal-based explanation evaluation is needed.

> Explainer goals determine which of the countless possible factors an explanation must include, and how those factors must be connected to the event being explained.

9.3   Major Explanation Purposes

In the preceding example, the goals of each explainer prompted efforts to include certain types of factors and connections in an explanation. Those efforts reflect 10 major explanation purposes triggered by anomalies:

1. Connect situation to expected/believed conditions.

2. Connect situation to previously unexpected conditions.

3. Connect situation to factors from which it can be predicted.

4. Connect undesirable state to possible repair points.

5. Connect situation to causes that show how a given actor can control its occurrence.

6. Connect situation to factors that suggest praise or blame for an actor.

7. Connect an action to the actor's motivations.

8. Connect situation to factors that discriminate between alternative responses.

9. Connect situation to factors within a given theory.

10. Connect situation to types of factors that, when their influence is communicated to another agent, will cause a desired change in that agent's beliefs.

The first two purposes in this list are the purposes of an explainer seeking to resolve an anomaly, which we describe in Chapter 8. The third through ninth purposes reflect needs arising primarily from a system's internal information requirements; this is the class of needs that we concentrate on in this chapter. The tenth purpose, which reflects the goal to communicate particular types of information to another agent, has previously been addressed in other contexts such as expert-system explanation, and we only address it briefly here.

9.4   How Explanation Purposes Arise

Anomalies show flaws in system knowledge. When that knowledge is revised in response to the anomaly, the system may discover that its prior goals and plans need to be revised as well, in response to the system's new picture of the world. However, revising goals and plans depends on having appropriate information—information that may need to go beyond what is provided by the explanation that originally resolved the anomaly. When a system needs particular types of information from an explanation, its needs prompt explanation purposes that guide the explanation effort.

> Explanation purposes are goals to build a belief-support chain involving particular types of factors.

Explanation purposes correspond to types of links and beliefs that an explanation must include; in our system these are described in terms of basic *evaluation dimensions*. ACCEPTER has individual heuristics for evaluating along each evaluation dimension, and it combines the heuristics as needed to build tests reflecting the multiple dimensions that may be important. Thus in our model, the goal-based evaluation decisions are determined by the following chain:

$$\text{Anomaly} \Rightarrow \begin{array}{c}\text{Changes}\\\text{in world}\\\text{model}\end{array} \Rightarrow \begin{array}{c}\text{Info needs}\\\text{for new}\\\text{goals and}\\\text{plans}\end{array} \Rightarrow \begin{array}{c}\text{Explanation}\\\text{purposes}\end{array} \Rightarrow \begin{array}{c}\text{Groups of}\\\text{dimension}\\\text{checks}\end{array} \Rightarrow \begin{array}{c}\text{Evaluation}\\\text{decision}\end{array}$$

As a concrete example, we trace the beginning of this chain for an explanation of surprising layoffs. Suppose a worker is not layed off but is surprised nevertheless that the layoffs take place despite the managers' pledge. An explanation accounting for the failure of prior expectations might be *the managers lied*. That explanation shows the worker that management cannot be trusted to protect workers, which suggests that the worker's job could be threatened if hard times continue. This triggers a new goal for the worker: to protect his job.

To accomplish that goal, the worker might decide on the following plan: to punish those responsible for the layoffs, in order to deter anyone who might cause future layoffs. For example, if the person who made the decision were personally blamed in the press and by the layed off workers, the negative publicity might provide an incentive to try to avoid layoffs in similar future situations.

Carrying out the worker's plan depends on having certain information that may not be initially available: The worker needs to know who the perpetrator was. This gives rise to an explanation purpose: to connect the layoffs to factors that suggest blame for a particular actor. For other goals, other explanation purposes apply; Table 9.1 sketches examples of how each of our explanation purposes can be triggered by a goal and plan.

Sometimes an anomaly will trigger more than one goal, or a goal will trigger multiple plans, causing multiple explanation purposes to be active simultaneously. However, even when multiple goals apply, limits on resources for information gathering may force a choice between them, in order to focus explanation effort on purposes serving the system's highest priority goals.

After an explanation purpose has been chosen, explanations must be evaluated to see if they fulfill that purpose. Although it would be possible to devise independent evaluation procedures for each purpose, parsimony suggests analyzing the purposes to find a set of simple component requirements that can be combined in different ways to describe multiple purposes. ACCEPTER's checks for explanation purposes are built from simple procedures for judging the role of antecedents along 10 evaluation dimensions: predictive power, timeliness, routineness, distinctiveness, knowability, causal force, repairability, independence, achievability/blockability, and desirability.[2] Some of these dimensions measure properties of individual beliefs, given the current context (e.g., knowability); others measure properties of how a belief is connected to an explanation's consequent (e.g., causal force). After an initial set of dimensions was defined for a few purposes, we found that needs for many of our other purposes could be described by simply using different combinations of dimensions from the initial set, and we believe that only a small set of additional dimensions would be needed for adding other purposes to the system.

This chapter discusses how ACCEPTER judges the suitability of explanations for its explanation purposes, using combinations of tests for different evaluation dimensions. The question of how to decide that an anomaly should trigger a particular explanation purpose is beyond the scope of this book.

---

[2]Although the checks return yes/no decisions, the values for all dimensions actually fall along a continuum.

TABLE 9.1
Examples of how Explanation Purposes Arise

Goal $\implies$	Plan $\implies$	Explanation Purpose
Prevent bad effects that result from acting on false information.	1. Confirm reasonableness of new information.	Connect situation to expected/believed conditions.
	2. Find and correct flaws in prior knowledge.	Connect situation to unexpected conditions.
Minimize bad effects/ maximize good effects in similar future situations.	Predict similar situations in time to prepare.	Connect situation to predictive factors.
Use malfunctioning device.	Execute repair.	Connect undesirable state to repair points.
Re-achieve the good effects caused by anomalous event.	Re-cause event.	Connect to achievable causes.
Prevent recurrence of surprising bad state.	Punish current actors to deter future perpetrators.	Connect to factors suggesting blame.
Counter an adversary.	Predict and respond to adversary's actions.	Connect to adversary's motivations.
Protect current plans.	Deal with ramifications of new features.	Connect to factors that discriminate between alternative responses.
Refine/demonstrate a theory.	Use theory to account for unexpected data.	Connect to within-theory factors.
Have an action performed by another agent.	Convince other agent the action is desirable.	Connect situation to factors that will influence other agent.

9.5   How Goals Affect ACCEPTER's Evaluation

In a planning system that used ACCEPTER to maintain its world model, explanation purposes would be determined by needs of the overarching planner. In the current stand-alone version of ACCEPTER, explanation purposes are selected by a human user. The user can choose among five explanation purposes: connecting the situation to factors that will help predict it, connecting it to factors that will help prevent it, connecting it to factors that can be repaired, and connecting it to factors that allow the assignment of blame or responsibility.

To evaluate whether an explanation is sufficient for a given purpose, ACCEPTER tests the explanation's beliefs and links along relevant evaluation dimensions, beginning by applying dimension checks to the explanation's antecedents. If the original explanation does not have suitable antecedents, or its antecedents are not linked in suitable ways, ACCEPTER next applies its tests to the antecedents of each subchain contained in the original belief-support chain. This process allows it to determine whether any part of the explanation provides the needed information. (In what follows, when we refer to the antecedents of an explanation we are referring to the antecedents of the subchain currently under consideration.)

If the original explanation or one of its subchains passes ACCEPTER's tests, the program accepts it and outputs a description of the useful information it provides. If no subchain includes an adequate set of useful antecedents, ACCEPTER outputs a description of any useful information found and summarizes the missing information to guide adaptation.

The following sections discuss the information requirements arising from standard goals that drive explanation. Each section discusses a goal, the explanation purpose arising from the goal, and the evaluation dimensions relevant to the purpose. For our examples, validity is important, and our discussion assumes that the explanations under consideration have already been judged to be valid. However, for some goals validity would be unnecessary or even undesirable; see section 9.10.4.

ACCEPTER's heuristics for testing evaluation dimensions are generally very simple; a much richer model is needed. However, that issue is irrelevant to our main points, which are the explanation purposes themselves, and the fact that the purposes can be described along a small set of dimensions.

We begin our discussion by looking at a basic goal for explanation: learning how to predict the anomalous event, to avoid repeating the failure next time.

9.6   Explaining to Predict

When an understander's expectations fail, its knowledge needs to be updated to avoid future failures. To avoid failures, the understander needs to find out how to expect the new situation, rather than the one that it had mistakenly expected. To do this, it needs to find predictive features to look for next time—warning signs that the surprising feature or event will occur again. This prompts the explanation purpose *connect situation to events from which it can be predicted.* For example, when Challenger exploded, many people involved in the space program tried to explain the disaster, in order to predict potential future disasters and avoid them.

In order for a belief-support chain to be useful for prediction, it must satisfy four requirements, each tested by a test for a different evaluation dimension:

1. Occurrence of the chain's antecedents makes the event likely.

   This is tested by applying checks for the antecedents' *predictive power.*

2. The antecedents happen long enough in advance of the event for the prediction they trigger to be useful.

   This is tested by applying checks for the antecedents' *timeliness.*

3. One of the antecedents is unusual compared to the expected situation, so that it gives evidence for the surprising event occurring instead of the previously expected one.

   This is tested by applying checks for the antecedents' *distinctiveness.*

4. The antecedents are conditions the system is likely to be aware of in the future.

   This is tested by applying checks for the antecedents' *knowability.*

Note that the conditions do not specify that the explanation must be causal: Valid predictions are often based on noncausal reasoning. For example, a belief-support chain might make sense of the date of a shuttle launch by showing how the date could be expected from a newspaper article. Although the article does not cause the launch date, that belief-support chain could still suggest how to predict the dates of future launches.

We next elaborate on each of the dimensions relevant to prediction.

9.6.1   Predictive Power

Even if an explanation describes a group of factors that caused an anomalous event, recurrence of those factors might not be sufficient to cause the event in the future. For example, investigation of the Challenger disaster led to wide agreement about the basic causal chain leading to the explosion: Cold weather made the solid rocket booster seals brittle, preventing them from sealing properly, allowing the boosters to burn through and ignite the main fuel tank. (We call this the "cold seal" explanation.) However, despite agreement that cold weather on the launch day led to the explosion, many were unwilling to predict that the next launch in cold weather would result in an explosion as well.

Unlike the deductive proofs assumed by EBL, everyday explanations cannot prove the necessity of an outcome. All everyday explanations depend on implicit assumptions about the circumstances outside of the explanatory chain. Consequently, explanation evaluation for prediction must examine the individual links in the explanatory chain to decide whether they support prediction. Some links describe consequences that almost always follow from the links' antecedents (turning on a light switch almost always turns on the light); others describe noncausal conclusions that allow reliable predictions (a trusted spy's reports may allow anticipation of an enemy's actions); some links describe consequences that only rarely follow (the purchase of a lottery ticket sometimes leads to winning, but we would not predict winning based on the purchase).

To enable ACCEPTER to judge predictive power, each of its inference rules is annotated with information about whether it is reasonable to predict occurrence of the rule's consequent if it is known that its antecedents have occurred. (The annotations are static, and reflect neither context nor gradations in predictive strength, so they provide only a coarse approximation to the actual predictive power of a link.)

ACCEPTER determines antecedents' predictive power by examining the belief-support chain connecting them to the event to predict. If each link in the belief-support chain is annotated as predictive, the entire chain traces a reasonable path of prediction, and the antecedents are considered predictive.[3] Note that because the predictive power judgment depends not on properties of the antecedents in isolation but on the types of rules linking them to the event being explained, this property could not be captured by traditional EBL operationality criteria—those criteria base decisions exclusively on properties of the antecedents of the explanation, independent of the explanation's derivation.

An example of ACCEPTER's judgment of predictive power is shown in our extended ACCEPTER trace in section 2.2.2. When ACCEPTER evaluates the cold seal explanation, it checks whether the antecedents of the launch and cold seals are actually predictive of future explosions. In the following

---

[3]Research on reasoning under uncertainty has developed finer grained criteria for propagating belief along chains; Pearl [1988a] provides an overview of some of that work.

output segment, it verifies that the links making the connection from the launch to the explosion are all predictive.

```
Applying test for PREDICTIVENESS to CHALLENGER'S
SPACE-LAUNCH.

  Checking the connection between CHALLENGER'S
  SPACE-LAUNCH and CHALLENGER'S EXPLOSION.

    Testing if CAUSAL-MOP-SCENE:LAUNCH=>IGNITION
    satisfies test for LINK PREDICTIVITY.

    Testing if CAUSAL-MOP-SCENE:IGNITION=>HIGH-PRESSURE
    satisfies test for LINK PREDICTIVITY.

    Testing if BRITTLE-SEAL+CONTAINER-SEAL+CONTENTS-PRESSURE=>
    CONTAINER-EXPLOSION
    satisfies test for LINK PREDICTIVITY.

    Testing if EXPLOSION-IN-COMPONENT=>EXPLOSION-IN-WHOLE
    satisfies test for LINK PREDICTIVITY.
  ... All links are acceptable.

  ... test passed.
```

9.6.2   Timeliness

Predicting an event is only useful if the prediction allows more effective behavior. One of the factors affecting this is whether the prediction can be made long enough in advance to be useful. Soon after the Challenger explosion, for example, a preliminary explanation was formed—television footage showed that the boosters had burned through. However, although the boosters burning through allows us to predict an explosion, that prediction is useless for preventing future explosions: By the time the boosters burn through, there is no hope of saving the spacecraft.

> Predictions should be formed early enough for the predictor to benefit by responding.

Because the initial explanation was inadequate for preventing future disasters, NASA continued its investigation, elaborating on this original one.

Finally, it established the cold seal explanation: that the booster failure was caused by the cold weather before the launch making the seals brittle. This cause could be known long enough in advance to avoid future disasters by cancelling launches in cold weather, and some engineers suggested continuing shuttle launches as long as the weather was sufficiently warm.

Deciding how much warning is needed: In order to judge timeliness of an explanation's antecedents, we must first decide how much warning is needed. For some goals, this depends on information within the explanation. For example, if explanation is being done to prevent a bad outcome, the explainer needs to predict the outcome while there is still time to block one of its causes. When ACCEPTER's evaluation is aimed towards prevention of an event, the system decides for itself how much warning is needed, by examining the explanation's belief-support chain to find the earliest causes the explainer can prevent. (See section 9.8 for an example.)

For other types of goals, the amount of warning depends on factors external to the explanation. For example, the minimum warning NASA needed to safely abort a shuttle launch depends on aspects of the shuttle design that are not directly implicated in the explosion, such as whether the shuttle has an emergency escape system and the conditions under which it can be used. When the amount of prediction needed depends on factors outside of the explanation, ACCEPTER's user can input the amount of warning to require.

Calculating the warning an antecedent provides: To calculate how far in advance of the explanation's consequent an antecedent occurs, AC-CEPTER adds up temporal separations along the links of the explanation's belief-support chain. If the antecedent occurs long enough in advance of the consequent for prediction based on it to be useful, it passes the timeliness test. For example, when ACCEPTER evaluates the timeliness of the cold booster seals for predicting another space shuttle explosion, it first decides that warning is needed minutes before the launch, in order to allow the launch to be stopped. With that knowledge, it checks whether the cold seals precede the explosion by at least that delay. Because the cold weather precedes the brittleness by some time, it is a sufficiently timely cause.

```
Applying test for TIMELINESS (is fact at least
MINUTES before CHALLENGER'S EXPLOSION?) to SOLID-ROCKET-31'S
O-RING'S COLD TEMPERATURE.

   Summing temporal separations along belief-support
   chain connecting SOLID-ROCKET-31'S O-RING'S
   COLD TEMPERATURE to CHALLENGER'S EXPLOSION.
```

```
SOLID-ROCKET-31'S O-RING'S COLD TEMPERATURE
leads to SOLID-ROCKET-31'S O-RING'S LOW
FLEXIBILITY HOURS afterwards.

SOLID-ROCKET-31'S O-RING'S LOW FLEXIBILITY
leads to SOLID-ROCKET-31'S EXPLOSION immediately.

SOLID-ROCKET-31'S EXPLOSION leads to CHALLENGER'S
EXPLOSION immediately.

... SOLID-ROCKET-31'S O-RING'S COLD TEMPERATURE
is HOURS BEFORE CHALLENGER'S EXPLOSION.

... test passed.
```

9.6.3   Distinctiveness

Even if an explanation shows sufficiently timely factors leading to an event, and the system believes that those factors are predictive of the event occurring, the explanation may not make it possible for the explainer to make predictions. The problem is that the explainer may end up with two belief-support chains that it considers predictive—the one leading to the original expectation, and the one accounting for what actually occurred—and have no way to decide which one applies in a given situation. In order for the explainer to be able to decide, the new chain must include factors distinguishing the situation in which it applies from those in which the prior reasoning does.

For example, someone might explain the Challenger disaster by Challenger's multisegment booster design, and that explanation could lead to the belief that the design makes booster failure likely (even when the shuttle was being designed, some engineers pushed strongly for the boosters to be manufactured in a single piece, to obviate the problem of seal failure). However, the design explanation is not sufficient for knowing when to predict future explosions. Launches before Challenger went safely, so we need to know what distinguished Challenger's launch from the launches before—why the booster failed in this particular episode, *as opposed to the others* in which boosters did not. This requires identifying something distinctive about the circumstances of the Challenger launch, compared to circumstances of the normal safe launches, in order to use it to discriminate between situations in which a safe launch is or is not likely. In this example, the distinctive feature is the weather. Previous launch days were all warm, so the seals were flexible enough to work; the design only led to disaster on cold launch days.

To decide whether a factor is distinctive, ACCEPTER compares it to the conditions that routinely hold in situations for which the normal outcome occurs. To do so, it first builds a memory context reflecting the beliefs on which expectations for the normal outcome were based, and then uses its routine understanding process to check whether the factor either matches those beliefs or would be expected to hold in the situation with the normal outcome, due to standard patterns. If so, it does not account for there being a different outcome in the current case. However, if the factor is unexpected or anomalous compared to the knowledge on which the failed expectation was based, the factor distinguishes the new situation from the normal one. Consequently, it can be used to decide which outcome to expect. By this process, factors such as the booster design are judged not to be distinctive (all shuttle boosters have the same design), but the cold weather is: Challenger's launch day was unusually cold for the Florida launch site.

The following example shows part of ACCEPTER's distinctiveness judgment for antecedents of the Challenger explosion. Although the launch itself was a necessary condition for the explosion, the launch is routine, so it is not a feature that leads to predictions of an explosion instead of a safe mission:

```
Checking whether CHALLENGER'S SPACE-LAUNCH satisfies
test(s) for "DISTINCTIVENESS".

   Applying test for DISTINCTIVENESS to CHALLENGER'S SPACE-LAUNCH.

      Using routine understanding to check whether CHALLENGER'S
      SPACE-LAUNCH is standard in context of CHALLENGER'S
      ROCKET-DESIGN.

         Building up new memory context with expectations
         from CHALLENGER'S ROCKET-DESIGN.

         Integrating CHALLENGER'S SPACE-LAUNCH into
         that context.

      CHALLENGER'S SPACE-LAUNCH satisfies the role-filling
      pattern "ROCKETs routinely fill role SPACECRAFT
      in SPACE-LAUNCH", so it's routine.
      ... test failed.
```

However, the cold seals are unusual. Consequently, ACCEPTER judges them distinctive—their contribution accounts for the fact that Challenger exploded, when previous shuttles did not.

9.6.4 Knowability

Even if an antecedent has predictive power, is timely, and is distinctive, it cannot trigger predictions unless we know of its occurrence. For example, one factor contributing to the Challenger disaster was that an engineer's efforts to stop the launch were overruled. A possible lesson is that we should predict disaster when we learn that management has ignored safety warnings. However, this lesson is unlikely to help a NASA director prevent future disasters, because no one would know about the warnings except the engineer's manager.

> To be useful, predictions must be triggered by factors that the system will notice routinely or can check for with reasonable cost.

Knowability reflects how easily the system can notice or find out about future occurrences of a particular type of state or event.

ACCEPTER's Knowability Criteria

ACCEPTER groups states and events into three knowability classes: *observable* factors, which are likely to be previously known or noticed in routine understanding, *testable* factors, which can be known by carrying out inexpensive tests known to the system, and *undetectable* factors, which cannot be detected by known tests. Depending on the importance of predicting the outcome, the user selects which level of knowability to require. Of course, the actual effort required by different tests can vary considerably, and both observability and testability are strongly context-dependent—grouping the required effort into three levels is only a crude approximation to the needed dynamic criteria.

ACCEPTER uses the following heuristics to decide whether factors are observable or testable. When factors are not observable, and no tests for them are found, they are assumed to be undetectable.

Judging observability: Factors can be considered observable for either of two reasons. First, if a factor is known to hold, or routinely holds (according to stereotypes), it can be considered observable even if we have no way to directly observe it. For example, by this criterion the fact that the shuttle's boosters have rubber O-rings would be considered observable, even though we cannot actually observe the interior of the boosters.

The second reason actually reflects the ability of someone nearby to verify the factor by direct observation. Nodes in ACCEPTER's memory net representing objects and events are annotated with information on their usual observability. For example, most actions are observable to people who are present, but thoughts are not. Observability information about specific object and event features is also stored, indexed under the objects and events. For example, a person's hair color is usually observable, but blood pressure is not. When no observability information is indexed under the object or event type, observability information is inherited from higher level abstractions in the memory net.

In order for the cold seal explanation to be useful for prediction, all its antecedents must be things the system is likely to know about. One of the antecedents is that the seals are made of rubber, which makes them tend to become brittle in the cold. ACCEPTER has no specific information on whether the material of seals in rocket boosters is usually observable, but it assumes that a system will usually know or be able to observe the material of any physical object known to the system:

```
Applying test for KNOWABILITY to SOLID-ROCKET-31'S
O-RING'S RUBBER MATERIAL.

    Searching up abstraction net for observability information.
    ⋮
    SOLID-ROCKET-31'S O-RING'S RUBBER MATERIAL
    is probably observable, since it is a(n) MATERIAL
    of a(n) PHYSICAL-OBJECT.

    ... test passed.
```

Because these observability criteria are static and based only on object type, they are equivalent to the static operationality criteria used by many EBL systems. Consequently, they suffer from the same well known problems. As we discuss in section 9.11, we view them as place-holders for the dynamic criteria that are needed.

Judging testability: Sometimes predicting an outcome is worth the effort of performing tests. If a comparatively low-cost plan is known for checking a feature that could lead to important predictions, that plan can be performed periodically, to increase the likelihood of generating the prediction when needed. For example, an employee at Yale changed her behavior after explaining the cause of engine damage to her car:

> X burned out an engine by driving when her car was low on oil. After that incident, she started checking the oil level whenever she got gas, to make sure she would notice low oil in time.

People learn standard plans to test for features of situations that have important ramifications but are not directly observable—for example, we are taught early on that before leaving a room in a burning building, we should touch the door handle to see if it is hot, as a test for fire on the other side. ACCEPTER judges the testability of events and states by searching its memory for standard plans to test for their occurrence; it considers a factor testable whenever it finds a plan to test for it.[4] In general, however, testability criteria should consider both how easily the plan can be applied in the current context, and what resources the planner is willing to expend on the test. Whether a given amount of effort is reasonable depends both on the actor's resources, and on the importance of making the correct prediction: Few people would be willing to spend much more than the cost of a *TV Guide* subscription to predict what will be shown on television, but it is worthwhile to the United States to spend millions each year on tests to predict nuclear attack.

When ACCEPTER evaluates whether the cold seal explanation for Challenger allows prediction of future explosions, it determines that no tests need to be applied to use the explanation for prediction—all the explanation's antecedents are observable. However, when it evaluates explanations of Swale's death for predicting similar future deaths, it determines that tests will be needed.

Predicting deaths like Swale's might be important to a horse farm, in order to avoid buying the wrong horses. However, in the explanation *horse racing + heart defect causes fatal heart attack*, only the exertion is an observable feature—heart defects are not. Consequently, using the explanation for prediction depends on finding tests that can reveal the condition of a horse's heart.

The following output shows ACCEPTER's knowability evaluation for antecedents of *horse racing + heart defect causes fatal heart attack*. ACCEPTER decides that horse racing is observable, because it is a form of public performance, but a heart defect is not. To decide if the defect is a testable factor, it searches memory for possible tests, beginning by checking for tests indexed directly as revealing the important feature: the organic state of a heart. ACCEPTER finds electrocardiogram indexed as a test for hearts' states, and consequently it decides that the explanation does show factors that allow an owner to predict future deaths, assuming the owner is willing to expend the effort required for an EKG.

---

[4]The tests in its memory are simply placeholders to allow exercising the system's memory search; how to carry out the tests is not represented in the system.

Applying test for KNOWABILITY to SWALE'S M-HORSE-RACE.

Searching up abstraction net for observability information.

Looking under SWALE'S M-HORSE-RACE and its
abstractions for observability value.

Looking for observability value of M-HORSE-RACE.
... none found.

Looking for observability value of M-RACE.
... none found.

Looking for observability value of M-PERFORMANCE.

SWALE'S M-HORSE-RACE is probably observable,
since it is a type of M-PERFORMANCE, and M-PERFORMANCEs
are usually observable.

Applying test for KNOWABILITY to SWALE'S HEART'S
HEREDITARY-DEFECTIVE ORGANIC-STATE.

Searching up abstraction net for observability information.

Checking if the ORGANIC-STATE of generalized
HEARTs is a(n) OBSERVABLE-FEATURE.
... No information found.

Checking if the ORGANIC-STATE of generalized
INTERNAL-ORGANs is a(n) OBSERVABLE-FEATURE.
... Disconfirming information found.

SWALE'S HEART'S HEREDITARY-DEFECTIVE ORGANIC-STATE
is probably not observable, since it is a(n)
ORGANIC-STATE of a(n) INTERNAL-ORGAN.

Searching up abstraction net for pointers to standard tests.
⋮
SWALE'S HEART'S HEREDITARY-DEFECTIVE ORGANIC-STATE
is testable, since ORGANIC-STATEs of HEARTs
can be detected by the standard test ELECTROCARDIOGRAM.
... test passed.

In the preceding sections, we show that four evaluation dimensions must be considered when deciding whether an explanation is useful for prediction: predictive power, timeliness, distinctiveness, and knowability. The following box summarizes their roles in the evaluation decision.

An explanation is useful for prediction if:

1. The antecedents have predictive power.

2. The antecedents are timely.

3. At least one of the antecedents is distinctive.

4. All distinctive antecedents are knowable.

These requirements are satisfied by the cold seal explanation for Challenger: The engineers thought that the same combination of factors would make explosions likely in future launches; the weather conditions that affected the launch were established long before the launch order; equally cold weather in Florida is unusual; and weather conditions are easily observable.

9.7 Explaining for Repair

If the anomaly to be explained is an undesirable state, we may try to explain it in order to find how to effect a repair. This prompts the explanation purpose *connect undesirable state to possible repair points*.

Four evaluation dimensions are involved in checking to see whether a factor cited by an explanation is a good repair point. The most obvious requirements are that the factor have *causal force* (it must have caused the bad state), and that it be *repairable* by the explainer—both currently in effect, and something the explainer knows how to repair.

However, these criteria are incomplete—if someone carrying a television trips on uneven steps, dropping it and damaging it, the stairs would satisfy these criteria, even though repairing them does not fix the television. To make sure that the repair will actually improve the problem, we must also require that the factor we consider repairing be *predictive* of the device failure's recurrence (its predictive power can be judged as described previously).

Finally, if some original problem causes a cascade of secondary problems, it is pointless to repair the secondary problems until the original one is fixed (if we did, the original one would simply restore them again, undoing our repairs). Consequently, explanations for repair must trace problems back to the original sources of the problem—those with *independence* from other factors in the current situation.

We examine these dimensions in more detail in the following sections. In our discussion, we assume that only a single cause must be repaired, but the same basic considerations apply to problems requiring multiple repairs as well.

9.7.1 Causal Force

An antecedent of a belief-support chain has causal force if the chain traces a sequence of links through which it (combined with other antecedents required by the links) actually brings about the chain's consequent. For example, the design of Challenger's boosters was one of the causes of the explosion, unlike the engineer's warning—the warning was predictive of the explosion but did not affect whether the explosion actually occurred. ACCEPTER's judgment of a factor's causal force, like its judgment of predictive power, is based on the types of links existing between that factor and the explanation's consequent. Consequently, it too depends on the internal content of the explanation, rather than simply on the antecedent being considered.

9.7.2 Repairability

Even if we identify a cause of an undesirable situation, knowledge of that cause may not enable a repair. For example, if the undesirable situation is that our car is nonfunctional, identifying a collision as the cause does not help repair the problem—we need a current condition as the focus for repair. Yet even information about a current condition may fail to suggest a practical repair: many problems are beyond the repair abilities of the average driver.

To judge the usefulness of an explanation for suggesting a repair, ACCEPTER examines its antecedents for potential repair points. Past events are not repairable, because there is no way to undo their occurrence; states continuing in the present and causing problems are sometimes repairable, depending on the repairer's knowledge and resources. To judge a state's repairability, ACCEPTER searches memory for repair plans indexed under the state involved. For example, if a television has an anomalously bad picture, and the picture is explained by a particular kind of atmospheric condition (e.g., stormy weather), ACCEPTER would look for repair plans for the atmospheric conditions, would find none, and would decide that the explanation was insufficient for repair. Consequently, additional elaboration of the explanation would be needed.

Additional elaboration might suggest another factor contributing to the bad picture: that because we had changed channels after last adjusting the antenna, it was now pointed in the wrong direction. A standard repair plan exists for fixing orientations of small objects—grabbing them and moving them—so the new explanation would be sufficient to guide the repair.

The following output gives a sample of ACCEPTER's repairability judgments, taken from the program trace of ACCEPTER's processing of an Audi recall in Chapter 1 (see page 26). In that trace, the anomaly being explained is that Joe's Audi has a defect, and two explanations have been presented to ACCEPTER for evaluation:

1. The mechanical problems resulted from the car being manufactured by Acme Car Company, under contract as a supplier. Acme has bad quality control, leading to the defect.

2. The defect resulted from a flaw in the transmissions, which are not checked by Audi's quality control department.

ACCEPTER determines that the antecedents in the first explanation are not repairable, because there is no way to retroactively have the car manufactured by another maker. To evaluate whether the second explanation is suitable for repair, ACCEPTER searches for repair plans. None are found indexed under the specific problem, the transmission defect, nor under abstractions of transmissions:

```
Applying test for REPAIRABILITY to TRANSMISSION-743'S
LOW MECHANICAL-CONDITION.

   Searching up abstraction net for pointers to standard
   repair plans.

   ... test failed.

TRANSMISSION-743'S LOW MECHANICAL-CONDITION is probably
not repairable, since no standard repair plans are
stored under any of its abstractions.
```

Because ACCEPTER finds no standard repair plans for the transmission itself, it checks for other causes worth repairing. The XP's belief-support chain shows that the engine defect is caused by both the transmission's defect, and by the role of that particular transmission as an engine component. Consequently, another potential repair point is the component relationship, and ACCEPTER searches for repair plans for that. It finds a repair plan for repairing any component relationship that causes problems: replacing the component.

Applying test for REPAIRABILITY to TRANSMISSION-743'S
PART-OF-RELATIONSHIP to AUDI'S ENGINE.

    Checking repairability of features of TRANSMISSION-743'S
    PART-OF-RELATIONSHIP to AUDI'S ENGINE.

        Searching up abstraction net for pointers to standard
        repair plans.

        AUDI'S ENGINE AS CONTAINER OF TRANSMISSION-743'S
        PART-OF-RELATIONSHIP to AUDI'S ENGINE is repairable, since
        CONTAINERs of PART-OF-RELATIONSHIPs can usually be repaired
        by the standard plan REPLACE-COMPONENT.

9.7.3   Independence

Device failures sometimes reflect cascades of problems, all arising from a single source. For example, if a television power supply develops problems, power fluctuations may also cause a fuse to blow out, rendering the television nonfunctional. Although the fuse prevents the television from working, repairing the fuse alone is pointless—as long as the bad power supply remains, replacement fuses will blow out as well. Consequently, in order to suggest appropriate repairs, explanations need to trace device failures back to a cause with *independence* from any prior causes of the problem that still hold. Once the independent cause is found and repaired, the problems it causes can be safely repaired as well. To judge independence, ACCEPTER uses a simple heuristic: It assumes that a cause is independent from prior causes unless it is caused by another state that is currently believed to hold.

The following box summarizes the evaluation dimensions ACCEPTER uses to decide whether an explanation connects a situation to appropriate repair points.

> An explanation is useful for repair if one antecedent:
>
> 1. Has causal force.
> 2. Is repairable.
> 3. Is predictive of the problem occurring.
> 4. Is independent of previous causes.

9.8   Explaining for Control

When an anomalous situation is undesirable, a system may want to prevent it in the future. Likewise, if the situation is desirable, an explainer may wish to find how to achieve it. Either effect may be sought either directly, by the actor itself taking action, or indirectly, by the actor influencing another actor who has control. Regardless of which strategy will be used, the goal to prevent or achieve an outcome in the future prompts the explanation purpose *connect situation to causes that are controllable by a given actor.*

In order to provide the information needed for an actor to achieve a situation, an explanation must link the situation to a set of its causes (i.e., factors with *causal force*). Occurrence of these causes must make the situation likely (i.e., have *predictive power*), and the causes must either be expected to usually hold in the future (have *routineness*) or be achievable by the actor (have *achievability*).

In order to provide the information for an actor to prevent a situation's future occurrence, explanations must show a cause that the explainer can block (that has *blockability*). Finding such causes may allow the explainer to prevent similar occurrences of the situation by permanently blocking one of the causes—for example, it might be possible to redesign the space shuttle boosters to eliminate the seals entirely; another option would be to simply cancel all future space shuttle launches, because the launch order is one of the causes of the explosion.

If it is impractical to permanently block any of an event's causes, it may still be possible to use the explanation to decide when to block them temporarily: If the explanation lets us predict an undesirable situation long enough in advance, we can take steps to prevent it after forming the prediction. This procedure is basically the *anticipate-and-avoid* strategy that Hammond [1989a] proposes for preventing failures in case-based planning. One use of the anticipate-and-avoid strategy was suggested by many people after the Challenger disaster. The cold seal explanation shows that explosions can be anticipated on cold days, so even though we would not want to cancel all future shuttle launches, we can avoid explosions by cancelling launches whenever the day is too cold.

9.8.1   Routineness

Routineness measures the likelihood of a state or event occurring in future similar situations, if the actor takes no action to achieve or prevent it; it determines which factors can be taken for granted when planning to achieve an outcome. For example, a saboteur trying to achieve another space shuttle explosion can use the cold seal explanation to decide that what is needed is a way to make the seals brittle again—other needed conditions, such as the fact that the shuttle uses seals and the fact of the launch order, will hold with no additional effort.

Routineness can be judged by comparing states and events to the stereo-typed patterns described in Chapter 4. Note that although distinctiveness and routineness are closely related, the context taken into account for the two judgments is different: Distinctiveness compares a factor only to the circumstances taken into account when forming prior expectations; routineness considers whether the factor seems likely to hold in the future, regardless of what was considered before the anomaly occurred.

9.8.2 Achievability/Blockability

Deciding what an explainer can achieve or block is difficult; factors that seem uncontrollable at first glance may actually be easy to influence. For example, whether a launch day is cold might seem outside of our influence, but it is probably controllable by scheduling launches only during summer months. Despite the difficulty of deciding controllability in general, however, a very simple heuristic is often sufficient for judging an actor's ability to control an event: Actors who voluntarily act in events can often achieve or block them, and suppliers of other role-fillers for the events probably have the power to block them by withholding those role-fillers.

The Challenger episode provides a real-world example of how different actors' roles in events affect the usefulness of explanations for blocking an outcome. After the explosion, each area of NASA attempted to find ways to prevent similar situations arising, and different divisions focused on different causes of the problem, depending on the explainers' influence. According to the astronaut John Creighton:

> "[Everyone had a different idea] of what we didn't think worked. If you're an engine man, you want the engine fixed; if you're in charge of something else, you want that fixed" [Adler et al., 1988, p. 31].

ACCEPTER's blockability checks reflect different types of involvement by considering three ways a person can be involved in an event: as an *actor* who is immediately involved; as a *director* of the action, who is not immediately involved, but who has authority over its progression; and as a *supplier* of the objects or actors that the director selects.

Actors in an event may be able to block it by refusing to participate. Directors may block it by ordering actors under their control not to participate, by controlling the setting for events (locale, time of occurrence, or features of the environment), by changing ways of selecting the objects used, to avoid using objects that are particularly likely to contribute to a bad outcome, or by changing object suppliers to avoid such objects. Suppliers can also block outcomes by controlling the objects they make available. Table 9.2 sketches how each of these means of explainer control entered into strategies that human explainers considered for preventing another space shuttle disaster.

ACCEPTER's basic procedure for deciding blockability by a given person has two steps. First, it examines the explanation's belief-support chain, to find causes of the situation being explained. It then checks whether those causes are blockable by the given actor, due to the actor being involved as an actor, director, or supplier of objects (which ACCEPTER checks by seeing if that person is the owner of any of the objects involved in the cause). If so, ACCEPTER assumes that the person could block the event.

Its second step, once it has found that an actor can block a situation, is to see if the explanation is useful for anticipating and avoiding the situation. To do this, it checks whether the explanation allows prediction in time for the actor to exert its influence and block any of the causes.

For example, the following output shows part of ACCEPTER's processing to decide whether the space shuttle's astronauts could prevent future explosions. One of the steps in which astronauts are involved is the launch itself, so ACCEPTER considers whether the launch is a cause of the explosion, to see if blocking launches would prevent future explosions:

```
Checking whether some antecedent satisfies the following tests:
CAUSAL FORCE TEST (does fact cause consequent?), and
BLOCKABILITY + TIMELINESS (can CHALLENGER'S SPACE-LAUNCH's
ASTRONAUT block after predicting outcome?).

   Applying test for CAUSAL FORCE (does fact cause
   consequent?) to CHALLENGER'S SPACE-LAUNCH.

      Checking the connection between CHALLENGER'S SPACE-LAUNCH
      and CHALLENGER'S EXPLOSION.

         Testing if CAUSAL-MOP-SCENE:LAUNCH=>IGNITION
         satisfies test for LINK CAUSATION.
         ... test passed.

         Testing if CAUSAL-MOP-SCENE:IGNITION=>HIGH-PRESSURE
         satisfies test for LINK CAUSATION.
         ... test passed.
```

TABLE 9.2
Strategies Suggested for Blocking Space Shuttle Explosions

Control by actors

- **Refuse to participate**

After the explosion, astronauts said that they would not fly until the shuttles were repaired.

Control by directors

- **Change setting for the event**

  - **Change locale for the event**

  Some people suggested changing the launch site to Hawaii, where the weather is warmer.

  - **Change the time of the event**

  Engineers advised delaying launching when the weather was below 53°.

  - **Change features of the environment**

  NASA installed heaters on the launch pad to warm boosters before launch.

- **Change role-filler choice**

  - **Apply tests to rule out bad objects**

  Some people suggested NASA should inspect the booster seals after delivery of the boosters. NASA rejected this because tests would require disassembly that might introduce new defects.

  - **Change supplier of object**

  Some advocated stopping using boosters made by Morton Thiokol, the manufacturer of the boosters that exploded.

Control by suppliers

- **Block access to a class of role-filler**

New shuttle manufacturing was frozen by congress while the Challenger investigation went on, in order to avoid future explosions.

- **Change design**

Morton Thiokol redesigned the boosters to improve the seals.

```
Testing if
BRITTLE-SEAL+CONTAINER-SEAL+CONTENTS-PRESSURE=>
CONTAINER-EXPLOSION
satisfies test for LINK CAUSATION.
... test passed.

Testing if EXPLOSION-IN-COMPONENT=>EXPLOSION-IN-WHOLE
satisfies test for LINK CAUSATION.
... test passed.

    ... All links are acceptable.

  ... test passed.
```

Because the explanation shows that the launch causes a rocket booster's explosion, which in turn causes the shuttle as a whole to explode, the launch has causal force.

ACCEPTER next checks whether an astronaut could block the launch. It first checks whether the astronaut controls the availability of objects required to fill roles in the launch (which the astronaut does not), or whether the astronaut has control over whether to participate in the launch:

```
Checking if CHALLENGER'S SPACE-LAUNCH is blockable.

  Checking if CHALLENGER'S SPACE-LAUNCH's ASTRONAUT
  controlled outcome by controlling a needed object.
  ... No actor-controlled objects found.

  Checking if CHALLENGER'S SPACE-LAUNCH's ASTRONAUT
  controlled outcome through a role he filled.

  CHALLENGER'S SPACE-LAUNCH's ASTRONAUT might
  have been able to prevent CHALLENGER'S SPACE-LAUNCH,
  by refusing to be its ASTRONAUT, since that
  is a voluntary actor role.
```

From this information, ACCEPTER concludes that the launch is a block-able cause. The next question is whether an explosion can be predicted before the launch, so the astronaut can stop the launch in time.

The latest cause of the explosion that the astronaut controls is the launch, so preventing future explosions is only possible if the explanation shows how to predict explosion before the launch occurs. To know how much warning this requires, ACCEPTER first uses the explanation to determine how far in advance of the explosion the launch occurs. It then applies checks for the explanation purpose *connect situation to events from which it can be predicted* to decide whether the explanation allows prediction with that amount of warning.[5]

```
Checking if XP allows prediction of outcome before
CHALLENGER'S SPACE-LAUNCH occurs.

    Calculating amount of warning needed to predict
    before CHALLENGER'S SPACE-LAUNCH occurs.

        CHALLENGER'S SPACE-LAUNCH leads to ROCKET-IGNITION-41
        immediately.

        ROCKET-IGNITION-41 leads to GAS-42'S HIGH PRESSURE
        MINUTES afterwards.

        GAS-42'S HIGH PRESSURE leads to SOLID-ROCKET-43'S
        EXPLOSION MINUTES afterwards.

        SOLID-ROCKET-43'S EXPLOSION leads to CHALLENGER'S
        EXPLOSION immediately.

Predicting before CHALLENGER'S SPACE-LAUNCH requires
finding a predictive feature at least MINUTES
before CHALLENGER'S EXPLOSION.

Checking detail for predicting CHALLENGER'S
EXPLOSION MINUTES before it happens.
:
```

The coldness of the seal occurs early enough to provide sufficient warning, and it is also distinctive, predictive, and knowable. Consequently, ACCEPTER accepts the explanation as being useful for an astronaut's prediction, allowing the astronaut to anticipate and avoid future disasters: On cold days, the astronaut can refuse to fly. The following box summarizes the evaluation dimensions relevant to control.

---

[5]Recall that ACCEPTER uses a coarse-grained temporal representation, with temporal separations represented as NONE, MINUTES, HOURS, DAYS, WEEKS, and YEARS.

An explanation is useful for achieving a situation if its antecedents:	An explanation is useful for blocking a situation if:
1. Have causal force.	1. One antecedent is a blockable cause.
2. Have predictive power.	2. The explanation allows prediction in time to block the cause.
3. Are routine or achievable.	

9.9   Explaining to Assign Praise or Blame

When a surprisingly good or bad outcome occurs, a system may benefit by explaining who contributed to the event. By identifying the actors involved and assigning praise or blame for their roles, it may be possible to influence their future performance in similar situations, or to influence those who find themselves in similar roles in the future. For example, when the Challenger disaster occurred, some relatives of the victims considered bringing lawsuits against those responsible for inadequate safety procedures, both as punishment and to deter NASA from policies they considered unsafe. Other people wished to reward the engineer who tried unsuccessfully to prevent the launch. Goals to reward or punish appropriate actors prompt the explanation purpose *connect situation to factors that suggest praise or blame for an actor.*

Three considerations affect whether praise or blame can be assigned to a particular actor. The first is whether that actor had a significant effect on the situation: whether the explanation shows that the actor could have blocked the outcome, or contributed to causing its occurrence. To establish this, we can apply the basic criteria for control from the previous section.[6]

The second consideration is whether the actor could reasonably be expected to anticipate that the situation would occur due to the actor's action or inaction. Someone who could have cancelled the Challenger launch, but had no reason to expect it would lead to disaster, could not be blamed for allowing the launch to proceed. We approximate this criterion by judging whether the explanation allows the outcome to be predicted.

The third consideration is the merit of the situation itself, and of the actor's actions affecting it. This dimension is *desirability.*

---

[6] A difficult question for assigning responsibility is when to decide, from the fact that an actor is not implicated in an explanation, that an actor was really uninvolved in the event. Because explanations focus on a limited part of a situation, it is difficult (or impossible) to establish that an actor not mentioned in an explanation was not involved in another way. Nevertheless, ACCEPTER assumes that if a given actor is not mentioned, that actor is uninvolved.

9.9.1 Desirability

An actor can often be blamed for actions that have undesirable results and be praised for actions that have desirable ones. (In general, the positive and negative aspects must be balanced against each other, to determine whether an action was justified [Flowers et al., 1982], but we ignore that consideration.) In addition, an actor can also be blamed, even if it was impossible to predict or control an outcome, if that actor contributed to the outcome through an undesirable act: For example, we might blame a drug dealer for an addict's death by overdose, even if deaths from overdose are relatively unlikely. ACCEPTER's current criterion for desirability of actions is one simple check: whether the action is a type of illegal activity.

The next output shows ACCEPTER's evaluation, for assigning blame, of the explanation that Swale died because a trainer gave him a large dose of performance-enhancing drugs. ACCEPTER first checks whether the trainer had control over his role in the drugging. Because the drugger is normally in control of the drugging, it decides that the trainer did. It then checks whether he should have predicted the result of giving the drugs in time to prevent the bad outcome. Because performance-enhancing drugs are usually not fatal, ACCEPTER would normally predict that administering them is safe, so it assumes that the trainer would also and considers the fatal result unintentional:

```
Checking PERFORMANCE-DRUG-OVERDOSE-BY-TRAINER for ASSIGNING-BLAME.
  :

  Applying test for BLOCKABILITY + TIMELINESS (can
  ATHLETIC-TRAINER-1497 block after predicting outcome?) to
  ATHLETIC-TRAINER-1497'S M-PERFORMANCE-ENHANCEMENT-DRUGS.
  :

    ATHLETIC-TRAINER-1497 could have prevented initiation
    of ATHLETIC-TRAINER-1497'S M-PERFORMANCE-ENHANCEMENT-DRUGS
    since its DRUGGER controls initiation.

    Outcome cannot be predicted in time to block it.

    ... test failed.
```

Nevertheless, because drugging race horses to improve performance is itself undesirable, the explanation still shows cause to blame the trainer:

```
Applying test for UNDESIRABILITY to ATHLETIC-TRAINER-1497'S
M-PERFORMANCE-ENHANCEMENT-DRUGS.

    The event type M-PERFORMANCE-ENHANCEMENT-DRUGS is normally
    considered undesirable.

    ATHLETIC-TRAINER-1497's involvement in ATHLETIC-TRAINER-1497'S
    M-PERFORMANCE-ENHANCEMENT-DRUGS is voluntary, so blamable.

    ... test passed.

PERFORMANCE-DRUG-OVERDOSE-BY-TRAINER has sufficient detail for
ASSIGNING-BLAME.
```

The following box summarizes the factors ACCEPTER considers when evaluating explanations for assigning blame.

> An explanation is useful for assigning blame to an actor if:
>
> 1. It connects the situation to a cause over which the actor had control (either achieved, or could have blocked).
> 2. It either shows that the situation should have been predicted, or that the controllable cause was undesirable in itself.

9.10   Sketch of Requirements for Other Goals

The following sections sketch four additional goals, their explanation purposes, and the evaluation requirements for those purposes. The point of these sections is to emphasize the dynamic nature of explanation evaluation: Many different goals can underly explanation, and each one carries with it particular requirements for information.

The following explanation purposes are not implemented in ACCEPTER, but the preceding evaluation dimensions give building blocks for many of the checks that would be needed.

9.10.1   Explaining to Learn a New Plan

People often learn new plans by explaining others' surprising actions. If someone seems to take a wrong turn on the way home, explaining the turn may reveal a shortcut. For learning new plans, the explanation purpose is *connect an action to the actor's motivations.* This requires that an explanation trace the anomalous action to the goals it serves, showing the plan's potential use, and to express the plan steps at a specific enough level for the system to execute them. For discussions of evaluation criteria for this purpose, see DeJong [1986], Segre [1988], and Mooney [1990].

9.10.2   Explaining to Choose a Response

When many alternative plans are available to deal with a situation, a planner may need to explain aspects of the situation to decide how to choose between the possible plans. This prompts the explanation purpose *connect situation to factors that discriminate between alternative responses.*

For example, a doctor explaining symptoms would try to explain them in terms of physical causes, generating explanations detailed enough to distinguish between ailments with different treatments. For this purpose, the distinctions an explanation must establish depend entirely on the factors that determine which plans are appropriate—a policeman explaining the same symptoms might only need to know whether the symptoms could be a sign of poisoning, in order to decide whether to investigate.

9.10.3   Explaining to Test a Special-Purpose Theory

If we have a causal or predictive theory for a domain, we may try to test it by checking whether it can account for situations that are anomalous in a different theory. This prompts the explanation purpose *connect to within-theory factors.*

For example, a physicist might try to use a new theory to account for anomalous experimental results, in order to test its applicability. To account for an event according to a theory, the explanation needs to explain it using factors and links within the scope of that theory.

9.10.4   Explaining to Influence Another Agent's Beliefs

Many explanations are built to be communicated to other agents. These explanations are tailored towards their effects on the other agents' beliefs, reflecting the purpose to *connect situation to factors that will influence another agent.* Explaining to assign praise or blame, which was described previously, is often used to this end. Explanations can also be used in other ways to affect people's interpretations of events. For example, we can decrease people's negative opinions of events by showing that the events were side-effects of achieving a greater good: If a patient is irate because of waiting in a doctor's office, a nurse might assuage the patient by explaining that the doctor was called away to save the life of an accident victim.

The goal that motivates an explainer's choice of information may also be a more neutral goal to transfer needed information—teachers explain in order to fill particular gaps in students' knowledge, or in response to questions. Information requirements for this purpose have been studied both in the context of answering and asking questions [Lehnert, 1978; Ram, 1989], and in the context of how to provide users of expert systems with the right information in response to their queries (see section 2.3.9).

In considering the aforementioned purposes, we implicitly assumed that the explanations being evaluated were valid. However, when the goal is to influence another agent, explanations that deviate from reality may be more useful, as long as the recipient believes them. For example, if the real reason for delays in a doctor's waiting room was that the doctor was playing golf, the nurse might decide to avoid patients' outrage by attributing the delays to a fictitious emergency instead. Likewise, our example of a used-car salesman's explanation of a car breakdown in the movie *Breaking Away* (see page 15) shows an explanation that is useful to the salesman, because it transforms a car's defect into a selling point, but that also happens to be a lie. In addition, explainers seeking humorous effects may intentionally select explanations that will be recognized as highly implausible.

9.11   Summary of Evaluation Dimensions

Table 9.3 summarizes the evaluation dimensions used by ACCEPTER, and the simple heuristics that the system uses to test along them. For each evaluation dimension, it sketches ACCEPTER's method for evaluating an event or state A in an XP along that dimension.

Although ACCEPTER evaluates some dimensions using criteria that depend dynamically on current context and knowledge (e.g., timeliness, distinctiveness, and repairability), its evaluation criteria for other dimensions are static (e.g., the observability component of knowability). However, we strongly agree with the arguments of DeJong and Mooney [1986] against static criteria; tests for all evaluation dimensions should be able to dynamically reflect current system knowledge. The reason we do not formulate dynamic tests along all dimensions, or attempt to provide a richer characterization of what each involves, is simply that developing such formulations is beyond the scope of our main goal: illustrating the wide range of possible explanation purposes and establishing the practicality of describing those purposes in terms of a restricted set of evaluation dimensions.

Thus in general, refined descriptions of evaluation criteria remain a topic for future study. However, some of the issues involved in defining checks for particular evaluation dimensions arise in other contexts, and approaches from those areas could be applied to formulating more refined evaluation criteria.

TABLE 9.3
Summary of Evaluation Dimensions

Predictive power and causal force	Check whether the XP derives the outcome from A by a sequence of predictive or causal links, respectively.
Timeliness	Trace along the XP's derivation of outcome from A, summing the standard delays from antecedent to consequent of each inference rule.
Routineness	Compare A to stereotyped patterns.
Distinctiveness	Use routine understanding mechanism to build up standard expectations from the background situation, and integrate A into that context. A is distinctive if it is unexpected or anomalous in that context.
Knowability	Check whether A, or an abstraction in memory, is annotated as usually observable, or search for a plan in memory that can be applied to determine whether A has occurred.
Repairability	Search memory for a standard repair plan for any abstraction of A.
Independence	Check if A is caused by a state still in effect. If not, assume A is independent from prior causes.
Achievability/ blockability	Look for direct involvement of the actor as an actor, director, or (for blockability only) supplier of A.
Desirability	Check if action described by A is an instance of illegal activity.

For example, a richer characterization of knowability would have to involve reasoning about competing ways to gather information, their likely costs, and their chance of success; Hunter [1990] considers some of these issues in the context of knowledge planning.

9.12   Goal-Based Adaptation

The previous sections describe requirements that explanations must satisfy in order to serve different explanation purposes. However, the intent of our evaluation procedures is not to simply reject inadequate explanations: It is to identify any useful information they provide, and to show what further elaboration is needed. In case-based explanation, the explanations that are retrieved simply give a head start to the explanation construction process. If the retrieved explanations are inadequate in any respect, the explanation construction process is continued by adapting the explanation to repair its flaws.

For example, suppose a driver is surprised that his car will not start and retrieves the explanation *the gas is contaminated, clogging the fuel line.* This explanation leaves out information such as how the clogging occurred, which might be useful for repairing the clog; it also leaves out information about how the gas became contaminated, which might be useful to investigate if the driver suspects that someone sabotaged the car and wants to assign blame. These two different needs for information would suggest different adaptations of the explanation: finding how the clogging occurs requires expanding on the internal structure of the explanation, to show how contaminants caused the clog; accounting for what made the gas contaminated leaves the internal structure of the explanation untouched but involves trying to add a new cause that explains the antecedent of the current chain.

The adaptation process itself is beyond the scope of this work, but Kass [1990] provides a thorough discussion of how to tailor adaptation towards providing appropriate information. After each incremental adaptation, the explanation is again evaluated, providing additional goal-based guidance for further adaptation. In this way, case-based explanation can take goals into account throughout the adaptation process.

9.13   Conclusion

Goal-based explanation evaluation is needed because of the complexity of real-world situations. No real-world explanation can include *all* the factors that are relevant to a situation; explanations necessarily highlight a few factors. If those factors are irrelevant to the explainer's goals, the explanation will be useless, regardless of its validity. Likewise, for some uses, a very vague or incomplete explanation may be sufficient; for others, explanations will need to include considerable detail. In order for explanation-based processing to be effective in complex situations, artificial intelligence systems must be able to require that their explanations satisfy their information needs. Being able to do so depends on knowing what information needs are triggered by possible goals, and being able to judge whether an explanation satisfies them.

We have established 10 basic purposes for explanation and shown how they arise from common types of goals. In order for these explanation purposes to influence explanation evaluation, we must also establish how they translate into requirements on explanations. In the preceding sections, we examine this question in detail for four divergent goals: learning to predict similar situations in the future, repairing undesirable states, controlling recurrence of situations, and assigning praise or blame. In addition, we show that their information needs can be characterized along a limited set of evaluation dimensions, simplifying the design of goal-based evaluation procedures, and illustrate with examples from ACCEPTER. The range of information requirements for these purposes, and for others we sketched more briefly, demonstrates that judgments of explanations' goodness cannot be context neutral: They must depend dynamically on changing system goals.

10 Conclusions and Future Directions

10.1 Summary and Significance of the Theory

This book develops a theory of how to detect and describe problems in explanations—both in the standard explanations generated during routine understanding, and in the more complex explanations built to account for novel situations. The theory focuses on how to make it practical to detect the anomalies that signal flaws in routine explanation, how to characterize the anomalies in order to guide a case-based explanation system's search for relevant explanations, and how to decide whether candidate explanations resolve the current anomaly and provide adequate information for the explainer to accomplish its goals. These questions are central to effective use of explanation, because the effectiveness of explanation-based methods depends both on knowing when to explain and on efficiently generating good explanations as their starting point.

The following paragraphs summarize our approach to the issues above, highlighting the major differences between our approach and other methods.

Evaluating routine explanations: Schema-based understanding systems do routine explanation by connecting new information to schema-based expectations, and activating new schemas when no active schema applies. This gives good performance when the right schemas are used, but problems may arise. Erroneous schemas, faulty schema selection, and changes in the world can lead to flawed knowledge. Repairing flawed knowledge depends on first noticing that it is flawed: understanders must be able to detect anomalies.

However, detecting anomalies may be arbitrarily expensive. A conflict between new and old information may only be revealed by inferring and comparing their distant ramifications, and inferring those ramifications is an explosive inference task. To overcome the cost of chaining as a method for anomaly detection, we argue for an alternative approach: replacing inference with table lookup. Rather than searching for conflicts by comparing ramifications, our approach restricts its tests to comparisons of new information to stereotyped patterns stored explicitly in memory. This avoids the cost of inference but introduces new questions of its own: What is the content of the tables and is their coverage sufficient? We answer these questions with a theory of the needed patterns and show that they account for a wide range of anomalies.

Directing nonroutine explanation: Previous explanation-based understanders explain each situation not accounted for by stored schemas. However, in everyday domains there may be an enormous number of such situations to explain, and many of the explanations will provide no useful information. Consequently, we argue that explanation should only be done when it is needed: when anomalies show that system knowledge is flawed. Likewise, we argue that to be worthwhile, explanations must be focused on resolving those anomalies. Rather than simply providing a neutral explanation of the *event*, explanations must address the *anomaly*—both why the event occurred and why prior knowledge was wrong.

Constructing explanations is in general a difficult task, and the requirement of accounting for anomalies rather than only events complicates it further. In other explanation-based systems, explanations are built from scratch, by backwards chaining through a space of operators, but even if the cost of this method is ignored, there is no assurance that the results will be relevant to the current anomaly.

We argue that problems of explaining from scratch can be overcome by a case-based explanation process that uses knowledge of the content of anomaly and explanation to guide search. We develop a vocabulary of anomaly types and show how it can facilitate the search for explanations. Vocabulary elements organize explanations stored in memory, as well as more general explanatory information; when anomalies are found, they are characterized according to the same vocabulary, and the characterization is used to suggest explanatory information. The relevance of the suggestion depends on whether situations characterized in the same way also have similar explanations, which we substantiate by showing that our anomaly vocabulary groups anomalies to which similar abstract explanation strategies apply.

Evaluating nonroutine explanations: Explanations are often treated as neutral to the circumstances in which explanation is done, and evaluation procedures are often based only on the form of candidate explanations. We argue instead that context and content are crucial.

Our evaluation scheme uses three criteria to judge explanations. The first criterion, just mentioned, is relevance to the anomaly: whether the explanation both addresses the surprising aspects of the situation, and resolves the underlying reasoning problems that an anomaly reveals.

The second criterion is plausibility. Everyday explanations are chains of plausible inference rules that depend on many implicit assumptions, so not all explanations with the correct structure will be valid. We show how the anomaly detection process can be used to judge the reasonableness of an explanatory chain, in light of prior system knowledge.

The third criterion is usefulness for current system goals. We demonstrate that explanation evaluation must be task dependent: that the goodness of explanations depends on what the explainer already knows, and what it needs to find out to satisfy its goals.

All the processes just described have been given a preliminary implementation in ACCEPTER. This work has firmly established many parts of our approach and identified other open areas for future research. We next discuss a sampling of some of those open areas.

10.2   Future Directions

Anomaly detection and explanation evaluation are rich research areas. In this section, we first highlight some of the main focuses of future research suggested by our current theory. We then sketch a natural extension to our approach: integrating a system's components for explanation and action.

Partial matching: As we discuss in section 3.4.1, anomaly detection depends on partial matching: being able to decide whether prior beliefs or expectations share enough important features to merge them with new information, despite the differences between them. If they are relevant to each other, their differences are anomalous; if not, differences are insignificant. ACCEPTER uses extremely simple heuristics for doing its partial matching, and a richer theory is needed.

Indexing to reflect additional goals: We argue that explanation search should be guided by the anomaly to be explained. Whereas this guidance is all that is needed to retrieve explanations that resolve relevant anomalies, Chapter 9 shows that there are many other purposes for explanation, each requiring different information. Rather than retrieving any explanation accounting for a similar anomaly, and adapting it to provide the needed information, it would be useful to take additional information needs into account at explanation retrieval time in order to retrieve explanations likely to be useful with less adaptation. For example, a student who misses a homework deadline might want to search for different explanations depending on whether the goal is to learn how to prevent future missed deadlines or to make excuses. Preventing future problems might suggest seeking explanations built to show controllable factors leading to other episodes of missed deadlines (e.g., starting the task too late); making excuses might suggest looking for explanations to absolve personal blame (e.g., "the dog ate my homework").

Evaluation of the utility of pursing a candidate explanation: The evaluation process of this book decides which parts of an explanation must be adapted, but does not attempt to judge how hard the adaptation would be to perform or how likely the adaptation is to result in a useful explanation. Estimates of the utility of pursuing an imperfect explanation could focus the adaptation process in case-based explanation: When multiple candidate explanations are available and none precisely fit the explainer's needs, the system could pursue the explanation believed most likely to lead to a useful result. Estimating utility of adapting an explanation, or of verifying its likelihood, is particularly important when the cost of adaptation or verification can be high—for example, when adaptation strategies are expensive or numerous strategies can be tried, or when verification of an explanation requires carrying out plans to gather additional information.

In general, any theory of which explanations to adapt first would have to be based on a theory of *adaptability* for explanations, that would estimate how easy a given type of problem usually is to repair.[1] Given an evaluator like ACCEPTER, one possibility would be to estimate adaptability of inapplicable parts of an explanation in terms of their plausibility, assuming that less believable explanations are usually harder to adapt. However, it is not clear that less plausible explanations are actually always harder to repair.

Deciding whether to store an inapplicable XP: When SWALE generates multiple explanations for an anomaly, ACCEPTER only stores the explanation that is finally accepted. A beneficial result is that the system's XP library reflects actual experience, giving the support of experience to the explanations the system applies in the future. However, especially in comparatively well-understood domains, it may be useful to retain some explanations

---

[1]Hammond [1989a] and Kambhampati [1990] present two approaches to judging the adaptability of plans.

even if they fail to fit the facts of the current situation. For example, if a doctor expends much effort to find two competing explanations that can account for particular symptoms, it is probably worthwhile to remember both, because the one that does not fit current circumstances may be useful in a future case. To determine whether it is reasonable to retain an explanation that does not apply, an evaluator should distinguish between explanations that are reasonable in themselves, but that fail to fit the current circumstances, and explanations that have defects that make them unlikely ever to apply; it must also have criteria for estimating their usefulness in the future.

Reflecting the influence of competing explanations: ACCEPTER's plausibility evaluation assigns plausibilities to each candidate explanation individually. However, the certainty with which an explanation is accepted depends not only on the plausibility of that explanation in isolation, but on the other alternatives that are available. If one plausible explanation is much stronger than all other alternatives, it seems reasonable to accept it; if its plausibility is roughly the same as that of competing explanations, the choice is more difficult, and additional information may be needed. Thus selection of explanations should involve a process of differential diagnosis between competing explanations, until a clearly superior explanation has been found.

Deciding when two explanations are contradictory: Sometimes ruling out a candidate explanation is as important as finding an explanation that applies. For example, a parent whose teenager was involved in a car accident will be interested in knowing whether the teenager was to blame. ACCEPTER's criteria can identify whether an explanation gives grounds to blame a given actor, but, if the explanation does not, ACCEPTER cannot decide whether it absolves the actor from blame. Criteria are needed for deciding that some explanations tend to rule out others—for example, to be able to decide that if the accident was caused by brake failure, the driver is probably not at fault.

Deciding whether one explanation rules out others is difficult because, as we have pointed out before, each explanation considers only a small subset of the factors actually involved in an outcome. In principle, ACCEPTER could notice that two explanations were factually contradictory, by first integrating one into memory, and then using its anomaly detection to notice conflicts while integrating the second. However, this would not help to decide that the teenager was guiltless if the brakes gave out, because there is no direct contradiction between the brakes giving out and the teenager being at fault. (In fact, the teenager could be at fault even if the brakes failed: He might have continued driving after realizing that the brakes were unsafe.) To deal with such cases, an explanation evaluator needs heuristics for deciding whether one explanation makes another unlikely.

Reconstruction of prior system reasoning: ACCEPTER maintains only very limited records of the sources of its beliefs and expectations. In order to check explanations' relevance to resolving a wider range of failures, an evaluator needs access to traces of the reasoning underlying each contradicted belief or expectation. When this information is not available, the evaluator needs to reconstruct that reasoning [Collins & Birnbaum, 1988], which raises questions of how to guide search for explanations of why a belief or explanation was originally formed.

Triggering and learning explanation purposes: We have described the information required for particular explanation purposes, but have not addressed how a system should notice that particular new information affects its goals. Nor have we considered how a system can learn new explanation purposes, by reasoning about the information that it requires to accomplish its goals. This requires a system to model its own reasoning process and capabilities, in order to note when its performance is inadequate and determine the additional knowledge that an explanation must provide. (Similar questions have begun to be investigated in other contexts; see for example Birnbaum et al. [1990] and Krulwich [1991].)

Integrating the processes that evaluate and use explanations: Our goal-based evaluation process moves beyond previous models of explanation that attempt to judge the "best" explanation in the abstract, without considering how it will be used. Yet despite the emphasis on goals in ACCEPTER's evaluation procedure, we view our model as only an approximation to the needed integration of explanation and action components.

When a planner seeks explanations, it does so in specific circumstances and for specific goals. To faithfully reflect the information needs of a planner, the evaluator must know the planner's capabilities, how it plans, and the circumstances in which it functions. Integrating planner and explainer would allow the planner itself to monitor the progress of explanation towards providing the needed information, in order to change the focus of explanation if new information in a partial explanation changed its goals, and to help explanation construction by seeking additional information when necessary. Consequently, we view this integration as a particularly important topic for future research.

10.3   Final Notes

This book presents a theory of the needs that motivate explanation, and how those needs are reflected by the explanation evaluation process. In response to the need of an understander to efficiently recognize flaws in its routine understanding, we develop a model of anomaly detection that replaces traditional inference chaining with pattern-based checks. The knowledge flaws detected by anomaly detection reveal another need for information—the need for information to repair flawed system beliefs—and we show how case-based explanation can guide search towards appropriate explanations. Finally, we develop a theory of how the resultant explanations can be evaluated according to whether they fulfill current needs for information, both to resolve the anomaly and to satisfy other overarching goals. In our theory, evaluation criteria are dynamic: context and overarching goals determine the information that explanations must provide.

To illustrate the theory's claims, we have discussed their ramifications in an initial computer model. The program ACCEPTER is a story understanding system whose explanation effort is motivated by gaps in its knowledge, and whose explanation search is focused towards explanations that address those gaps. Once explanations are found, they are judged both by whether they fill the original knowledge gap and whether they provide the information needed to respond to the unexpected situation. Consequently, ACCEPTER may retrieve very different explanations for a given event, depending on context, and the same explanation of an event can receive very different evaluations depending on the program's current knowledge and goals.

A key point in our approach, which sets it apart from other work, is that it is not only a theory of the *process* of explanation, but also of the *content* of the knowledge involved in that task. In order to substantiate our pattern-based approach to anomaly detection, we need a theory of the patterns used; in order to guide explanation search by organizing explanations according to the anomalies they explain, we need a theory of the types of anomalies there are; in order to guide goal-based explanation evaluation, we need a theory of the goals that explanations can serve, and the types of information needed for those goals.

Building a content theory of everyday explanation requires working in complex real-world domains. Because these domains are messy and uncontrollable, standard evaluation methods cannot at this point be used to test the theory. However, we demonstrate that the focusing mechanisms we present are needed to overcome problems with traditional approaches, and show that our theory has promising properties, both for its coverage and effectiveness.

In AI, any answers worth finding also raise new questions—both about their current ramifications and about how they might be extended. This book presents a preliminary model of dynamic problem detection for both explanations built during routine understanding, and explanations built in response to anomalies. That model is a starting point for future research on need-driven explanation.

References

Adler, J., Gibney, F., Hurt, H., Hager, M., Murr, A., & Calonius, E. (1988). After the Challenger. *Newsweek*, 112(15):28–36.

Ahn, W., Mooney, R., Brewer, W., & DeJong, G. (1987). Schema acquisition from one example: Psychological evidence for explanation-based learning. In *Proceedings of the Ninth Annual Conference of the Cognitive Science Society*, Seattle, WA. Cognitive Science Society.

Anderson, J. (1938). The problem of causality. *Australasian Journal of Psychology and Philosophy*, 16(2):127–142.

Ashley, K. (1990). *Modeling legal argument : reasoning with cases and hypotheticals*. MIT Press, Cambridge.

Bareiss, R. (1989). *Exemplar-Based Knowledge Acquisition: A Unified Approach to Concept Representation, Classification, and Learning*. Academic Press, Inc., San Diego.

Bhatnagar, N. & Mostow, J. (1990). Adaptive search by explanation-based learning of heuristic censors. In *Proceedings of the Eighth National Conference on Artificial Intelligence*, pages 895–901, Boston, MA. AAAI.

Birnbaum, L., Collins, G., Freed, M., & Krulwich, B. (1990). Model-based diagnosis of planning failures. In *Proceedings of the Eighth National Conference on Artificial Intelligence*, pages 318–323, Boston, MA. AAAI.

Bower, G., Black, J., & Turner, T. (1979). Scripts in memory for text. *Cognitive Psychology*, 11:177–220.

Carbonell, J. (1979). *Subjective Understanding: Computer Models of Belief Systems.* PhD thesis, Yale University. Computer Science Department Technical Report 150.

Carbonell, J. (1986). Derivational analogy: A theory of reconstructive problem solving and expertise acquisition. In Michalski, R., Carbonell, J., & Mitchell, T. (Eds.), *Machine Learning: An Artificial Intelligence Approach*, volume 2, pages 371–392. Morgan Kaufmann Publishers, Inc., Los Altos, CA.

Carbonell, J. & Gil, Y. (1990). Learning by experimentation: The operator refinement method. In Kodratoff, Y. & Michalski, R. (Eds.), *Machine Learning: An Artificial Intelligence Approach*, volume 3, pages 191–213. Morgan Kaufmann Publishers, San Mateo.

Charniak, E. (1978). On the use of framed knowledge in language comprehension. *Artificial Intelligence*, 11(3):225–265.

Charniak, E. (1986). A neat theory of marker passing. In *Proceedings of the Fifth National Conference on Artificial Intelligence*, pages 584–588, Philadelphia, PA. AAAI.

Chien, S. (1989). Using and refining simplifications: Explanation-based learning of plans in intractable domains. In *Proceedings of the Eleventh International Joint Conference on Artificial Intelligence*, pages 590–595, Detroit, MI. IJCAI.

Collins, G. (1987). *Plan creation: using strategies as blueprints.* PhD thesis, Yale University. Computer Science Department Technical Report 599.

Collins, G. & Birnbaum, L. (1988). An explanation-based approach to the transfer of planning knowledge across domains. In *Proceedings of the 1988 AAAI Spring Symposium on Explanation-based Learning*, Stanford, CA. AAAI.

Cress, D. (1984). Clot suspected in Swale's death. *The Washington Post*, page E1. June 19.

Crist, S. (1984a). Questions on Swale's death. *The New York Times*, page B11. June 20.

Crist, S. (1984b). Swale, who won Kentucky Derby and Belmont, collapses and dies. *The New York Times*, page A1. June 18.

Crist, S. (1984c). Tests find flaws in heart of Swale. *The New York Times*, page B7. July 11.

Cullingford, R. (1978). *Script Application: Computer Understanding of Newspaper Stories.* PhD thesis, Yale University. Computer Science Department Technical Report 116.

Dasigi, V. (Ed.) (1991). *Towards Domain-Independent Strategies for Abduction*, Anaheim, CA. AAAI. Workshop notes from the Ninth National Conference on Artificial Intelligence.

DeJong, G. (1979). *Skimming Stories in Real Time: An Experiment in Integrated Understanding*. PhD thesis, Yale University. Computer Science Department Technical Report 158.

DeJong, G. (1986). An approach to learning from observation. In Michalski, R., Carbonell, J., & Mitchell, T. (Eds.), *Machine Learning: An Artificial Intelligence Approach*, volume 2, pages 571–590. Morgan Kaufmann Publishers, Cambridge, MA.

DeJong, G. & Mooney, R. (1986). Explanation-based learning: An alternative view. *Machine Learning*, 1(1):145–176.

Dietterich, T. & Flann, N. (1988). An inductive approach to solving the imperfect theory problem. In *Proceedings of the 1988 AAAI Spring Symposium on Explanation-based Learning*, Stanford, CA. AAAI.

Dietterich, T. & Michalski, R. (1983). A comparative review of selected methods for learning from examples. In Michalski, R., Carbonell, J., & Mitchell, T. (Eds.), *Machine Learning: An Artificial Intelligence Approach*, pages 41–81. Tioga Publishing Company, Cambridge, MA.

Doyle, J. (1979). A truth maintenance system. *Artificial Intelligence*, 12:231–272.

Doyle, R. (1986). Constructing and refining causal explanations from an inconsistent domain theory. In *Proceedings of the Fifth National Conference on Artificial Intelligence*, pages 538–544, Philadelphia, PA. AAAI.

Dyer, M. (1983). *In-Depth Understanding: A Computer Model of Integrated Processing For Narrative Comprehension*. MIT Press, Cambridge.

Etzioni, O. (1990). Why PRODIGY/EBL works. In *Proceedings of the Eighth National Conference on Artificial Intelligence*, pages 916–922, Boston, MA. AAAI.

Flowers, M., McGuire, R., & Birnbaum, L. (1982). Adversary arguments and the logic of personal attacks. In Lehnert, W. & Ringle, M. (Eds.), *Strategies for Natural Language Processing*, pages 275–294. Lawrence Earlbaum Associates, Hillsdale, NJ.

Gentner, D. & Collins, A. (1981). Studies of inference from lack of knowledge. *Memory and Cognition*, 9(4):434–443.

Goldman, R. & Charniak, E. (1990). Incremental construction of probabilistic models for language abduction. In O'Rorke, P. (Ed.), *Working Notes of the 1990 Spring Symposium on Automated Abduction*. AAAI. Technical Report 90-32, Department of Information and Computer Science, University of California, Irvine.

Granger, R. (1980). *Adaptive Understanding: Correcting Erroneous Inferences.* PhD thesis, Yale University. Computer Science Department Technical Report 171.

Hammond, K. (1987). Learning and reusing explanations. In *Proceedings of the Fourth International Workshop on Machine Learning*, pages 141–147, Irvine, CA. Machine Learning, Morgan Kaufmann.

Hammond, K. (1989a). *Case-Based Planning: Viewing Planning as a Memory Task.* Academic Press, San Diego.

Hammond, K. (Ed.) (1989b). *Proceedings of the Case-Based Reasoning Workshop.* Morgan Kaufmann, Inc., San Mateo.

Hanson, N. (1961). *Patterns of Discovery.* Cambridge University Press, Cambridge, England.

Harman, G. (1965). The inference to the best explanation. *Philosophical Review*, 74:88–95.

Hayes-Roth, F. (1983). Using proofs and refutations to learn from experience. In Michalski, R., Carbonell, J., & Mitchell, T. (Eds.), *Machine Learning: An Artificial Intelligence Approach.* Tioga Publishing Company, Cambridge, MA.

Heider, F. (1958). *The Psychology of Interpersonal Relations*, volume XV of *Current Theory and Research in Motivation.* John Wiley and Sons, New York.

Hempel, C. (1966). *Philosophy of Natural Science*, chapter 5. Prentice-Hall, Englewood Cliffs.

Hirsh, H. (1987). Explanation-based generalization in a logic-programming environment. In *Proceedings of the Tenth International Joint Conference on Artificial Intelligence*, Milan, Italy. IJCAI.

Hirsh, H. (1990). Conditional operationality and explanation-based generalization. In Kodratoff, Y. & Michalski, R. (Eds.), *Machine Learning: An Artificial Intelligence Approach*, volume 3, pages 383–395. Morgan Kaufmann Publishers, San Mateo.

Hobbs, J., Stickel, M., Appelt, D., & Martin, P. (1990). Interpretation as abduction. Technical Report 499, SRI International.

Hunter, L. (1990). Planning to learn. In *Proceedings of the Twelfth Annual Conference of the Cognitive Science Society*, pages 261–268, Cambridge, MA. Cognitive Science Society.

Josephson, J. (1991). Abduction: Conceptual analysis of a fundamental pattern of inference. Technical Research Report 91-JJ-DRAFT, Laboratory for Artificial Intelligence Research, The Ohio State University.

Kahneman, D., Slovic, P., & Tversky, A. (1982). *Judgement under uncertainty: Heuristics and biases.* Cambridge University Press, Cambridge.

Kambhampati, S. (1990). Mapping and retrieval during plan reuse: A validation structure based approach. In *Proceedings of the Eighth National Conference on Artificial Intelligence*, pages 170–175, Boston, MA. AAAI.

Kass, A. (1986). Modifying explanations to understand stories. In *Proceedings of the Eighth Annual Conference of the Cognitive Science Society*, Amherst, MA. Cognitive Science Society.

Kass, A. (1990). *Developing Creative Hypotheses by Adapating Explanations.* PhD thesis, Yale University. Northwestern University Institute for the Learning Sciences, Technical Report 6.

Kass, A. & Leake, D. (1987). Types of explanations. Technical Report 523, Yale University Department of Computer Science.

Kass, A. & Leake, D. (1988). Case-based reasoning applied to constructing explanations. In Kolodner, J. (Ed.), *Proceedings of the Case-Based Reasoning Workshop*, pages 190–208, Palo Alto. Defense Advanced Research Projects Agency, Morgan Kaufmann, Inc.

Kass, A., Leake, D., & Owens, C. (1986). SWALE: A program that explains. In *Explanation Patterns: Understanding Mechanically and Creatively*, pages 232–254. Lawrence Erlbaum Associates, Hillsdale, NJ.

Kautz, H. & Allen, J. (1986). Generalized plan recognition. In *Proceedings of the Fifth National Conference on Artificial Intelligence*, pages 32–37, Philadelphia, PA. AAAI.

Kedar-Cabelli, S. (1987). Formulating concepts according to purpose. In *Proceedings of the Sixth Annual National Conference on Artificial Intelligence*, pages 477–481, Seattle, WA. AAAI.

Keller, R. (1988). Defining operationality for explanation-based learning. *Artificial Intelligence*, 35(2):227–241.

Kelley, H. (1967). Attribution theory in social psychology. In Levine, D. (Ed.), *Nebraska Symposium on Motivation*, pages 192–238. University of Nebraska Press, Lincoln.

Kolodner, J. (1984). *Retrieval and Organizational Strategies in Conceptual Memory.* Lawrence Erlbaum Associates, Hillsdale, NJ.

Kolodner, J. (1987). Extending problem solving capabilities through case-based inference. In *Proceedings of the Fourth International Workshop on Machine Learning*, Irvine, CA. Machine Learning, Morgan Kaufmann.

Koton, P. (1988). Reasoning about evidence in causal explanations. In *Proceedings of the Seventh National Conference on Artificial Intelligence*, pages 256–261, Minneapolis, MN. AAAI, Morgan Kaufmann Publishers, Inc.

Krulwich, B. (1991). Determining what to learn in a multi-component planning system. In *Proceedings of the Thirteenth Annual Conference of the Cognitive Science Society*, pages 102–107, Chicago, IL. Cognitive Science Society.

Krulwich, B., Birnbaum, L., & Collins, G. (1990). Goal-directed diagnosis of expectation failures. In O'Rorke, P. (Ed.), *Working Notes of the 1990 Spring Symposium on Automated Abduction*, pages 116–119. AAAI. Technical Report 90-32, Department of Information and Computer Science, University of California, Irvine.

Lalljee, M. & Abelson, R. (1983). The organization of explanations. In Hewstone, M. (Ed.), *Attribution Theory: Social and Functional Extensions*. Blackwell, Oxford.

Lalljee, M., Watson, M., & White, P. (1982). Explanations, attributions, and the social context of unexpected behavior. *European Journal of Social Psychology*, 12:17–29.

Leake, D. (1988a). Evaluating explanations. In *Proceedings of the Seventh National Conference on Artificial Intelligence*, pages 251–255, Minneapolis, MN. AAAI, Morgan Kaufmann Publishers, Inc.

Leake, D. (1988b). Using explainer needs to judge operationality. In *Proceedings of the 1988 AAAI Spring Symposium on Explanation-based Learning*, pages 148–152, Stanford, CA. AAAI.

Leake, D. (1989). Anomaly detection strategies for schema-based story understanding. In *Proceedings of the Eleventh Annual Conference of the Cognitive Science Society*, pages 490–497, Ann Arbor, MI. Cognitive Science Society.

Leake, D. (1991). An indexing vocabulary for case-based explanation. In *Proceedings of the Ninth National Conference on Artificial Intelligence*, pages 10–15, Anaheim, CA. AAAI.

Leake, D. & Owens, C. (1986). Organizing memory for explanation. In *Proceedings of the Eighth Annual Conference of the Cognitive Science Society*, pages 710–715, Amherst, MA. Cognitive Science Society.

Lebowitz, M. (1980). *Generalization and Memory in an Integrated Understanding System*. PhD thesis, Yale University. Computer Science Department Technical Report 186.

Lehnert, W. (1978). *The Process of Question Answering*. Lawrence Erlbaum Associates, Hillsdale, NJ.

Lytinen, S. (1984). *The Organization of Knowledge In a Multi-lingual, Integrated Parser*. PhD thesis, Yale University. Computer Science Department Technical Report 340.

Mackie, J. (1965). Causes and conditions. *American Philosophical Quarterly*, 2(4):245–264.

McDermott, D. (1974). Assimilation of new information by a natural language-understanding system. Master's thesis, Massachusetts Institute of Technology, Artificial Intelligence Laboratory, Cambridge, MA. Technical Report 291.

McDermott, D. (1982). A temporal logic for reasoning about processes and plans. *Cognitive Science*, 6:101–155.

McDermott, D. & Sussman, G. (1973). The CONNIVER reference manual. AI Technical Report 259, MIT AI Laboratory.

Minsky, M. (1975). A framework for representing knowledge. In Winston, P. (Ed.), *The Psychology of Computer Vision*, chapter 6, pages 211–277. McGraw-Hill, New York.

Minton, S. (1988). *Learning Search Control Knowledge: An Explanation-Based Approach*. Kluwer Academic Publishers, Boston.

Mitchell, T., Keller, R., & Kedar-Cabelli, S. (1986). Explanation-based generalization: A unifying view. *Machine Learning*, 1(1):47–80.

Mooney, R. (1990). *A General Explanation-based Learning Mechanism and its Application to Narrative Understanding*. Morgan Kaufmann Publishers, Inc., San Mateo.

Moore, J. & Swartout, W. (1989). A reactive approach to explanation. In *Proceedings of the Eleventh International Joint Conference on Artificial Intelligence*, pages 1504–1510, Detroit, MI. IJCAI.

Mostow, J. (1983). Machine transformation of advice into a heuristic search procedure. In Michalski, R., Carbonell, J., & Mitchell, T. (Eds.), *Machine Learning: An Artificial Intelligence Approach*. Tioga Publishing Company, Cambridge, MA.

Mostow, J. & Bhatnagar, N. (1987). Failsafe—a floor planner that uses EBG to learn from its failures. In *Proceedings of the Tenth International Joint Conference on Artificial Intelligence*, Milan, Italy. IJCAI.

Ng, H. & Mooney, R. (1990). On the role of coherence in abductive explanation. In *Proceedings of the Eighth National Conference on Artificial Intelligence*, pages 337–342, Boston, MA. AAAI.

Norvig, P. (1983). Frame activated inferences in a story understanding program. In *Proceedings of the Eighth International Joint Conference on Artificial Intelligence*, pages 624–626, Karlsrhue, Germany.

Norvig, P. (1989). Marker passing as a weak method for text inferencing. *Cognitive Science*, 13(4):569–620.

O'Rorke, P. (1983). Reasons for beliefs in understanding: Applications of non-monotonic dependencies to story processing. In *Proceedings of the National Conference on Artificial Intelligence*, Washington, DC.

O'Rorke, P. (1990). Working notes of the 1990 spring symposium on automated abduction. Technical Report 90-32, Department of Information and Computer Science, University of California, Irvine.

Owens, C. (1991). *Indexing and retrieving abstract planning knowledge*. PhD thesis, Yale University.

Paris, C. (1987). Combining discourse strategies to generate descriptions to users along a naive/expert spectrum. In *Proceedings of the Tenth International Joint Conference on Artificial Intelligence*, pages 626–632, Milan.

Pazzani, M. (1988). Selecting the best explanation for explanation-based learning. In *1988 Spring Symposium Series: Explanation-Based Learning*, pages 165–169, Stanford, CA. AAAI.

Pazzani, M. (1990). *Creating a Memory of Causal Relationships: An Integration of Empirical and Explanation-Based Methods*. Lawrence Erlbaum Associates, Hillsdale, NJ.

Pearl, J. (1988a). Evidential reasoning under uncertainty. In Shrobe, H. (Ed.), *Exploring Artificial Intelligence: Survey Talks from the National Conferences on Artificial Intelligence*. Morgan Kaufmann, Palo Alto.

Pearl, J. (1988b). *Probabilistic Reasoning in Intelligent Systems: Networks of Plausible Inference*. Morgan Kaufmann, San Mateo.

Peng, Y. & Reggia, J. (1990). *Abductive Inference Models for Diagnostic Problem Solving*. Springer Verlag, New York.

Pennington, N. & Hastie, R. (1988). Explanation-based decision making: Effects on memory structure and judgement. *Journal of Experimental Psychology: Learning, Memory and Cognition*, 14(3):521–533.

Pierce, C. (1948). Abduction and induction. In Buchler, J. (Ed.), *The Philosophy of Pierce: Selected Writings*, chapter 11. Harcourt, Brace and Company, New York.

Rajamoney, S. (1988). Experimentation-based theory revision. In *Proceedings of the 1988 AAAI Spring Symposium on Explanation-based Learning*. AAAI.

Rajamoney, S. & DeJong, G. (1988). Active explanation reduction: An approach to the multiple explanations problem. In *Proceedings of the Fifth International Conference on Machine Learning*, pages 242–255. Machine Learning.

Ram, A. (1989). *Question-driven understanding: An integrated theory of story understanding, memory and learning.* PhD thesis, Yale University, New Haven, CT. Computer Science Department Technical Report 710.

Ram, A. & Leake, D. (1991). Evaluation of explanatory hypotheses. In *Proceedings of the Thirteenth Annual Conference of the Cognitive Science Society*, pages 867–871, Chicago, IL. Cognitive Science Society.

Read, S. & Cesa, I. (1991). This reminds me of the time when ...: Expectation failures in reminding and explanation. *Journal of Experimental Social Psychology*, 27:1–25.

Rieger, C. (1975). Conceptual memory and inference. In *Conceptual Information Processing.* North-Holland, Amsterdam.

Riesbeck, C. (1975). Conceptual analysis. In *Conceptual Information Processing.* North-Holland, Amsterdam.

Riesbeck, C. (1981). Failure-driven reminding for incremental learning. In *Proceedings of the Seventh International Joint Conference on Artificial Intelligence*, pages 115–120, Vancouver, B.C. IJCAI.

Schank, R. (1972). Conceptual dependency: A theory of natural language understanding. *Cognitive Psychology*, 3(4):552–631.

Schank, R. (1975). The structure of episodes in memory. In *Representation and Understanding*, pages 237–272. Academic Press, New York.

Schank, R. (1982). *Dynamic Memory: A Theory of Learning in Computers and People.* Cambridge University Press, Cambridge, England.

Schank, R. (1983). The current state of AI: One man's opinion. *The AI Magazine*, 4(1):3–8.

Schank, R. (1986). *Explanation Patterns: Understanding Mechanically and Creatively.* Lawrence Erlbaum Associates, Hillsdale, NJ.

Schank, R. & Abelson, R. (1977). *Scripts, Plans, Goals and Understanding.* Lawrence Erlbaum Associates, Hillsdale, NJ.

Schank, R., Collins, G., & Hunter, L. (1986). Transcending inductive category formation in learning. *Behavioral and Brain Sciences*, 9(4).

Schank, R. & Leake, D. (1989). Creativity and learning in a case-based explainer. *Artificial Intelligence*, 40(1-3):353–385. Also in Carbonell, J., editor, *Machine Learning: Paradigms and Methods*, MIT Press, Cambridge, MA, 1990.

Segre, A. (1987). On the operationality/generality tradeoff in explanation-based learning. In *Proceedings of the Tenth International Joint Conference on Artificial Intelligence*, Milan, Italy. IJCAI.

Segre, A. (1988). *Machine learning of robot assembly plans*. Kluwer Academic Publishers, Boston.

Shortliffe, E. (1976). *Computer-based medical consultations: MYCIN*. American Elsevier, New York.

Simpson, R. (1985). *A Computer Model of Case-based Reasoning in Problem-solving: An Investigation in the Domain of Dispute Mediation*. PhD thesis, School of Information and Computer Science, Georgia Institute of Technology. Georgia Institute of Technology, Technical Report GIT-ICS-85/18.

Snyder, C., Higgens, R., & Stucky, R. (1983). *Excuses: Masquerades in Search of Grace*. Wiley, New York.

Sussman, G. (1975). *A computer model of skill acquisition*, volume 1 of *Artificial Intelligence Series*. American Elsevier, New York.

Swartout, W. (1983). Xplain: a system for creating and explaining expert consulting programs. *Artificial Intelligence*, 21(3).

Sycara, K. (1987). *Resolving Adversarial Conflicts: An Approach Integrating Case-based and Analytic Methods*. PhD thesis, School of Information and Computer Science, Georgia Institute of Technology. Georgia Institute of Technology, Technical Report GIT-ICS-87/26.

Tadepalli, P. (1989). Lazy explanation-based learning: A solution to the intractable theory problem. In *Proceedings of the Eleventh International Joint Conference on Artificial Intelligence*, pages 694–700, Detroit, MI. IJCAI.

Thagard, P. (1989). Explanatory coherence. *The Behavioral and Brain Sciences*, 12(3):435–502.

Tversky, A. & Kahneman, D. (1982). *Judgement under uncertainty: Heuristics and biases*, chapter 1. Cambridge University Press, Cambridge.

Van Fraassen, B. (1980). *The Scientific Image*, chapter 5. Clarendon Press, Oxford.

Vecsey, G. (1984). 'That funny sound'. *The New York Times*, page C1. June 18.

Wilensky, R. (1978). *Understanding Goal-Based Stories*. PhD thesis, Yale University. Computer Science Department Technical Report 140.

Wilensky, R. (1983). *Planning and Understanding*. Addison-Wesley, Reading, MA.

Winston, P., Binford, T., Katz, B., & Lowry, M. (1983). Learning physical descriptions from function definitions, examples, and precedents. In *Proceedings of the National Conference on Artificial Intelligence*, Washington, DC.

Zukier, H. (1986). The paradigmatic and narrative modes in goal-guided inference. In Sorrentino, R. & Higgins, E. T. (Eds.), *Handbook of Motivation and Cognition: Foundations of Social Behavior*, chapter 16, pages 465–502. Guilford Press.

Author Index

Subject Index